BLINDSIDED:

The Radical Islamic Conquest

BLINDSIDED:

The Radical Islamic Conquest

Michael Youssef, Ph.D.

ISBN 978-0-9848108-2-6

First Edition

Printed in the United States of America

1 2 3 4 5 6 7 — 06 05 04 03 02 01

Blindsided is dedicated

in memory of

U.S. Army Private William Andrew Long,

and to all of the brave men and women

and their families

who have suffered

at the hands of Islamic extremists.

CONTENTS

PREFACE

In writing this book, I have deliberately chosen not to be scholarly or technical because I want to spare readers the need to refer constantly to a lexicon or dictionary. I have used Westernized spellings of Arab names, as those names are commonly found in popular American periodicals.

I was born in the Middle East, spent my early years in the culture of the Middle East, and I return to the Middle East often. I have had many long, revealing conversations in Arabic with Muslims in general and Islamist hardliners in particular. I know the Middle East and have had much firsthand experience with Islamic practices and thought processes.

My love for the freedom and democracy I enjoy here in America compelled me to write this book. I am also compelled by my love for Muslim people.

Throughout this book, I have tried to distinguish between Islamic ideology and Muslims as people. I have many dear friends and acquaintances who embrace Islam. While I risk being criticized for my sociological, economical, and political assessments, my ardent desire is that no one misunderstand my genuine affection and appreciation for Muslim people.

From my perspective as a Christian, I see all other religious systems as less than whole. The God who revealed Himself in the person of Jesus Christ tells us that without this one Savior, no one can be accepted by the Father.

I do not look down on Muslims. On the contrary, I humbly yearn for them to know the fullness of life that comes only through Jesus Christ.

THE SEARCH FOR ANSWERS

On September 11, 2001, nineteen young men shattered the peace and security of the most powerful nation on earth. Each of these men was armed with nothing but a box cutter—a simple tool that can be purchased at a hardware store for a few dollars. These nineteen terrorists from the Middle East represent a way of life that has remained largely unchanged since the seventh century A.D., yet their coordinated attacks on that day stunned and paralyzed the greatest economic and military power on the planet.

As Americans, we were blindsided. We watched in horror as airliners flew into the twin towers of the World Trade Center in Manhattan. We saw the billowing flames, the people leaping out of upper-story windows to escape being burned alive, the buildings collapsing into clouds of debris and piles of rubble. Then we heard about another plane crashing into the Pentagon in Washington DC, and yet another plane diving into a field in Pennsylvania. We wondered if there was still more death and destruction yet to come.

We were wounded to the depths of our souls, and we asked ourselves: Why did the terrorists attack us? Why do they hate us so? What do they want from us? What's next? When will the next attack come—and where? What is their ultimate goal?

As the dust settled and the soul-searching began, we realized that we had been targeted *not* because of any crimes we had committed against the Muslim world, but simply because of who we are, what we believe, and the values we embrace. Above all, we are a super power, and all super powers must be subjected to Islam.

Prior to 9/11, many Americans viewed terrorism by Islamic extremists as directed against our political system, our military, and our government. In the past, the terrorists had primarily targeted U.S. government facilities and assets overseas—the October 1983 bombing of the Marine barracks in Beirut, the June 1996 Khobar Towers bombing in Saudi Arabia, the August 1998 bombings of two U.S. embassies in distant Africa, and the October 2000 attack on the destroyer USS *Cole*. These were evil acts, but they seemed to be aimed at our government—not at civilians.

But 9/11 changed that. Ordinary people got up one morning, showered, had breakfast, dropped off their kids at school, went to work or set off on business trips—totally unaware that their lives were about to end in fiery horror. On that day, the same enemy who had attacked those distant embassies and an American warship had struck again. But this time, the enemy had turned two of America's greatest cities into war zones.

This was hard for Americans to understand. It wasn't just our government that came under attack that day. We, the American people, were targeted for indiscriminate slaughter. This extremist enemy hated *us* and targeted *us* to be butchered and terrorized. We were stunned and disoriented.

Suddenly, the name "Al-Qaeda" was on everyone's lips. We learned that this shadowy organization, which specializes in coordinated bombings and suicide attacks, operated out of training camps in Afghanistan, Pakistan, Sudan, and Iraq—and even had a major presence in the United States. The ideological vision of Al-Qaeda, we learned, was to eradicate all foreign influence from Islamic countries and to create a new Islamic empire—a Caliphate. Under the rules of engagement of this ideology, the indiscriminate killing of civilians—men, women, and children—is religiously permissible as an act of *jihad* (war against unbelievers).

In response to the 9/11 attacks, then-President George W. Bush launched what he called "The War on Terror." In the course of that war, a number of high-ranking Al-Qaeda leaders were captured, including Khalid Sheikh Mohammed, the chief planner of 9/11, and Abd al-Rahim al-Nashiri, who plotted the *Cole* bombing and other attacks.

Al-Qaeda founder Osama bin Laden eluded capture throughout the Bush years, but was located and killed by Navy SEALs at his compound in Abbottabad, Pakistan, on May 1, 2011. On September 30, 2011, Anwar al-Awlaki, Al-Qaeda's top recruiter and terror instigator, was killed by a CIA drone attack in Yemen. With each capture or killing of a high Al-Qaeda leader, Americans celebrated.

The killing of bin Laden brought cheering crowds into the street in New York's Times Square and in front of the White House. But no sooner had the celebrations ended than reality set in: The threat hasn't gone away. The world is still dangerous, and Westerners are still targets of terrorism. We still have to take our shoes off and endure intrusive pat-downs at airports. Every day, more Islamic extremists are stepping up to replace the fallen.

The deaths of Osama bin Laden and Anwar al-Awlaki may have slowed Al-Qaeda's plans—but nothing has truly changed. The hatred among militant Middle Eastern extremists grows. The world can never return to the way it was before 9/11.

So we are left to wonder—what next? Is there any hope for peace in the world—or is terror our destiny? How can we even begin to understand an ideology so fanatical that its adherents are willing to kill themselves in order to slaughter and terrorize us? Is it even possible for us to understand such an alien way of thinking?

I believe we can understand this ideology. And I'm convinced that we must.

This book offers answers to all of those questions. The answers I offer here are not intended to be exhaustive and scholarly. Rather, I want to provide answers that are concise, accurate, and targeted on the challenges that confront us from militant Islamists. In these pages, I will be as factual and objective as possible, but I want to state at the outset that the perspective of this book is unabashedly pro-American ideals and Christian.

Westerners in general, and Americans and Christians in particular, are the targets of these terrorist attacks. So, as Americans and Christians, we must seek to understand who is attacking us, why they hate us, and how we should appropriately respond.

The search for answers begins with a clear-eyed examination of Islam and the Middle Eastern culture.

1

THE WAR WE ARE LOSING

Mohamed Bouazizi was a twenty-six-year-old street vendor in Sidi Bouzid, a rural village in central Tunisia. His father died when he was three, and his stepfather was unable to work. So from the time he was ten, Mohamed had worked hard to provide for his family. In his twenties, he found it harder to find work, and he was rejected by the army, so he bought a vendor's cart. He earned a little more than a hundred dollars a month selling produce from the cart, which was not much bigger than a wheelbarrow. He budgeted his money carefully, using it to support his mother, stepfather, and siblings. He even put one sister through college. He managed to set aside a small amount each month, hoping to someday buy a used van to replace his cart.[1]

According to a close friend, Hajlaoui Jaafer, Mohamed had been bullied almost daily by the police. They demanded bribes and confiscated his produce when he couldn't pay. "Since he was a child, they were mistreating him," said Jaafer. "He was used to it. I saw him humiliated."

Mohamed's customers loved him. Jaafer said, "Mohamed was a very well-known and popular man. He would give free fruit and vegetables to very poor families."[2]

On the morning of December 17, 2010, Mohamed went out into the street to sell his wares. A little after 10:30 a.m., the police stopped him and demanded to see his vendor's permit, even though street vending is legal without a permit in Tunisia. It was yet another shakedown for a bribe. Not only did Mohamed have no money for a bribe, he had borrowed $200 to buy the produce he sold from his cart.

When Mohamed refused to pay the bribe, a woman named Faida Hamdi, a municipal official, came out to confront him. Witnesses say she confiscated his weighing scales (valued at $100). When he protested, she slapped him, spat at him, insulted his dead father, and overturned his produce cart. In Mohamed's culture, being publicly humiliated by a woman was the most shameful thing that could happen to a man.

Worse still, his produce was ruined. Now he had no way to pay back the $200 loan—and he could not buy more produce on credit. The police told him he would be fined, and he had no money to pay the fine. He went to the governor's office to ask for his scales back, but the governor refused to see him. Mohamed believed he was ruined; his life was over.

So he got a can of gasoline and stood in the intersection in front of the governor's office. As he doused himself with gasoline, he shouted, "How do you expect me to make a living?"[3]

Then he flicked a match and set himself ablaze.

Minutes later, an ambulance arrived and took Mohamed to a hospital in Sfax, more than an hour away. Severely burned over 90 percent of his body, he lived for eighteen days, then died on January 4, 2011.

More than five thousand people attended Mohamed Bouazizi's funeral. Some were grieving. Others were full of rage toward the corrupt government that had steadily, relentlessly destroyed the twenty-six-year-old street vendor's hope.[4]

Expressions of anti-government anger didn't end with Mohamed's funeral. Word of the young man's self-immolation spread across Tunisia, galvanizing the Tunisian people—especially the young. They expressed their rage in the form of mass demonstrations and revolts from one end of Tunisia to the other. The unrest was so widespread that Tunisian president Ben Ali and his family fled to exile in Saudi Arabia.

The mood of revolution spread quickly across the region. In Egypt, thousands of protesters poured into historic Tahrir (Liberation) Square in Cairo. The protests quickly spread to Alexandria, Suez, and other cities. The demonstrations began as nonviolent displays of civil disobedience. But as the government of Egyptian President Hosni Mubarak tried to quell the demonstrations, clashes broke out, killing hundreds and injuring thousands. Demonstrators demanded an end to the repressive Mubarak regime, with its corruption and police brutality. On February 11, after eighteen days of protests and violence, Hosni Mubarak resigned, ending a presidency that had lasted for thirty years.

Civil uprisings were reported in Bahrain, Yemen, Oman, Algeria, Jordan, Syria, Iraq, Morocco, Kuwait, Lebanon, Mauritania, Saudi Arabia, Sudan, and Western Sahara. Palestinian protestors demonstrated along the borders of Israel. Several Arab nations, including Jordan, Kuwait, Lebanon, Oman, and Morocco, implemented government reforms in order to prevent the protests from getting completely out of control. The Syrian government, by contrast, doubled its repressive measures, executing as many as two thousand unarmed civilians.

A full-fledged civil war broke out in Libya. After NATO forces formed a no-fly zone over Libya, rebel forces advanced on the capital, Tripoli, and Libyan dictator Muammar al-Gaddafi scurried into hiding. The Libyan National Transitional

Council took control of Bab al-Azizia—Libya's primary military barracks and compound in Tripoli—and seized control of the entire nation except for a few pockets of resistance. One of those pockets was Gaddafi's hometown of Sirte.

On October 20, 2011, while a battle raged for control of Sirte, NATO forces spotted a convoy of vehicles fleeing the city. A NATO air strike blew up the convoy, killing many loyalist fighters. Gaddafi, who was in one of the vehicles, escaped and hid in a drainpipe under a road. Rebels found him, dragged him out of the drain, then beat and tortured him. He died a tyrant's death at the hands of the people he had brutalized.

All told, an estimated 35,000 people died in these uprisings during the spring of 2011—a time which has come to be known as the "Arab Spring." Yet the repression and violence of the state could not quell the demonstrations, strikes, marches, and rallies. In country after country across the Arab world, people chanted, "*El Shaab yurid iskat el Nizam!* The people want the fall of the regime!"[5]

THE FALSE HOPE OF THE ARAB SPRING

Ayman Anwar Mitri is a Coptic Christian, a middle-aged man living in the Egyptian town of Qena. Employed as a school administrator, Mitri owned an apartment, which he rented to two Muslim sisters referred to him by a rental agent. In early 2011, soon after Egyptian President Hosni Mubarak was deposed in the so called Arab Spring uprisings, Mitri learned that the two sisters who rented his apartment were indicted for prostitution. As a Christian, he refused to allow his property to be used for immoral purposes. He asked the women to move out, and they did.

A few days later, Ayman Mitri was awakened at four in the morning by a phone call informing him that his apartment was on fire. By the time he arrived at the apartment, firemen had extinguished the blaze. As Mitri inspected the damage, a Muslim appeared at the door, shouting accusations that he had brought prostitutes into the building. Mitri tried in vain to calm the man down. Finally, the angry Muslim man suggested they go to the apartment of a policeman to talk the matter over. Mitri agreed, and when the two men reached the policeman's apartment, he found a dozen Muslim men inside waiting for him. The fire had been a setup to lure Ayman Mitri into a trap.

Once the Muslims dragged Mitri into the apartment, they began beating him and shouting, "We will teach you a lesson, Christian!" Then they brought in one of the prostitute sisters and told her she was to claim she had committed adultery with Ayman Mitri. When she refused, they beat her. Finally, she agreed to accuse the Christian man of adultery.

Then the Muslims shoved Ayman Mitri in a chair. One of them cut off his right ear, then gashed the back of his neck, slit his other ear and face, and cut his arms. Finally, several of them decided to throw Mitri out of the window of the fifth-floor apartment—but the policeman wouldn't let them because it would get them into trouble. The men demanded that Mitri convert to Islam, but he refused.

Finally, the men called the police station and told the police to come get Mitri. "We have applied the law of Allah," they said. "Now come and apply your civil law." So the police arrived and took Ayman Mitri and the prostitute away.

At first, Mitri wanted justice and compensation from his attackers. But he backed off and withdrew the police report after receiving calls threatening to kill him and kidnap his daughters. No one was ever arrested for the attack on Ayman Mitri.[6]

This incident is symbolic of the dark and dangerous underside of the so-called "Arab Spring." Western news agencies mainly have painted a rosy picture of the Arab Spring as a peaceful outbreak of pro-democracy passions throughout the Arab world. And it's true that, at the beginning, these uprisings were an expression of a desire for freedom, especially among the student class.

In the early stages of the uprisings in Egypt, large numbers of Coptic Christians (who comprise about 15 percent of Egypt's 85 million people) joined the pro-democracy demonstrations against President Mubarak. The Copts trace their Christian heritage back to St. Mark the Evangelist, who founded the Egyptian church in Alexandria around A.D. 42. The Coptic Christians joined the popular uprising, believing it would bring about a less oppressive state that would protect the rights of all Egyptians.

What the Copts didn't realize was that the Arab Spring demonstrations were being subtly co-opted by Islamic fundamentalists, including the Salafi sect (followers of the Salafiyyah Islamic movement), who take an extreme puritanical view of Islamic theology. The Salafis view vigilante acts of Sharia "justice" as a legitimate form of Islam. (*Sharia* literally means "the straight path," and Muslims believe that Sharia—Islamic law—governs all aspects of life.)

The Arab Spring in Egypt began as a popular pro-democracy movement under the slogan of, "The people want the fall of the regime!" Before it was over, gangs of Muslim men swarmed through Cairo and other cities, armed with stones, clubs, and torches. Their slogan had changed: "The people want to bring down the Christians!"[7]

During those days, I called Christian leaders in Cairo, and they told me they were very anxious because roving gangs of thugs were looting shops and banks. In many neighborhoods, young men stood guard in front of homes and shops, protecting their families and possessions against the thugs and looters.

An Egyptian-Canadian friend told me she had gotten through to her family and learned that her father was sick and bleeding in the hospital, but there was no medical care being provided in the hospital. The janitor and other low-level hospital workers had armed themselves with knives and sticks and were trying to defend the patients from the thugs and looters. It was anarchy, and the police could not protect the people.

I also got word that the police were guarding the Ministry of the Interior in Cairo as if it were the Alamo. The building contained many police files that the Islamists wanted to get their hands on, so the police were defending the building against the militants.

Young pro-democracy reformers set the Arab Spring movement into motion—but they were leaderless and disorganized. By contrast, the Islamists and hardliners within the movement were a well-coordinated force. The largest Islamist group is the Muslim Brotherhood, a political organization founded in Egypt in 1928, and now operating throughout the world, including Europe and the United States. The slogan of the Muslim Brotherhood: "Islam is the solution." The credo of the Brotherhood: "Allah is our objective. The Prophet is our leader. Koran is our law. Jihad is our way. Dying in the way of Allah is our highest hope."[8] The Muslim Brotherhood quickly seized these demonstrations for their own purposes.

As Walid Phares, the Beirut-born American expert on the Middle East, put it, "The region's mostly-Sunni Islamist movements gradually rose from the bottom and seized the initiative. . . . While masses, and particularly real revolutionary youth, were exploding against dictators from Egypt to Libya and Yemen to Syria, Islamist networks were systematically climbing the ladder of each national revolt."[9]

In the early stages of the Egyptian uprising, there were a number of instances of cooperation between Egyptian Christians and Muslims. For example, after a New Year's Day 2011 car bomb destroyed the Saints Church in east Alexandria, killing twenty-five worshipers, thousands of grassroots Muslims attended Mass alongside the Coptic Christians later that week as a show of support. One Muslim Egyptian told the *Los Angeles Times*, "I'm here to tell all my Coptic brothers that Muslims and Christians are an inseparable pillar of Egypt's texture. Copts have to know that we will share any pains or threats they go through."[10]

The following month, as the anti-Mubarak demonstrations were in full swing in Cairo, thousands of Muslims gathered in Tahrir Square to protest and pray. At the same time, hundreds of Coptic Christians encircled their Muslim compatriots, joining hands to form a protective cordon around the Muslims against police and military forces.[11] As the Associated Press reported:

> *At Tahrir Square, the epicenter of the revolution against Mubarak, there were glimpses of a fleeting utopia where coexistence and mutual respect between Muslims and Christians was the rule. The iconic image of Christians forming a human shield around Muslim worshippers during Friday prayers to protect them from thugs and pro-Mubarak loyalists spoke volumes to the dream.*[12]

These heartwarming examples of cooperation between Christians and Muslims in Egypt were tragically short-lived. Just one month after Christians defended Muslims in Tahrir Square, clashes between Christians and Muslim thugs broke out in that same square, killing thirteen people.[13]

Soon after Hosni Mubarak resigned on February 11, cooperation between Egyptian Christians and Muslims disintegrated. Religious tensions flared and clashes erupted. In late February, a Coptic priest was stabbed to death by masked men shouting "Allah is greater!"[14] On March 12, the Shahedin Church in Helwan Province was torched by a Muslim mob, setting off a street battle that killed thirteen Christians.[15] In May, a dozen Egyptians were killed in attacks on Coptic churches.[16] On September 20, a Muslim mob partially destroyed the al-Marenab Church in the southern Aswan Province.[17]

Copts believed that the military government, which had replaced the Mubarak dictatorship, was permitting Muslim extremists to burn churches and kill Christians with impunity. The destruction of the church in Aswan Province prompted a peaceful demonstration by Copts in front of the Maspero, the Egyptian TV headquarters on the bank of the Nile in Cairo. The Christian protestors staged a peaceful sit-in, but were attacked by Egyptian security forces.

A disturbing video report on TheRealNews.com shows Egyptian Christians, who were beaten and bloodied, holding up crosses and Egyptian flags or carrying off their wounded, saying, "We're not going to back down." One unarmed man was on the ground in a fetal position, trying to protect his head as more than a dozen policemen clubbed him with nightsticks. Armored military vehicles weaved through the crowd, deliberately mowing people down and bouncing over their bodies.

The video also shows that, once again, a few brave young Muslims came out to support the Coptic Christians against the government. One Muslim man in his early twenties shook his fist and shouted, "We the Muslims are with the Christians! We will die today! The military council is the second Mubarak! . . . The Egyptian people are 85 million people—don't provoke them!" Other young Muslim men added their impassioned voices to his, and the man next to him shouted, "The

Egyptian army is running over the Copts with their tanks! Before our eyes, they are running them over! Blasphemy!"

The Egyptian military fired tear gas canisters and sent plain clothed thugs into the crowd to disperse the demonstrators, but the crowd only grew larger during the night. Muslim women, many of them wearing traditional hijabs, added their voices to the protest. The crowd chanted that Muslims and Christians were "one hand" raised against the military government. The video also showed dead protesters laid out side-by-side, some bloodied from beatings, others crushed under the tread of military vehicles. In all, twenty-six civilians were dead and four hundred were injured.

One of the final images showed a wounded, bandaged Coptic Christian youth. He spoke emotionally about the wrongs the Egyptian people had suffered from their government, then added, "But also we say thank God, and He will bring us justice."[18]

It's important to remember that there are Muslims—especially the youth—who are not caught up in the extremism and anti-Christian hatred demonstrated by the Salafis, the Muslim Brotherhood, and the military hard-liners. The Arab Spring genuinely began as a movement of mostly young people demanding freedom and democracy. But these protesters have found that the new military dictatorship is even more cruel and repressive than the old Mubarak regime.

The hope of the Arab Spring has proven false. The movement has been infiltrated and subverted by extremists. The promise of the Arab Spring was a cruel hoax.

THE PATTERN REPEATS ITSELF

During the early stages of the uprisings, I accepted invitations to appear on CNN, Fox News, the Christian Broadcasting Network, and other outlets to talk about these momentous events throughout the Arab world. While most of the Western media celebrated the Arab Spring as a wave of freedom sweeping through the Arab world, I was one of the few voices sounding a warning. I predicted that these changes would result in violence and persecution for Christians—and sure enough, as Egyptian military vehicles barreled into the crowds of peaceful Christian demonstrators, everything I predicted came to pass.

As Americans, we must understand that our tax dollars funded the Egyptian army's industrial establishment. You and I paid for the military assault vehicles that crushed the bodies of the protesters in Cairo. Our tax money subsidized the slaughter of innocent Christians in Egypt. This is not a partisan issue; Republicans and Democrats are equally responsible for funding these power-mad Egyptian generals, and we must demand that our government stop sending billions of our tax dollars so that foreign governments can more efficiently kill and oppress their own people.

As I told Governor Mike Huckabee when I appeared on his Fox News Channel show, "I'm not here to defend former President Hosni Mubarak. During his thirty-year tenure, state corruption grew and political dissidents were often imprisoned without trial. At the same time, Mubarak made a number of positive reforms. For example, he privatized the banks and grew the economy, which in turn helped create a large Egyptian middle class."

In 2011, when I saw student protestors waving signs that read, "Down with the tyrant Mubarak," I thought, "Those kids don't know what a *real* tyrant is." I grew up in Egypt under Gamal Abdel Nasser. When I was around my friends in high school, I chose my words very carefully and avoided talking about politics or the government, because I never knew which of my friends might be a government informant. It seemed like every other person was a potential informant, and every once in a while, you heard that someone you knew had been denounced and arrested. It was an atmosphere of fear, much like living in the world of George Orwell's *1984*. Life under Mubarak was no utopia, but it was a far cry from the repressive Egyptian society I grew up in.

The young university-educated demonstrators in Tahrir Square were sincere. They wanted freedom, and they demonstrated in the streets for democracy. But they were unaware that there were hidden hands working in the shadows, exploiting their youthful fervor. The hidden Islamists were using and exploiting these well-meaning young people who genuinely wanted Western-style democracy. The goal of the Islamists was to seize control of the revolution, just as the Ayatollah Khomeini seized control of the Iranian Revolution more than three decades ago.

During the Iranian Revolution of 1979, the Islamists stirred up revolutionary passions and pushed the Iranian students out into the streets of Tehran to demonstrate against the shah of Iran, Mohammad Reza Pahlavi. When the shah gave up power and left the country, the Ayatollah Khomeini came in and took over the revolution. All of the freedom-loving protesters who dreamed of a secular, democratic Iran were soon silenced, imprisoned, or killed. The last thing the Islamists wanted was freedom and democracy.

The Ayatollah Khomeini became the supreme leader of Iran, and to give the *appearance* of democracy in Iran, Khomeini arranged for Abulhassan Banisadr, the son of one of his closest friends, to run for president of Iran. Banisadr won election to a four-year term—but a year and a half later, Khomeini dismissed Banisadr, began impeachment proceedings against him, and claimed the power of commander in chief for himself. Banisadr fled to France, where he lives in exile to this day.

That is the pattern followed by many revolutions in the Arab world. The hidden Islamists stir the pot and keep the idealistic young university students inflamed and angry. Then, once the revolution is in full swing, the Islamists seize power, round up the activists, and chop off their heads—either figuratively or literally. After the revolution, the Islamists refer to the original demonstrators and figurehead leaders like Banisadr as *hemir al-thawra* ("stooges") or "donkeys of the revolution"—people to be used, and then discarded.

Hamas, the Sunni Palestinian terror organization and political party, followed the same pattern in coming to power in the Gaza Strip. An offshoot of Egypt's Muslim Brotherhood, Hamas gained power by exploiting the revolutionary passions of the demonstrators during the First Intifada, the Palestinian uprising against Israel in 1987.

Today, the same pattern is playing out in Egypt. As I told Governor Huckabee on Fox News, "Every year for the past twenty years, I have been in Egypt, preaching in Egyptian churches. . . . I have seen how Mubarak tried to appease the Islamists by tightening the leash on the Christians, taking away their freedoms, and arresting some of the Christian leaders. And for a long time, I've been reading the Arab-language Islamic press in Egypt. I've seen this crisis building for a long time. The Islamists have been stirring the pot and stirring the pot . . . and Iran, make no mistake about it, is playing a role in all this. The Islamic hardliners are trying to tighten the noose around Israel, and we know what will happen if that takes place."

Governor Huckabee asked me, "If Mubarak is forced out, what should be our primary concern about the new government [that comes after Mubarak]?"

I replied that there is no safety net to catch the Egyptian political system if the Mubarak regime collapses. "If the system falls," I said, "it will be a free-for-all, and the extremists and militants will move in for the kill. Make no mistake, they will use the secular-educated Muslims to get the power, but once they get to power, they are going to get the dissidents out of the way. . . . Their number-one goal is to break the accord with Israel, create an alliance with Hamas in Gaza, and then reignite the conflict and enmity with Israel again. . . . The Arab world is in ferment all around the nation of Israel, and is working all around the borders of Israel. Once Israel falls, their vision, their third wave of jihad, is Europe and then the United States."

Everything I have seen in the weeks and months that followed have only served to confirm that view.

"OUR MISSION: WORLD DOMINATION"

What is the Muslim Brotherhood? Where did it come from and what are its goals for the Arab world? What are its goals for the West?

The Muslim Brotherhood was founded in 1928 by a school teacher named Hassan al-Banna. He was angry and frustrated over Western political influence and the declining influence of Islam in Egypt. A brief history lesson is needed to explain Hassan al-Banna's anger:

In the 1860s, Egypt was building the Suez Canal in partnership with France—and racking up a mountain of debt to European banks. Ultimately, the only way Egypt could discharge the debt was by selling its share of the Suez Canal to Great Britain. (There's a lesson here for nations that pile up debt that can never be repaid.) This arrangement gave Britain controlling seats in the Egyptian cabinet—and Egypt became a *de facto* protectorate of the British Empire. In 1922, the government of the United Kingdom issued a declaration of Egyptian independence—but Egypt was not entirely free. The British government reserved four areas for itself—communications in Egypt, the defense of Egypt, the protection of foreigners and minorities in Egypt, and the administration of the Sudan. Though technically "independent," Egypt remained largely under colonial rule.

That was the situation in Egypt when Hassan al-Banna arrived on the scene in the 1920s. Strongly influenced by the radical Wahabi Islamist movement in Saudi Arabia, al-Banna declared that he and his fellow Muslims had to liberate Egypt from British rule and erase all non-Islamic influence. Al-Banna founded the Muslim Brotherhood in the ancient city of Ismailia, on the west bank of the Suez Canal. In March 1928, the Brotherhood consisted of just seven men, al-Banna and six men who worked for the Suez Canal Company. He taught them that the only way to defeat the corrupting influence of the Christian West was to return to Sharia law, based on the Koran. One of the key requirements of Sharia law is an Islamic Caliphate as the form of government. From this small beginning, the Muslim Brotherhood grew to an estimated 2 million members by the late 1940s.[19]

Hassan al-Banna emphasized actions over words. So, in 1939, he and the Brotherhood's inner circle created a military wing called the Secret Apparatus. During World War II, the Brotherhood cooperated with Amin al-Hussaini, the Grand Mufti of Jerusalem in British Mandate Palestine. Al-Hussaini worked closely with the Nazis from 1933 to the end of the War, meeting personally with Hitler and Mussolini, and recruiting Muslims soldiers to fight in the Nazi military. Al-Hussaini also tipped off the Germans to a secret plan to rescue Jewish children from eastern Europe and send them to Palestine; as a result, those children ended up in Nazi extermination camps.[20] Al-Banna and the

Brotherhood helped Amin al-Hussaini recruit Muslims to join the Arab armies that attacked the fledgling nation of Israel in 1948,[21] and also helped distribute Arabic-language versions of anti-Jewish writings, including *Mein Kampf* and *The Protocols of the Elders of Zion*.[22]

After the War, the Brotherhood's Secret Apparatus carried out assassinations and acts of terror against Coptic Christians, politicians, and others who (in their view) posed a hindrance to achieving an Islamic state under Sharia law. In November 1948, Egyptian Prime Minister Mahmud Fahmi Nokrashi ordered a crackdown on the Muslim Brotherhood because of these bombings and shootings. Angered by the crackdown and believing the prime minister to be a puppet of the British, the Brotherhood assassinated Nokrashi on December 28, 1948. In response, agents of the Egyptian government ambushed and killed Hassan al-Banna in Cairo in February 1949.

In 1952, the Muslim Brotherhood supported a military coup that overthrew the monarchy. The Brothers believed that they had finally won the right to a place of power in the Egyptian government—but they soon discovered that the military junta that now controlled the government had just used the Brotherhood to stage a revolution. The junta had no intention of sharing power or lifting martial law in Egypt.

In October 1954, the Brotherhood attempted to assassinate Colonel Gamal Abdel Nasser, who was then vice-chairman of the Egyptian Revolutionary Command Council (the ruling military junta). Nasser was in Alexandria, giving a speech to celebrate Britain's final withdrawal from the Egyptian government. Suddenly, a Brotherhood member, standing just twenty-five feet from Nasser, pulled a gun and fired eight shots. Every shot missed. The audience panicked, but Nasser maintained his composure and appealed for calm. "My countrymen," he said, "I will live for your sake and die for the sake of your freedom and honor. Let them kill me; it does not concern me so long as I have instilled pride, honor and freedom in you. If Gamal Abdel Nasser should die, each of you shall be Gamal Abdel Nasser."[23] Nasser's courage in the midst of an assassination attempt helped solidify his power and popularity.

The assassination attempt proved to be the Muslim Brotherhood's undoing. Nasser rounded up the Brothers, put some to death and sent others to hard-labor prisons. The imprisoned Brotherhood members remained there until Nasser died in 1971 and his successor, Anwar Sadat, released them.

Since 1971, the Muslim Brotherhood has been reorganizing itself in order to disguise its true objectives. By doing various forms of charitable work, the Brotherhood is able to adopt the guise of a humanitarian agency, and it is even able to attract donations from people who are fooled by this charitable pose. The charitable work, however, has only one purpose, and that is to make the Muslim Brotherhood appear harmless and well-intentioned while it methodically goes about its business of undermining democracy and pushing for Sharia law. Many of the Brothers whom Sadat released from prison in the early 1970s left Egypt and settled in other Arab countries, especially Qatar. In fact, a large number of the operatives of Al Jazeera—the huge satellite TV and Internet communications network headquartered in Doha, Qatar—have been members of the Muslim Brotherhood.

The Muslim Brotherhood has spread throughout the world, even forming chapters in major European capitals and across the United States. The logo of the Muslim Brotherhood consists of a green disk with two crossed swords and the command (in Arabic script), "Get Ready." This is a statement that the Brothers are to always be ready for jihad. Until 2001, the Muslim Brotherhood's publication in London, *Risalat Al-Ikhwan* (Message of the Brotherhood), declared on its front page, "Our Mission: World Domination." In 2004, the former Supreme Guide of the Muslim Brotherhood, Muhammad Mahdi Othman Akef, declared, "I have complete faith that Islam will invade Europe and America, because Islam has logic and a mission."[24]

IS AMERICA FUNDING JIHAD?

During the Arab Spring uprisings, a reporter asked me, "Why should we in America care about what happens in Egypt—or in Tunisia, Jordan, Libya, and the rest of the Arab world?" The answer is simple: The Muslim Brotherhood and their fellow militant Islamists are bent on world domination. The Western mind-set cannot comprehend the extreme militant Muslim mind-set, even though the Islamists have repeatedly told us this was their intention. There is a sense of denial in our government, our media, and our social institutions. When you suggest that these militant extremists are actively working to destroy our democracy and our Western way of life, people say, "Don't be paranoid. America is too strong. That could never happen."

But consider this: Long before 9/11, Osama bin Laden had repeatedly declared war against America. The World Trade Center had already been bombed once before, in 1993. FBI counterterrorism specialist John O'Neill repeatedly warned that Islamists would make another attempt on the World Trade Center, but his warnings went unheeded (O'Neill himself died in the 9/11 attacks).[25]

In the months leading up to 9/11, the FBI was repeatedly warned by flight schools in California, Arizona, Minnesota, and Florida, that Middle Eastern men were taking lessons in how to fly Boeing passenger jets, yet showed no interest in learning to take off or land. Just weeks before 9/11, the FBI received reports of planned hijackings of U.S. airliners. The FBI even arrested an Al-Qaeda suspect, Zacarias Moussaoui, at a flight school in St. Paul because he appeared to be planning to hijack a plane and crash it into the World Trade Center. That arrest came just days before 9/11.[26]

America was warned again and again that 9/11 was coming—yet the warnings went unheeded. Why? Because Westerners live in a state of denial and can't comprehend the militant Islamist mind-set. Our leaders could not imagine that anyone would ever hijack an airplane and fly it into a building, deliberately killing himself in order to inflict death and terror on America. Such an act was beyond their comprehension, so when the warnings and reports came in, our leaders responded, "Let's not be paranoid. America is strong. This could never happen."

Those who ignored the warning signs were wrong about 9/11—and our leaders and media pundits are just as wrong about Islamist extremists today. Our enemy is patient and determined. Our nation is vulnerable and our people are unaware and ignorant of the danger. This threat to our nation and our way of life is every bit as real as the threat of 9/11.

For years, Muslim journalists have been writing openly of the jihadist intentions of the Muslim Brotherhood. But here in the West, we refuse to listen, we live in denial. Our "politically correct" news media not only ignores these warnings, but actually shills for the Islamists. For example, liberal American media pundits have vigorously defended Park51, the stealth-jihadist "Ground Zero Mosque" in Manhattan—and they have attacked and ridiculed opponents of Park51 as "bigots" and "Islamophobes."

On June 25, 2007, Egyptian columnist Tariq Hasan published an article in the *Al Ahram* newspaper stating that the Muslim Brotherhood was preparing for a violent takeover in Egypt, using its masked militia to replicate Hamas' seizure of power in Gaza. Tariq Hasan's warnings went unheeded. In all the Western media's exuberance over the Arab Spring uprisings, few reporters noticed that Hasan's predictions were being fulfilled right before their eyes. While Egyptian pro-democracy forces were disorganized and in disarray, the Muslim Brotherhood launched a political party and a media campaign to seize the momentum and mount a political offensive for the coming parliamentary and presidential elections.[27]

We are watching as a beautiful country—the cradle of an ancient civilization, the Land of the Pharaohs—is falling into the hands of authoritarian hardliners. Even more alarming, the fall of Egypt is only a harbinger of things to come. What the Muslim Brotherhood and its jihadist allies are already achieving in Egypt is exactly what they have planned for America and Western civilization. Their plan is already being implemented.

In 2004, the FBI raided a suspected terrorist safe house in Annandale, Virginia, and discovered a secret basement containing a treasure trove of jihadist and Muslim Brotherhood documents. One of those documents was called "An Explanatory Memorandum: On the General Strategic Goal for the Group." That document, written by a top-level official of the Brotherhood and a senior Hamas leader, Mohammed Akram, was adopted by the Muslim Brotherhood's Shura Council and Organizational Conference in 1987. It contained this chilling mission statement:

> *The process of settlement [of Islamists in Western countries] is a "Civilization-Jihadist Process" with all the word means. The Ikhwan [the Arab name for the Brotherhood] must understand that their work in America is a kind of grand jihad in eliminating and destroying the Western civilization from within and "sabotaging" its miserable house by their hands and the hands of the believers so that it is eliminated and God's religion is made victorious over all other religions.*[28]

Clearly, the Muslim Brotherhood is pursuing a strategy of collapsing the United States from within. The Brotherhood is using our own political leaders and opinion leaders to do their bidding and advance the jihadist cause in America.

Evidence of the ongoing success of the Brotherhood's efforts in the United States came in February 2011, at the height of the Arab Spring uprisings, when President Obama's Director of National Intelligence, James Clapper, testified before the House Intelligence Committee. When Congresswoman Sue Myrick of North Carolina asked if the Muslim Brotherhood posed a threat to democracy and freedom in Egypt, Director Clapper gave this astonishing reply: "The term 'Muslim Brotherhood' . . . is an umbrella term for a variety of movements, in the case of Egypt, a very heterogeneous group, largely secular, which has eschewed violence and has decried Al-Qaeda as a perversion of Islam. They have pursued social ends, a betterment of the political order in Egypt, et cetera. . . . In other countries, there are also chapters or franchises of the Muslim Brotherhood, but there is no overarching agenda, particularly in pursuit of violence, at least internationally."[29]

"Largely secular"? "Has eschewed violence"? "No overarching agenda"? How could President Obama's director of National Intelligence make such statements which are completely at odds with history, evidence, and common sense? How could the Muslim Brotherhood—which was founded as a means to impose Sharia law on the world—be considered "largely secular" and without an "overarching agenda"? Certainly a man whose very title says "intelligence" cannot be a stupid man. It is impossible to know what was going on in Mr. Clapper's mind, but we do know that what he told this House committee was utter nonsense.

We are also learning that the Obama White House has appointed people with Muslim Brotherhood ties to influential positions in the administration. For example, Rashad Hussain, the U.S. Special Envoy to the Organization of the Islamic Conference (OIC), has given speeches at Brotherhood-affiliated events and has spoken in support of Professor Sami Al-Arian, a Muslim Brotherhood member who pled guilty in 2006 to conspiracy to contribute aid to the Palestine Islamic Jihad, a terrorist organization.[30]

Another example: Dalia Mogahed, of President Obama's Advisory Council on Faith-Based and Neighborhood Partnerships, has spoken in favor of Sharia law, saying that Muslim women prefer living under Sharia law because they associate it with "gender justice." She is also a vocal defender of two Muslim Brotherhood front groups, the Council on American-Islamic Relations (CAIR) and the Islamic Society of North America (ISNA). In 2010, *Tablet Magazine* called Dalia Mogahed "the most important person shaping the Obama Administration's Middle East message."[31]

Also troubling is the fact that President Obama chose Ingrid Mattson, then-president of the Muslim Brotherhood front group ISNA, to offer an Islamic prayer at the National Cathedral as part of his Inauguration Day ceremonies. Ingrid Mattson is a Catholic-raised Canadian who left the Christian faith in her teens and converted to Islam while in Paris in the 1980s. ISNA, the organization she headed in 2009, was named an unindicted co-conspirator in a plot to funnel millions of dollars to the terror group Hamas. Even so, President Obama sent his senior advisor, Valerie Jarrett, to give the keynote speech at the national convention of ISNA in 2009.[32]

In June 2011, President Obama appointed a Muslim professor, Azizah al-Hibri, to the United States Commission on International Religious Freedom. The granddaughter of a Saudi sheik, she has said, "Islamic *fiqh* [law] is deeper and better than Western codes of law." She once held a leadership role in the now-defunct American Muslim Council, which was a front group of the U.S. branch of the Muslim Brotherhood.[33]

Former FBI special agent John Guandolo states that the last three presidential administrations—Clinton, Bush, and Obama—have been penetrated to varying degrees by the Muslim Brotherhood. For President Obama, however, "it even goes back to his campaign." According to Guandolo, who served as an officer in the Marines, the Muslim Brotherhood has placed several sympathizers and operatives in key positions in Homeland Security and the U.S. military. All of this, he adds, is consistent with the Brotherhood's strategy of "eliminating and destroying the Western civilization from within," as outlined in the document seized in the 2004 Annandale raid.[34]

To be fair, there is no "smoking gun" evidence that there are actual Muslim Brotherhood members serving in the White House. But there are murky connections between the Brotherhood and White House officials that are troubling at best and which should not exist.

Equally troubling is the fact that, during the Arab Spring uprisings in Egypt, the Obama White House declared that *all opposition groups*—including the Muslim Brotherhood, the largest opposition group in Egypt—should be represented in the post-Mubarak Egyptian government. By making this statement, President Obama has strengthened the hand of a fanatical anti-Israel, anti-American organization that has declared its intent to undermine America from within. And, of course, President Obama's statement comes a year and a half after he invited Muslim Brotherhood leaders to attend his speech to the Muslim world in Cairo, June 4, 2009.[35] Why does President Obama nurture ties to an organization that has sworn to destroy America from within?

Walid Phares warns that American taxpayer dollars will likely be used to fund the Islamist agenda in the Middle East:

> *The Muslim Brotherhood . . .with Washington's stealthy backing . . . seized the revolution's microphone, positioned itself at the center of the uprising, and branded itself as the "soul" and "future" of the movement, even though the Muslim Brotherhood did not make up more than 15 percent of the mass of demonstrators. . . . Mr. Obama has sent billions in economic aid to a government controlled or significantly influenced by Islamists who . . . remain loyal to jihadi ideology.*[36]

By funding the Islamists in Egypt and elsewhere in the Arab world, we are subsidizing jihad and the oppression of pro-democracy populations—and we are contributing to our own ultimate demise. We can see America's future in recent events in European nations, which have permitted a massive flow of Muslim immigrants into their borders. London, Paris, Amsterdam, Madrid, Brussels, Milan, Rome, and other European cities have been shaken by demonstrations, lootings, fires, rock-throwing, and synagogue burnings perpetrated by Islamist mobs.

In London in 2010, the 2nd Battalion Royal Anglian Regiment arrived at London Luton Airport after being deployed in Iraq. While most of the citizens waved flags and honored the returning soldiers, a group of Islamist protestors waved signs and shouted taunts and jeers of "Baby killers," "British soldiers go to hell," "Rapists, all of you," and more. One of the signs they waved proclaimed:

> *ISLAM WILL DOMINATE THE WORLD—*
> *FREEDOM CAN GO TO HELL!*

A number of the Islamist demonstrators later bragged to reporters that they were "on benefits" (that is, they were taking full advantage of Britain's generous welfare state), and that they wanted to see Sharia law imposed on Great Britain. They were telling the British taxpayer, in effect, "We will destroy your culture and your way of life, and you will support us with your tax money as we do so."[37]

To those naïve individuals who think the Islamists can be reasoned with, who think that militant Islamists just want the same things we all do—the freedom to live their lives in peace—I urge you to think about that slogan, which has been popping up in Islamist demonstrations across Europe: "Islam will dominate the world—freedom can go to hell." If that doesn't prove to you how alien the Islamist hardliner mind-set is to yours, I don't know what will.

IS IT ALREADY TOO LATE?

Western civilization prizes ideals of intellectual enlightenment, liberty, tolerance, progress, compassion, and peace. Militant Islamists demand conformity to an ancient and merciless code of laws; they are intolerant of other faiths, their worldview is stuck in the seventh century, their way is not peace or compassion, but jihad. Even though the worldview of the militant jihad is a throwback to another millennium, Middle Eastern oil wealth, foreign aid, and Western technologies have given these extremists enormous power to destabilize the world.

With a handful of hardware store box cutters, nineteen extremists brought war, death, and terror to the heart of our two greatest cities. They changed the direction of American foreign policy. Today, the American people are surrounded by surveillance cameras wherever they go. They submit to humiliating searches before boarding an airplane. Over the ten-year period from 9/11 through 2011, the War on Terror has cost taxpayers more than $1 trillion, and has taken the lives of six thousand U.S. troops and 2,300 civilian contractors.[38]

After ten years and so many lives and so much money expended, you'd think the world would be safe for democracy. But as you look at Iraq, Afghanistan, and Pakistan, as you look around the Arab world, does it seem that freedom and democracy are winning? Or are we losing the War on Terror—the war against Islamic extremism?

One of the unintended consequences of American support for the Arab Spring revolt in Libya is that the U.S. and its NATO allies were unprepared for the sudden collapse of the Gaddafi government—and the resulting loss of security over Colonel Gaddafi's massive weapons stockpile. There were thought to be as many as twenty thousand shoulder-fired heat-seeking surface-to-air missiles in Libyan warehouses—but when the Libyan government fell, no one guarded the missiles.

Unknown people began driving up in trucks and taking whatever weaponry they wanted. Many of those missiles, capable of knocking commercial airliners out of the sky, may have been transported far beyond Libya's borders. Many could be in the hands of Al-Qaeda terrorists right now.[39]

America has been fighting the wrong war, and that's why we are losing the War on Terror. That's why the world is becoming more dangerous, not less. America and the West are losing the war of ideas. How can we turn this war around? Or is it already too late?

I believe there is still time to win the war of ideas between Western civilization and the forces of jihadist extremism. That is what we shall explore in the pages to come.

2

WHO ARE WE FIGHTING?

Much of the Islamic extremism and terrorism that afflicts our world today can be traced back to one man whose name is virtually unknown in America: Sayyid Qutb.

Born in Egypt in 1906, Sayyid Qutb was a Sunni Muslim writer and intellectual. In 1949, he came to America and pursued studies at Colorado State Teachers College in Greeley, Colorado. His views on America and Western culture were profoundly shaped during that time. Greeley in the late 1940s was a quiet, peaceful town populated by moral and religious people, a "dry" town where alcohol was banned. Yet, Qutb viewed Greeley (and by extension, all of America) as a cesspool of immorality, materialism, and injustice.

Many of Qutb's impressions were the result of simple culture shock. For example, he saw the lush green lawns in front of American homes as a symbol of greed and materialistic excess. It offended this son of the parched Egyptian desert to see gallons and gallons of water showered on lawns, and to see Americans spending their weekends mowing and edging and manicuring those useless patches of grass.

He was rightly offended by the segregation he saw in America in 1949, but he also expressed some extremely twisted views on American history. For example, in his Arab-language article "Amrika allati Ra'aytu" ("The America I Have Seen"), he described the American Revolution as "a destructive war led by George Washington." He was also offended by American support for the Jews and the newly founded state of Israel.

Why did Qutb view quiet little Greeley, Colorado, as such a wide-open cesspool of depravity and sin? I think the answer lies within Sayyid Qutb himself. He was an introverted and socially isolated man who never married, claiming he could never find a woman of true "moral purity and discretion." In other words, he rationalized his awkwardness with the opposite sex as moral and spiritual superiority.

Every American woman he met seemed, to his distorted perception, like a wanton temptress. "The American girl," he wrote, "is well acquainted with her body's seductive capacity. She knows it lies in the face, and in expressive eyes, and thirsty lips. . . . She shows all this and does not hide it." He described a dance held in a church basement as being "replete with tapping feet, enticing legs, arms wrapped around waists, lips pressed to lips, and chests pressed to chests. The atmosphere was full of desire." These sound like the words of a man who projects his own lusts onto other people, who condemns a church social because he doesn't dare acknowledge the sinful urges within himself.

His writings drip with loathing for American entertainment, music, and sports. He saw American men as brutal and obsessed with sports. He wrote of "the spectacle of the fans as they follow a game of football . . . or watch boxing matches or bloody, monstrous wrestling matches." He called American churches "entertainment centers and sexual playgrounds." Immediately upon returning to Egypt, he joined the fundamentalist Muslim Brotherhood.

Qutb strongly rejected democracy and nationalism as Western ideas incompatible with Islam. He was the first Sunni Muslim to find a way around the ancient prohibition against overthrowing a Muslim ruler. His rationale: such rulers were no longer Muslims but infidels who allowed Western modernization.

Sayyid Qutb's views on America are profoundly influential in the Muslim world today. He has been called "the father of modern Islamic fundamentalism" and "the most famous personality of the Muslim world in the second half of the twentieth century." His writings have profoundly shaped the worldview of Islamic extremists—and especially the views of Al-Qaeda leaders Osama bin Laden and Ayman al-Zawahiri.

Qutb's description of American culture in the late 1940s is a bizarre caricature of the American reality. Yet we cannot deny that American culture today has more than caught up with Qutb's caricature. The blatant immorality and brutality of American popular culture today seems to confirm Qutb's description. Moreover, the Hollywood version of America is the only America most Muslims have ever seen. It's an image of outrageous corruption, immorality, violence, and brutality—and it's extremely offensive to the Islamic mind.[1]

THE SLAUGHTER OF INNOCENTS

In October 1954, while Colonel Gamal Abdel Nasser was giving a speech in Alexandria, a Muslim Brotherhood member fired eight shots at him and missed. The nation of Egypt heard the failed assassination attempt live by radio—and Nasser's calm, defiant response caused his popularity to soar. With popular support behind him, Colonel Nasser acted swiftly, ordering a mass roundup of Muslim Brothers. Six ringleaders were tried and hanged, and thousands of Brothers were tossed into prison.

One of those arrested was Sayyid Qutb. He was charged with being a member of the Muslim Brotherhood's Secret Apparatus. With the arrest of so many Muslim Brotherhood members, Nasser believed he had eliminated them as a threat. In *The Looming Tower*, Lawrence Wright explains what the imprisonment of Sayyid Qutb actually accomplished:

> *Stories about Sayyid Qutb's suffering in prison have formed a kind of Passion play for Islamic fundamentalists. It is said that Qutb had a high fever when he was arrested; nonetheless, the state-security officers handcuffed him and forced him to walk to prison. He fainted several times along the way. For hours he was held in a cell with vicious dogs, and then, during long periods of interrogation, he was beaten. . . .*
>
> *Three highly partisan judges, one of them Anwar al-Sadat, oversaw these proceedings. They sentenced Qutb to life in prison, but when his health deteriorated, the sentence was reduced to fifteen years.*[2]

While in prison, Qutb wrote his militant Islamic manifesto called *Ma'alim fi al-Tariq* (*Milestones*), and smuggled it out with the help of family and friends. For years, Qutb's book writings were mimeographed and circulated, becoming an instant underground classic. Finally, in 1964, the different pieces of Qutb's manifesto were edited together and published in book form. The Egyptian government banned the book—but could not suppress it.

In his writings, Sayyid Qutb divided the world into two parts—Islam and *jahiliyya* (pre-Islamic ignorance). Before the Prophet Muhammad delivered his "divine message," the entire world was steeped in *jahiliyya*. Muslims, Qutb said, must reject all aspects of modern, non-Islamic culture, art, literature, law, government, science, and reason. He called Muslims to return to pure, primitive, seventh century Islam. "We need to initiate the movement of Islamic revival in some country," he wrote. "There should be a vanguard which sets out with this determination and then keeps walking the path. I have written *Milestones* for this vanguard, which I consider to be a waiting reality about to be materialized."[3]

Young Muslims reading those revolutionary words were galvanized. They believed they heard the voice of Allah calling them to be that vanguard, and to play that decisive role in history.

Qutb was released from prison, and went right to work rebuilding the Secret Apparatus of the Muslim Brotherhood. Only six months after his release, he was arrested once more and charged with plotting to overthrow the government. As a defendant, Qutb was defiant. During his three month trial, he declared, "The time has come for a Muslim to give his head in order to proclaim the birth of the Islamic movement." He was convicted and sentenced to death. In response, Qutb thanked Allah and told the court, "I performed jihad for fifteen years until I earned this martyrdom."[4]

Sayyid Qutb was executed by hanging on August 29, 1966. His writings and ideology, however, live on. In fact, Qutb's influence remains so strong that his ideology of armed jihad has become known as Qutbism (or Qutbiyya), a radical fundamentalist form of Sunni Islamist ideology. Today, Sayyid Qutb is a hero and a martyr to Islamic fundamentalists, and his writings are studied across the Muslim world, from Morocco to Malaysia. It would not be an exaggeration to say that the 9/11 attacks had their genesis in Sayyid Qutb's strange American odyssey in Greeley, Colorado.

Qutb's writings were a major source of inspiration to Sheik Omar Abdel Rahman, the "blind sheik" who was convicted in 1995 of conspiring to blow up the World Trade Center, the United Nations, and other New York City landmarks. Sayyid Qutb's writings also inspired and influenced Osama bin Laden, the founder of Al-Qaeda, and Ayman al-Zawahiri, who succeeded bin Laden as leader of Al-Qaeda after bin Laden's death. Two other Islamists who influenced bin Laden—Abdallah Azzam (a Palestinian who was killed by a car bomb in 1989) and Saf al-Hawaii, a Saudi revolutionary—were both steeped in the writings of Sayyid Qutb.

One of Qutb's most influential ideas was his interpretation of *takfir*, the principle of excommunication. Qutb came to the conclusion that any Muslim who did not live out his radical interpretation of Islam and the Koran was simply not a genuine Muslim. *Takfir* gave Qutb a way to circumvent the ancient prohibition against overthrowing a Muslim ruler. If a ruler didn't measure up to Qutb's high standards of Islamic perfection, then that ruler was no longer a true Muslim, but an infidel who permits Western-style modernization and pollution of Islam. This gave him the right to kill any Muslim who fell short of his standards of Islamic purity—including a ruler.[5]

The principle of *takfir* explains why Osama bin Laden came to the conclusion that the Islamic government of Saudi Arabia was "illegitimate" on the basis that the Saudis had allowed American troops to walk on sacred Arabian soil. *Takfir* also explains why Islamic terrorists like bin Laden and Zawahiri have killed far more Muslims than Christians or Jews.

For example, on November 19, 1995, Ayman al-Zawahiri carried out a massive car bomb attack against the Egyptian embassy in Islamabad, Pakistan. Sixteen innocent people died in the blast, plus two Al-Qaeda suicide bombers. Sixty were injured. It was Zawahiri's first successful terror attack, and all of the victims were

Muslim. The death of so many innocent Muslims alienated some of Zawahiri's followers, but he offered a Qutbist rationalization, as Lawrence Wright reveals:

> *[Zawahiri] explained that there were no innocents inside the embassy. Everyone who worked there, from the diplomats to the guards, was a supporter of the Egyptian regime, which had detained thousands of fundamentalists and blocked the rule of Islam. Those who carry out the duties of the government must shoulder responsibility for its crimes. No true Muslim could work for such a regime. In this, Zawahiri was repeating the takfir view. . . . Yes, he admitted, there might have been innocent victims—children, true believers—who also died, but Muslims are weak and their enemy is so powerful; in such an emergency, the rules against the slaughter of innocents must be relaxed.*[6]

We should note that Zawahiri was also implicated in the successful plot to assassinate Egyptian President Anwar Sadat in 1981—an historically significant act of *takfir*.

THE WARNING WE IGNORED

Osama bin Laden, a wealthy young Saudi, got his start in the jihadist struggle after the Soviet Union invaded Afghanistan in 1979. He was a scion of the bin Laden family which owned the Saudi Binladin Group, a global oil, construction, and equity management conglomerate with reported earnings of $5 billion annually. Osama bin Laden used his own wealth (and raised millions from other wealthy Arabs) to fund the Afghan Mujahideen insurgents in their struggle against the Soviet occupation. The United States also contributed money, weapons, and intelligence to aid the Mujahideen against the Soviets (the term *mujahideen* means "fighters engaged in jihad").

Osama bin Laden operated a mujahideen training camp in Peshawar, Pakistan, called Maktab al-Khadamat. At the same time, Ayman al-Zawahiri worked as a physician at a Kuwaiti-financed Red Crescent hospital in Peshawar. The hospital was staffed and operated largely by members of the Muslim Brotherhood.[7] The two men met when bin Laden came to the hospital to lecture, and they quickly forged an alliance. Bin Laden was the wealthy, charismatic, devout idealist; Zawahiri was the propagandist and political strategist. Lawrence Wright explains:

> *The dynamic of the two men's relationship made Zawahiri and bin Laden into people they would never have been individually; moreover, the organization they would create, Al-Qaeda, would be a vector of these two forces, one Egyptian and one Saudi.*[8]

On August 11, 1988, bin Laden met with a number of senior leaders of a group called Egyptian Islamic Jihad. Much of the discussion centered on turning Egypt into a fundamentalist Islamic state. But the most momentous decision made at that meeting was a vote to form a new organization to maintain the forward momentum of jihad after the collapse of the Soviet occupation of Afghanistan. That meeting was the first place the name of the new organization was mentioned: Al-Qaeda, which means "the base."[9]

Six months after that meeting, in February 1989, the Soviets left Afghanistan in defeat. Osama bin Laden returned to his hometown of Jeddah, Saudi Arabia, as a conquering hero. Only thirty-one years old, he believed his own press clippings which claimed that he had toppled the Soviet superpower.[10] He gave no credit to American aid and the American-supplied Stinger missiles that knocked scores of Soviet planes and helicopters out of the air. Instead, bin Laden took the credit himself—and he was convinced it was time to take on the next superpower—America.

When Saddam Hussein launched the Iraqi invasion of Kuwait on August 2, 1990, the Saudi royal family feared that Saudi Arabia might be Iraq's next target. Brimming with self-confidence, Osama bin Laden met with Prince Sultan bin Abdelaziz al-Saud, the Saudi defense minister, and told him not to rely on the American unbelievers for defense. Instead, let bin Laden and his army of mujahideen followers (he claimed they numbered a hundred thousand men) defend the border. The prince was skeptical and pointed out that the Iraqis had four thousand tanks, plus missiles and chemical weapons. Besides, there were no mountains and caves in the desert as there were in Afghanistan. How, asked the prince, did bin Laden propose to fight Saddam Hussein?

"We fight him with faith," bin Laden replied.[11]

The Saudi government refused bin Laden's offer, and turned to the U.S. for help. The presence of American troops on Saudi soil enraged bin Laden. He denounced the "unjust American occupation of the land of the two mosques" (Mecca and Medina) and denounced the Saudis for profaning the sacred soil of Arabia.[12] From that point on, Osama bin Laden turned his attention primarily to plotting attacks against the West, especially the United States.

In August 1996, bin Laden issued a *fatwa*, or religious edict, against the United States. Published in *Al Quds Al Arabi*, a London-based Arabic newspaper, the *fatwa* was called "Declaration of War against the Americans Occupying the Land of the Two Holy Places." It was a declaration of jihad to expel American troops from Islamic lands.[13] And in February 1998, bin Laden and Zawahiri issued another fatwa calling on Muslims to "kill the Americans and plunder their money wherever and whenever they find it." They also said that the slaughter of Americans and their allies was "an individual duty for every Muslim."[14]

"Bin Laden declared war on us," former New York City Mayor Rudy Giuliani said on NBC's *Meet the Press*. "We didn't hear it. I thought it was pretty clear at the time, but a lot of people couldn't see it."[15] And because we didn't hear and see it when Osama bin Laden declared war against our entire culture, we were caught napping when 9/11 exploded on our collective consciousness.

Osama bin Laden warned us. We didn't believe him.

WHY DO THEY HATE US?

One of the most admirable aspects of America's collective response to the 9/11 attacks on the United States has been that we refused to allow the War on Terror to become a religious war. On September 17, six days after the attacks, President Bush went to the Islamic Center in Washington and said, "These acts of violence against innocents violate the fundamental tenets of the Islamic faith. And it's important for my fellow Americans to understand that. . . . The face of terror is not the true faith of Islam."[16]

A few days later, President Bush addressed a joint session of Congress and said, "I also want to speak tonight directly to Muslims throughout the world. We respect your faith . . . and those who commit evil in the name of Allah, blaspheme the name of Allah. The terrorists are traitors to their own faith, trying, in effect, to hijack Islam itself. The enemy of America is not our many Muslim friends. . . . Our enemy is a radical network of terrorists, and every government that supports them. Our War on Terror begins with Al-Qaeda, but it does not end there. It will not end until every terrorist group of global reach has been found, stopped, and defeated."[17]

Americans need to realize that an extreme sect of Islam has declared war on Western civilization, on the United States of America, and on Christians and Jews. While the War on Terror is not a religious war—that is, not a war of one religion versus another religion—we must recognize that religious beliefs and ideology drive the hostility at the heart of the conflict.

We, as Americans and as Christians, are not at war with Islam. But an extremist form of Islam clearly chooses to be at war with us. To pretend otherwise is to be in denial of the facts—and denial is deadly, as the events of 9/11 have shown. Though we do not choose to be at war with Islam, reality is in the perception of the perpetrators—the Islamists themselves.

Again and again, we Americans have taken up the cause of oppressed Muslim people. In the 1980s, America helped the Muslim Mujahideen defend themselves against the Soviet occupation of Afghanistan. In the early 1990s, America defended Muslim Bosnians against genocidal attacks by Serbs in the former Yugoslavia. In the late 1990s, America defended Muslim Kosovo Albanians against Serb-instigated genocide in Kosovo. When America stationed troops in Saudi Arabia during the first Gulf War, we did so to prevent Muslims from killing Muslims. America liberated Muslim Kuwait and Muslim Iraq from the tyrannical regime of Saddam Hussein. Most recently, America and its NATO allies helped liberate Muslim Libya from the tyranny of Colonel Muammar Gaddafi.

In spite of all the American blood and treasure that has been sacrificed to defend oppressed Muslim people around the world, the Muslim extremists still hate America and want to do us harm. The extremists don't just hate our government. *They hate US.* Osama bin Laden and Ayman al-Zawahiri issued *fatwas* ordering all Muslims to kill *all* Americans, and *all* American allies, wherever they might be found. Radical Islamist hatred toward Americans is rooted in ignorance, false perceptions, culture clash, and a deep religious divide—but we must never forget that their hatred is very real and it threatens each of us.

Radical Islamists resent the West for a variety of reasons—including some quite valid reasons. There is a history of Western (mostly European) nations colonizing and exploiting parts of the Arab world, especially for its oil resources. But much of the Islamist hatred toward us is rooted in emotion and prejudice, not reality. One reason radical fundamentalist Muslims say "Freedom can go to hell" is that they believe American-style freedom has produced immorality, irreligion, and outright blasphemy in our culture. They envy America's economic success—but they hate what they see as American greed, arrogance, and exploitation. They hate America's power and influence in the world because we use that power to support the state of Israel—and in their thinking that amounts to the oppression of the Muslims in Palestine.

The radical Islamists also despise Americans for being (in their minds) weak, soft, decadent, and impatient. Muslim extremists have shown a willingness to work patiently for decades and even centuries to achieve an Islamic victory over Western civilization. Americans, by contrast, demand immediate results—or immediate withdrawal. They have heard American media pundits and congressional leaders saying that "America should declare victory in Iraq and Afghanistan and go home," without regard to whether victory has been secured. To the Muslim mind, such statements stand as proof of a yellow stain of weakness in the American character.

The religious divide between the West and the Muslim world should not be underestimated—even though much of the Islamists' views of America and Western culture are wildly distorted. Osama bin Laden's statements about America are saturated with religious imagery and theological language. In May 1998, just two months before the U.S. embassy bombings in Kenya and Tanzania, bin Laden told ABC News reporter John Miller:

> *The call to wage war against America was made because America has spear-headed the crusade against the Islamic nation, sending tens of thousands of its troops to the land of the two Holy Mosques over and above its meddling in its affairs and its politics, and its support of the oppressive, corrupt and tyrannical regime that is in control. These are the reasons behind the singling out of America as a target.*[18]

Osama bin Laden's use of the word "crusade" is an explicitly religious term. It demonstrates his twisted view that America today is carrying on the tradition of the Crusades—a series of wars for control of the Holy Land. Those wars were conducted during the 11th through 13th centuries, and were ended long before the United States ever came on the scene—and even before Columbus discovered America. The notion that America is a theocratic "Christian nation" still carrying out "the crusade against the Islamic nation" would be laughable if it weren't such a dangerous notion.

When bin Laden speaks of "the Islamic nation," he does not mean one specific political entity, such as Iraq or Saudi Arabia. *All* the nations and peoples of the Muslim world are, in the Muslim mind, "the Islamic nation." Islam is comprised of many nations and ethnicities, and the boundaries between nations are nothing but territorial divisions imposed by Western colonial mapmakers. Once the entire world is united under Sharia law and Islamic religion, there will only be one nation—the Islamic nation.

To bin Laden and his fellow Muslim fundamentalists, the war against Western civilization has always been a war of Islam versus unbelief and unbelievers—and this war is regarded by the Islamists as a noble cause. As bin Laden went on to say:

> *Our call is the call of Islam that was revealed to Muhammad. It is a call to all mankind. We have been entrusted with good cause to follow in the footsteps of the Messenger [Muhammad] and to communicate his message to all nations. It is an invitation that we extend to all the nations to embrace Islam, the religion that calls for justice, mercy and fraternity among all nations. . . . We are entrusted to spread this message and to extend that call to all the people. We, nonetheless, fight against their governments and all those who approve of the injustice they practice against us. We fight the governments that are bent on attacking our religion and on stealing our wealth and on hurting our feelings.*[19]

Bin Laden also stated that Al-Qaeda's acts of terrorism were "of the commendable kind" that were "directed at the tyrants and the aggressors and enemies of Allah. . . . Tyrants and oppressors who subject the Arab nation to aggression ought to be punished."[20] We have to wonder how many actual "tyrants and oppressors" of Muslims actually died in the World Trade Center and the Pentagon on 9/11. The ability of the radical Islamists to rationalize the slaughter of innocent people as some sort of holy service to Allah is beyond the comprehension of Western minds.

OTHER VOICES FROM THE ISLAMIC WORLD

Some voices in our culture have been quick to point out that the radical Islamists do not represent all of Islam. That's true—but it is equally true that mainstream Muslim society has not been vocal in condemning 9/11 and other acts of terror. One prominent Muslim group that claims to speak out against terror is the Council on American-Islamic Relations (CAIR). The group has waged a vigorous public relations campaign on behalf of the Islamic faith and culture in the wake of 9/11. CAIR claims on its website that it has engaged in "persistent and consistent condemnation of terror" from 1994 until the present day. "CAIR is a natural enemy of violent extremists," the organization says.[21]

Yet a statement released by CAIR just three days after the 9/11 attacks said, "If such attacks were carried out by a Muslim—as some biased groups claim—then we, in the name of our religion, deny the act and incriminate the perpetrator." The executive director of CAIR's New York branch claimed that the 9/11 attacks were part of a conspiracy to discredit Islam, explaining, "I believe that many of the names of the terrorists are people impersonating innocent Muslims and Arabs." And CAIR spokesman Ibrahim Hooper told Salon.com just days after the attacks, "We condemn terrorism. We condemn the attacks on the buildings. If Osama Bin Laden was behind it, we condemn him by name." When ABC News reporter Jake Tapper asked why Hooper qualified his statement about bin Laden with the word "if," Hooper replied that he resented the question. It wasn't until December 2001, when bin Laden himself claimed credit for the attacks, that CAIR finally acknowledging Al-Qaeda's role in 9/11.[22]

In November 2001, CAIR sponsored a "Know Your Rights" workshop for Muslims in San Diego. At the event, Muslim attorney Randall Hamud said, "There's still no evidence that Muslims carried out 9/11." He also said that anti-terrorism statements released by the Fiqh Council of North America (an organization which interprets Islamic law in North America and endorsed by CAIR) were nothing but public relations gestures. If Muslim religious leaders in America wanted to sign those statements, fine. "You just need to read it and sign it and decide what you want to do with it. But it's a *fatwa* I think for popular consumption in the United States," an attempt to "get the [Muslim] religion off the hook with the media." Hamud didn't expect these public relations gestures to do much good, however, because the American media "is controlled by basically Zionists."[23]

Though CAIR portrays itself as a moderate Muslim advocacy group, CAIR and its leaders are part of the Palestine Committee, which was created by the Muslim Brotherhood in the United States to generate support and fund-raising for the Palestinian political party and terror group Hamas.[24]

Queen Rania Al-Abdullah of Jordan appeared on the Oprah Winfrey program on October 5, 2001. Oprah asked her, "When this first happened on September 11, I think it came as a shock to so many of us that other people in the world hated us so much. Can you help explain that to us?" The thirty-one-year-old queen of Jordan responded:

> *I think it's very important that you realize that for the majority of Muslims, they do not hate Americans. They do not hate the American way of life. In fact, many countries look at the American model as one that needs to be replicated, one that they aspire to achieve.*
>
> *We are talking about a minority of people who feel that they have been unjustly treated by the United States. Some of them feel that U.S. foreign policy might have been partial and not completely fair to all parties involved, and they wanted their voice to be heard. Unfortunately, the means that they have used are ones that are condemned all over the Arab world.*[25]

It's true that terrorist acts are perpetrated by an extremist minority within the Muslim community—but where is the voice of the majority? Where is the condemnation of terrorism that we should hear from the moderate, mainstream Muslim community? Are the moderates afraid to speak up and condemn the extremists in their midst? Are they afraid of what the Islamists will do to them or their families if they speak out against extremism? Whatever the reason, Muslim condemnation of extremism and terrorism has been muted—yet Muslim advocacy groups like CAIR have been quick to accuse the American government and American society of acts of bigotry and "Islamophobia."

Even in mainstream Muslim communities, young Muslim-Americans are being indoctrinated in some very un-American ways of thinking. A month after the 9/11 attacks, *Washington Post* reporter Marc Fisher talked to young American-born Muslims, all U.S. citizens, at the Muslim Community School in Potomac. They had no conception of why America is an exceptional nation, no conception of how great and rare it is to enjoy American-style freedom, no conception of how blessed they were to live under the protection of the American Constitution and Bill of Rights.

One Muslim seventh-grader named Miriam shrugged off the specialness of being an American citizen, asking, "What does it really mean to be an American? Being American is just being born in this country." Ibrahim, an eighth-grader, added, "Being an American means nothing to me. I'm not even proud of telling my cousins in Pakistan that I'm American." An eleventh-grader named Kamal, however, said, "I love being an American," but added that he felt ambivalent, wondering if "maybe we might have done things to [the terrorists'] country that weren't right, that led to" the 9/11 attacks.[26]

Reporter Marc Fisher interviewed the principal of the Muslim school, asking if he thought that Osama bin Laden was responsible for 9/11. The principal responded by shifting the discussion to the subject of Israel. "I don't know Osama bin Laden," he said. "But whatever is said about him, I want it said about the Israeli prime minister. If we're going after terrorism, let's go at it at the roots, not the branches."[27]

These were common responses from the Muslim community after 9/11: Muslims denied or expressed skepticism that Muslims were involved. Or they suggested that American foreign policy was really to blame for 9/11. Or they suggested that there is a moral equivalence between Israel and Al-Qaeda. Around the world, however, large parts of the Muslim community openly applauded the hijackers as heroes and martyrs in the cause of Islam:

- In Egypt, university students burned U.S. and Israeli flags and chanted, "Arrogant George Bush, tomorrow you will reap the fruits of your war!"[28]
- In Indonesia, hundreds of Islamic activists clashed with police outside the U.S. Embassy in Jakarta.[29]
- In Sudan, protesters tried to storm the U.S. Embassy in Khartoum.[30]
- In the Philippines, about 5,000 Muslim protesters chanted "Death to America" and "Long live Osama bin Laden" as they burned American flags and a picture of President Bush.[31]
- In Malaysia, the Pan-Malaysia Islamic Party called upon the United Nations to declare the United States a terrorist state.[32]
- In the Gaza strip, two Palestinians were killed and 76 injured in protests against America.[33]

As the United States geared up to respond to Al-Qaeda terrorist camps and the Taliban regime that harbored Al-Qaeda in Afghanistan, the secretary-general of the Arab League, Amr Moussa, said in Qatar, "Any military strike to any Arab country will lead to serious consequences and will be considered an aggression against Arab states."

ECHOES OF THE AYATOLLAH KHOMEINI

The response from the Arab world as a whole, and especially from certain militant factions of Islam, is reminiscent of the rhetoric heard during the Iranian Revolution of 1979. After the taking of fifty-two Americans as hostages in Tehran, the Ayatollah Khomeini declared, "This is not a struggle between the United States and Iran. It is a struggle between Islam and the infidels. . . . The governments of the world should know that Islam cannot be defeated. Islam will be victorious in all the countries of the world, and Islam and all the teachings of the Koran will prevail all over the world."

Khomeini was not expressing some perverted view of Islam. He was expressing what lies at the heart of all fervent believers in Islam. The global supremacy of the Koran is basic Islamic doctrine.

Though the words of Khomeini made little sense to Westerners, to Muslims he made perfect sense. Some Islamic moderates wish Khomeini had not been so blunt and candid about Islamic teachings. But Islamic moderates are becoming a minority on the world scene. It is the extremist Muslims who grab the headlines and set the course of events. As never before, extreme Islamists are affirming their spiritual identity and flexing their political and economic muscles. Their goal is the same as the Ayatollah Khomeini's goal—to take part in the struggle between Islam and the infidels, to see that the teachings of the Koran prevail across the world.

Islam is spreading faster today than at any other time in history, and currently boasts about 1.5 billion adherents. Roughly one out of five people in the world are Muslims. Islam reigns as the dominant religion in forty-five nations. The spread of Islam as a whole has encouraged the rise of militant Islam—and militant Islam is the original and authentic Islam of the seventh century.

WE MUST OPEN OUR EYES

We can no longer afford to be ignorant and naïve about the world around us. The 9/11 attacks have taken away our innocence about the world. We must open our eyes to see that the real cause of terrorism is *hate*. This hate is a belief system, a way of seeing the world. People attack what they hate, and they seek to either destroy the object of their hate or subjugate it. And that is what the Islamists seek to do to Western civilization.

Militant Islamists hate all that Christians believe, stand for, hope for, and love. They hate our freedom. They hate our message of Christlike love, which they see as weakness. They hate our Christian Gospel, which they see as blasphemy. The concept of a secular, tolerant society that guarantees religious liberty is alien to them. They are convinced that the entire world must come under the domination of the Koran and Sharia law. They seek the utter destruction of Christianity and the subjugation of Christians.

Even if the radical fringe of Islam could be silenced or defeated militarily, it would not go away. New expressions would emerge—and it is possible that some of these new expressions of the Islamist quest for world domination could produce even more violence than we have already seen. Imagine, for a moment, if some future version of Al-Qaeda possessed nuclear weapons and a means of delivering them or smuggling them into the United States—what would happen then?

It's not enough to defeat militant Islam on the battlefield. The War on Terror must ultimately be fought as a battle for the human mind and heart. We are not merely engaged in a war to dismantle funding sources, terrorist training camps, lines of communication, and command structure. Ultimately, we are in an ideological struggle of immense importance—and eternal significance.

We must open our eyes to understand who this enemy is and how this enemy intends to destroy us.

3

THE PROPHET AND THE KORAN

Relatively little is known about the people and culture of pre-Islamic Arabia—the peninsula now occupied by Saudi Arabia, Oman, the United Arab Emirates, Qatar, Bahrain, and Yemen. Ancient writings and inscriptions give us tantalizing hints—but few details—about the people who lived in Arabia during Old Testament times. We know hardly anything about the cultures of the Thamud tribes of the Iron Age, or the Minaean kingdom or the south Arabian kingdom of Sheba, whose queen visited King Solomon and witnessed the splendor of Jerusalem (see 1 Kings 10; 2 Chronicles 9).

Long before the birth of Islam in the seventh century A.D., a number of civilizations and kingdoms flourished on the Arabian Peninsula. Streams of caravan traders routinely crossed the vast Arabian Desert, making it the commercial land-link between the Mediterranean and Far East. Three major towns were settled in northern Arabia to service this trade route. The most prosperous and important of these towns was Mecca, which became a bustling city by 600 A.D.

The people of pre-Islamic Arabia practiced various forms of idolatry. Each of the nomadic Bedouin tribes living in the vast desert worshiped a variety of deities and nature spirits, although a few gods were revered in common. For centuries, the Arabians withstood every attempt by Christians from Syria and Egypt to convert them.

In A.D. 602, the declining Eastern Roman Empire (the Byzantine Empire) went to war against the faded power of the Sassanid dynasty of the Persian Empire. The long and devastating Byzantine–Sassanid War of 602–628 was the last gasp of these two once-great empires. Near the end of this war, both empires were bankrupt and weakened militarily. At the same time, a virulent plague swept through both empires (the plague of Justinian, probably a strain of the bubonic plague), killing thousands of people per day.

At the same time as the Byzantine–Sassanid War, a religious and military leader, Muhammad ibn Abd Allah, rose up in Arabia and founded the religion of Islam. Muhammad united the various warring tribes of Arabia, built up an army of 10,000 fierce warriors, and became revered by his followers as a messenger and prophet of Allah. As one historian observed, the "unnecessarily prolonged" Byzantine-Sassanid War created a power vacuum that "opened the way for Islam."[1]

THE KAABA AND THE WELL OF ZAMZAM

Muhammad was born in the city of Mecca in A.D. 570. At the time of his birth, the black stone cube known as the Kaaba had existed for about a thousand years as a shrine to the many tribal deities of the Arabian tribes. *Kaaba* literally means "cube" or "the heel of the foot." It is a large cubical structure in a massive courtyard in Mecca that once served as a site of pagan worship by Arabia's pagan tribes. Hubal, the most important deity of Mecca's ruling Quraysh tribe, was worshipped at the Kaaba.

According Muhammad's claim, he received revelations from Allah through the Archangel Gabriel in A.D. 610, and began preaching and calling for the people of Mecca to turn from paganism to his new monotheistic religion. Muhammad was persecuted for thirteen years, and finally left Mecca with his followers and moved to Yathrib (the city now known as Medina). Muhammad and his followers later returned and conquered Mecca, destroying the pagan images. Muhammad declared Mecca to be the holiest site in Islam, and ordered the city closed to all non-Muslims—a law that is enforced to this day. After conquering Mecca, Muhammad went on to unify the entire Arabian Peninsula under the banner of Islam.

After Muhammad expelled the former pagan deities from the Kaaba, he made the Kaaba the central shrine of the new Islamic religion. The Kaaba remains the focal point of Islamic worship today. Those who make the pilgrimage to Mecca must walk around the Kaaba seven times, kissing and touching the Black Stone. Muslims know this site as "the house of Allah."

According to tradition, the Kaaba was built by Abraham and his son Ishmael, after Ishmael moved to Arabia. Tradition states that when Ishmael's mother Hagar wandered in the desert with her son Ishmael, they reached Mecca nearly dead of thirst. While Hagar looked for water between two hills, Ishmael waited in the shade of a tree. Then, as Ishmael cried out with thirst, water bubbled up under his feet and became a stream of sweet, flowing water. The place where the spring supposedly appeared is known as the Well of Zamzam, located just twenty yards east of the Kaaba, within the enclosure of the Masjid al-Haram, the world's largest mosque. The well still gives water today.

The legend doesn't end there. Abraham supposedly made a visit to Zamzam to offer his son Ishmael as a sacrifice. This, of course, is a significant diversion from the Genesis account in which the son of sacrifice is Isaac, not Ishmael, and the place of sacrifice is Mount Moriah, not Zamzam. Islamic tradition holds that when Abraham was prevented from sacrificing Ishmael, Abraham and Ishmael together built the Kaaba at God's command.

However, we know that Jews, who lived in Arabia at the time the Kaaba was built, refused to participate in the pagan worship that took place there. The pagan origins of the Kaaba refute the Islamic claim that Abraham and Ishmael built the Kaaba. There is no evidence in the Bible that Abraham ever came as far south as Mecca. Nevertheless, the Kabba quickly became the focal point of early Islamic rituals.

THE SUPREME PROPHET OF ISLAM

The Arabian Peninsula was unusually resistant to the spread of the Christian Gospel during the early Christian era. There are two reasons for this.

First, the idolatry practiced in Mecca was a mixture of pagan and Hebrew ideas. The tenets of Judaism were familiar to the Arabians, and the worship at the Kaaba was based in part on Jewish patriarchal traditions. There was just enough watered-down Judaism in the religious legends of that region that the people were immune to the truth of Christianity, which is the fulfillment of Judaism.

Second, Arabian Christianity in the seventh century was corrupted and distorted by Gnostic heresies and divisions over the nature of Christ. Some of these heresies taught that Jesus was a mere human being who achieved divinity through mystical knowledge. Though some Arab Christians revered the New Testament as God's revealed Word, many embraced the Gnostic heresies, so that the "Christianity" they practiced was weak and unbiblical. So the Christianity of Arabia had little appeal to the pagans in that region.

Even though Arabia was largely closed to the Gospel, the people of Arabia were spiritually hungry and ready for a religious rebirth. The potential for a dramatic religious transformation existed. The only question was: Who would mold and shape that transformation—and in what direction?

In a cave at the foot of Mount Hira near Mecca, a man named Muhammad Ibn Abd Allah, from the Hashemite clan of the Quraysh tribe, stepped into this religious vacuum in 610 A.D. Muhammad stepped onto the scene with a vision and a message.

I can't help wondering: What if Muhammad had embraced genuine Christian truth as it was being preached in Europe and elsewhere? I think it's likely that Christian history might revere the memory of a "Saint Muhammad"—perhaps a "Muhammad the Martyr," an Arabian Apostle Paul, the man who laid the foundation stone of the Arabian church. But it was not to be. Instead, Muhammad founded a religion that has become one the fiercest enemies that Christendom has ever known.

Islam begins and ends with a two-fold proclamation called the *Shahada*: "There is no god but Allah, and Muhammad is the Messenger (Prophet) of God." To understand the first part of that confession, we must understand the nature of the Messenger.

Who, then, was Muhammad?

Born in Mecca in the autumn of A.D. 570, Muhammad received his name from his mother and grandfather. It is a rare name among Arabs, meaning "highly praised." His father, a trader named Abdullah, died before Muhammad was born. According to the custom of Meccan aristocracy, the infant Muhammad was sent to the desert to be wet-nursed by a Bedouin mother. Muhammad spent most of his childhood years with his nurse, Halima, among the Beni Saad tribesmen.

At age five Muhammad returned to his mother's home in Mecca, but she became ill and died. His care then became the responsibility of Abdul Muttelib, his grandfather. Abdul Muttelib loved Muhammad very much, but he died soon after Muhammad's arrival. Guardianship of the child went to Abu Talib, Muhammad's uncle.

When Muhammad was twelve, he took his first business trip to Syria with Abu Talib. The journey took several months and was filled with many rich experiences. During the journey, Muhammad visited Jewish settlements in Palestine and Christian communities in Syria. He undoubtedly saw Christian churches with their crosses and other symbols of the Christian faith.

In his youth in Mecca, Muhammad was also influenced by Jewish and Christian poets and preachers who expounded on the essence of their faith to the crowds at the annual fairs in the city. These recitations did not offer much theological depth, but they were emotionally powerful and served to give Muhammad a smattering of information (and misinformation) about Judaism and Christianity. Muhammad's later writings reveal far more familiarity with Judaism than with Christianity, probably because Judaism was more prominent in the region.

It's also important to note that there was very little religious tolerance in that culture and time. Christians and Jews regarded each other with disdain and suspicion—and both Christians and Jews spurned the Arab tribes as heathens who were destined to suffer the wrath of an offended God.

Little else is known about Muhammad's early years. Like other young men, he probably tended sheep and goats in the neighboring hills and valleys. Authorities agree that he was respected for his serious and thoughtful nature, and for his personal integrity. He was nicknamed al-Amin, "the trustworthy one." He appears to have lived a quiet, peaceful life with the family of Abu Talib.

At age twenty-five, while traveling the same route he had trekked earlier with his uncle, Muhammad led a caravan expedition to Syria on behalf of a widow named Khadija. On this journey, Muhammad took even more time to delve into the practices of the Syrian Christians and conversing with the monks and clergy he met. Later, while writing the Koran, he spoke of these Christians with respect and even praise. He had no sympathy, however, for their doctrine, and little genuine understanding of the teachings of Jesus Christ.

MUHAMMAD'S VIEW OF JESUS

Muhammad found two major stumbling blocks in the Christian message, as it was presented to him by the Syrian Christians. One stumbling block was the role of Mary. The other was the divinity of Jesus. Sir William Muir wrote that the Gospel Muhammad heard from the Syrian monks was tragically "altered and distorted." Muir writes:

> *Instead of the simple majesty of the Gospel—as a revelation of God reconciling mankind to Himself through His Son—the sacred dogma of the Trinity was forced upon the traveler with . . . misleading and offensive zeal . . . and the worship of Mary [was] exhibited in so gross a form as to leave the impression upon the mind of Mahomet [Muhammad] that she was held to be a goddess, if not the third Person [of the Trinity] and consort of the Deity.*[2]

The ancient Arab pagans believed that the gods could have sexual intercourse with human women, thereby producing children called "the sons of the gods" or "the sons of God." Muhammad rejected the idea that God could father a child through a human woman. Christians believe that Mary conceived Jesus, the Son of God—but her conception was not the result of sexual intercourse (as in the pagan myths) but the work of the Holy Spirit. Because Muhammad misunderstood the virgin birth, he rejected the belief that Jesus was born of God, and refused to call Jesus "the Son of God." Instead, he called Jesus "the son of Mary."

Upon his return from this commercial venture, which proved to be financially successful, Muhammad married Khadija. She was fifteen years older than Muhammad and had been married twice before. She remained Muhammad's only wife as long as she lived and she bore him two sons and a daughter. After her death, Muhammad took nine other wives and more concubines.

A MID-LIFE VISION IN A CAVE

As he approached forty, Muhammad spent more and more time pondering the age-old question, "What is truth?" His soul was perplexed, and he was also troubled by the social injustice he saw among the clans in his own tribe.

Muhammad's Hashemite clan was the poorer of two main clans in the Quraysh tribe. He was distressed to see the rival clan growing rich and strong, even as his own grew weaker. One of his aims was to create a more equitable social system that would protect the poor, the widows, and the orphans.

Troubled in spirit, Muhammad frequently went alone into the hills near Mecca to meditate in solitude. His favorite place was a cave about two or three miles north of the city. According to the account of Ibn Ishaq, the first biographer of Muhammad, the future prophet was sound asleep when the angel Gabriel appeared and commanded, "Recite!"

Startled and afraid, Muhammad asked, "What shall I recite?" He immediately felt his throat tighten as if the angel were choking him.

"Recite!" the angel commanded, and again Muhammad felt the angel's grip.

A third time the angel commanded, "Recite! Recite in the name of the Lord, the Creator who created man from a clot of blood! Recite! Your Lord is most gracious. It is he who has taught man by the pen that which he does not know." From that day forward, Muhammad felt compelled to preach the word of "Allah," his name for the Creator. The first section of the Koran has a title that literally means "recitation." Muhammad's own account of his revelation is worth noting. He said:

> *Inspiration cometh in one of two ways; sometimes Gabriel communicateth the Revelation to me, as one man to another, and this is easy; at other times, it is like the ringing of a bell, penetrating my very heart, and rending me; and this it is which afflicteth me the most.*[3]

Muhammad returned from this experience in the cave and told Khadija that God had commissioned him to preach. She immediately consulted with her *hanif* kinsman (a hanif is a holy man who holds to the pure monotheistic beliefs of the patriarch Ibrahim, or Abraham). The *hanif* listened to the story, and then declared that Muhammad had been chosen, like Moses, to receive divine inspiration and to be the prophet of his people. As long as Khadija lived, she gave unfailing support to Muhammad, even though many in Mecca rejected his message.

The people of Mecca initially scoffed at Muhammad because he was illiterate. But Muhammad turned his inability to read to his advantage by stating that his illiteracy substantiated his claim to have received his revelations directly from

Allah. Down through the centuries, Muslims have regarded Muhammad's vision as sacred and his recitation as a miraculous act of God, though Muhammad himself did not work any miracles. Muhammad also turned his lack of miraculous acts to his own advantage. He stressed his ordinary humanity as a prophet. As a result, Muslims take pride in the fact that they do not call themselves Muhammadans, because such a term would imply that they worship Muhammad as Christians worship Christ.

Even before his first revelation, Muhammad had a reputation for being wise and devout. One of the legends of Islam illustrates why he was considered wise. According to tradition, Muhammad looked out from his balcony one day to see members of four clans engaged in a dispute as to who would carry the sacred Black Stone, which Muslims claim descended from paradise during the time of Adam (some, in fact, believe it to be a meteorite). The Arabs wanted to place the Black Stone in its new niche in the Kaaba, but their bickering made it impossible to carry out the task. Muhammad came down from the balcony and proposed a compromise that was agreeable to all. He instructed the representative of each tribe to lift one corner of a blanket, then he placed the Black Stone on the blanket. So all four tribes carried the Black Stone, and when they reached the Kaaba, Muhammad himself set the Black Stone in its niche, where it remains today.

After receiving his initial revelation and recitation, Muhammad became fearful and depressed when he received no further messages from God. He became so distressed that he contemplated suicide. Accounts of the time of Muhammad's depression are a bit confused, and this period is thought to have lasted anywhere from six months to three years. During this period, Muhammad felt uncertain about himself and his mission.

MUHAMMAD EMERGES FROM OBSCURITY AND GOES TO MEDINA

By the time he was forty-four, Muhammad had emerged from both his doubts and his obscurity. He asserted unequivocally that Allah had ordained him as a prophet and had commissioned him to go to the people of Arabia. He recited his warnings, exhortations, and messages as coming directly from Allah. He taught that Allah was the one God and that men must thank him for their existence and worship him only. He preached equality and justice before God, and he warned that a Day of Judgment was coming for all men.

Muhammad's wife Khadija was his first convert, followed by his slave Zaid, whom he later adopted as a son. Then he converted two of his most trusted friends, Abu Bakr and Umar, who later succeeded him as leaders of the Muslim movement.

In Mecca, however, Muhammad met with stiff opposition from his own tribe. His people refused to acknowledge him as a prophet and refused to give up idol worship.

The Jews in the area, however, did not oppose Muhammad as much as his own tribesmen did. So Muhammad developed a close relationship with the Jews, some of whom acknowledged him as a prophet, others as the messiah descended from Abraham. The majority of Jews took a "wait and see" attitude. Muhammad incorporated into his new religion many Jewish traditions and a number of Old Testament stories—though it's not clear whether he was influenced by them or included Jewish traditions merely to gain favor with the Jews. In any case, the Koran includes the story of Abraham and Ishmael, Hagar and Ishmael, stories about Joseph and Jacob, and the account of the destruction of Sodom and Gomorrah. In the Koran, these stories are usually mixed with other stories, myths, and legends that come from non-biblical sources.

Muhammad's unsuccessful attempt to win the hearts of the Meccans was deeply frustrating to him. In his discouragement, Muhammad and his followers moved to the city of Medina in a mass migration known in Islamic history as the *hijra*. In Medina, Muhammad struck a more responsive chord in the people's hearts. The city had a large community of Jews; in fact, three of the five tribes living in the city were Jewish. The Jews of Medina had often warned the Arab tribes in the area that the coming Messiah would punish them for their wickedness and injustices. Unlike the more worldly Meccans, the people of Medina were ripe for Muhammad's message, especially his message of a monotheistic religion.

In Medina, Muhammad successfully brought Jews and pagans together under the banner of Allah. He managed to please the Jews by adopting some of their religious rites. The Jewish Day of Atonement became the Muslim fast day of Ashura. Prayer was increased from two to three times daily to accommodate the Jewish morning, midday, and evening prayers—and were later increased to five times daily. Muslims held a public service, such as the Jews had in their synagogues. The Muslims declared Friday to be their holy day, an accommodation to the Jewish Sabbath which began at sundown on Friday. Muhammad even adopted the Jewish call to prayer—but instead of using the trumpet of the Jews, he chose to use a human prayer-caller or *muezzin* who would cry out the call to prayer from the minaret of a mosque.

Later, when many of the Jews began to reject Muhammad's message, he became angry and accused the Jews of rejecting the truth. He claimed Jewish property as his own. By the time he left Medina, Muslim Arabs controlled the city, and the two Arab tribes that had lost virtually everything to the Jews were restored to power and prestige.

Muhammad never showed an interest in courting Christians to his cause, or in adopting Christian rituals and beliefs, yet he was not hostile toward Christians. In fact, he had a generally favorable attitude toward Christian people, even though he strongly disagreed with the tenets of their faith.

Tradition holds that shortly after Muhammad's initial revelation, Khadija's cousin, Waraqa ibn Naufal—a Christian scholar—translated portions of the New Testament into Hebrew and Arabic. Waraqa tutored Muhammad in the Christian faith, but he died soon after beginning his mentoring relationship with Muhammad. Some attribute Muhammad's "confused period" (which occurred soon after his initial revelation) to an intense personal struggle with the Christian ideas Waraqa tried to teach him.

THE PROGRESSION OF MUHAMMAD'S TEACHINGS

There was a step-by-step progression to Muhammad's teachings, and at each stage he became increasingly more extreme and grandiose:

First, Muhammad sought to warn and reform the pagan society of the Arabian Peninsula. He felt a burden to call people to turn to the one true God, the God of Abraham.

Next, he equated his revelation with that of Judaism and Christianity, perceiving himself to be on an equal footing with Moses and Jesus.

Finally, Muhammad saw himself and his message as the final word of God that superseded both Judaism and Christianity. He was convinced that, because the Jews and Christians had moved away from God's intended purposes, God had sent him to proclaim the ultimate revelation. He claimed that his teachings rose triumphant over both the Law and the Gospel.

In the end, Muhammad claimed that Islam was the universal faith—a faith that started with Abraham (whom Muhammad called the "first Muslim"). At the same time, Muhammad was strict in his belief that the new message of Allah was announced in the Arabic language and intended for Arabs, who henceforth would have a prophet and a holy book of their own.

To Muhammad, the Jew was to follow the Law and the Christian was to hold fast to the Gospel. Both Jews and Christians were to admit the apostleship of Muhammad and the authority of the Koran as being equal to their own respective prophets, teachers, and writings. As the Koran states: "Say: O People of the Book! Ye do not stand upon any sure ground until you observe both the Torah and the Gospel as well as that which has been now sent down unto you from your Lord" (Koran 5:68).

At first, the Jews living on the Arabian Peninsula saw Muhammad as their ally. This alliance between Muhammad and the Arabian Jews lasted as long as Muhammad saw his mission as a protest against error and superstition, because the Jews also opposed error and superstition.

But as Islam became more exclusive and demanded to have priority over other religions, the Jews backed away. By the time Muhammad began his farewell pilgrimage, he had barred Christians and Jews from visiting the Kaaba. He claimed that it was a "divine command" that non-Muslims be excluded until they confessed the supremacy of Islam or consented to pay tribute.

Muhammad initially used the ancient legend about Abraham and Ishmael to legitimize his new religion. He argued that Islam's relationship to Abraham made Islam the equal of Judaism and Christianity. Later in life, however, Muhammad revised this claim, stating that his revelation superseded both Judaism and Christianity and had become the final revelation of God.

THE KORAN—THE SUPREME BOOK OF ISLAM

Muslims believe that God has spoken to the human race throughout the ages, and specifically through those called prophets. Muslims regard Muhammad as the *final* prophet of God. Islam acknowledges other prophets before Muhammad's time, including the great figures of the Old and New Testaments such as Abraham, Moses, David, and Jesus. But Islam contends that God gave Muhammad the complete revelation of the final divine truth. This ultimate knowledge of God is found only in the pages of the Koran, the collection of Muhammad's proclamations that his followers memorized and recorded. It is through Muhammad that Allah allegedly made known the fullness of his laws and spelled out precisely what he expects from man, morally, ethically, and religiously.

Islam requires that the Koran be obeyed literally. Muslims believe that the Koran is explicit and literal, and human beings must obey the Koran literally in order to comply with God's rules. Islamic extremists and fundamentalists complain that the Koran has been interpreted figuratively by non-purists, and that any non-literal interpretation of the Koran is the equivalent of a compromise with Western godlessness. Islam contends that all mankind should seek to know Allah's will as revealed in the Koran, and then submit to Allah's will.

The enforcement of Islamic law—which Muslims view as God's law on earth—is of paramount importance to zealous Muslims. The enforcement of the Koran is at the root of all Islamic fundamentalist regimes, such as the Islamic Republic of Iran and Saudi Arabia. Islamic fundamentalists are growing in number and in influence in such nations as Iran, Egypt, Libya, Pakistan, Syria, and among the Palestinian people in Israel. The fundamentalist zeal to enforce the Koran is at the core of the radical Taliban in Afghanistan. Those who attain the power to impose Islamic law on society usually do so without mercy.

The Ayatollah Khomeini, for example, did not spare the lives of his closest friends and allies whom he suspected of disloyalty to the Islamic, Koran-based government of Iran. One historian writes:

> *Khomeini believed that spies and traitors were everywhere. In his zeal to root out enemies, Khomeini turned on his own loyal followers. In a series of spectacular trials, inner members of Khomeini's own circle gave forced confessions on national television. They confessed to spying and plotting to overthrow the Islamic government.*[4]

Are there "moderate Muslims"? If by "moderate" you mean less zealous and less extreme, then there certainly are moderate Muslims. Yet these moderate Muslims have good reason to be fearful when zealous, extremist Muslims take political control of the nation. Much of the freedom that moderate Muslims enjoy—including the freedom to interpret the Koran according to their own conscience—disappears under fundamentalist Islamic rule. And one reason moderate Muslims do not speak out against the excesses of the fundamentalists is that they know that the fundamentalists do not hesitate to respond with force and cruelty.

The fundamentalist Islamic threat to non-Muslims is even greater. The Koran has explicit rules for dealing with non-Muslims, and if those rules are interpreted literally and strictly, the lives of non-Muslims are subject to assault. (We will explore this issue in greater detail later in this book.)

The Koran is composed of 114 suras (chapters), beginning with the longest and ending with the shortest. The suras are not arranged in any historical or chronological order. As a result, it is impossible to determine at what stage in Muhammad's life these "revelations" came to him. The suras are simply arranged in order of length, beginning with the longest and progressing toward the shortest.

Muhammad, being illiterate, did not write these revelations down. He spoke his revelations, and his followers acted as scribes, writing down his revelation on any paper-like material that was handy—from leaves to dried bones, to scraps of parchment.

Several Muslim scholars have tried to put events in the Koran into a chronological order. One Muslim scholar, Ibn-Ishaq, gives this order: Creation; Adam and Eve; Noah and his offspring; Hud; Salih; Abraham; Lot; Job; Shu'ayb; Joseph; Moses; Ezekiel; Elijah; Elisha; Samuel; David; Solomon; Sheba; Isaiah; al-Khidr; Daniel; Hananiah; Azariah; Mishael and Ezra; Alexander; Zechariah and John (the Baptist); the family of Imran and Jesus, son of Mary; the Companion of the Cave; Jonah; the Three Messengers; Samson; and George of Lydda (whom Christians call "St. George").

As you read through this list, you notice that many of the so-called prophets from the Koran are not mentioned in either Old or New Testament texts. It is also apparent that many of the biblical characters listed are not in historical order. This is due to the fact that Muhammad had a sketchy knowledge of the Bible. If you read the Koran, you soon find that it differs significantly from the Bible with regard to various events. Here are a few of the differences:

- In the Koran, one of Noah's sons separated himself from the rest of the family and died in the floodwaters—the ark later came to rest on Mount Judi in the Anatolian range of modern Turkey (Koran 11:32-48). In the Bible, all members of Noah's family were spared, and the ark came to rest on Mount Ararat in the Armenian Highland of Turkey (Genesis 7:1-13; 8:4).
- In the Koran, Abraham dwelt in a "valley without cultivation" by the Kabah (Koran 14:37), a valley thought to have been the Meccan valley. In the Bible, Abraham dwelt in Hebron, nineteen miles south of modern Jerusalem (Genesis 13:18).
- In the Koran, the wife of Pharaoh plucked Moses from the river, saying, "It may be that he will be of use to us" (Koran 28:8-9). In the Bible, the daughter of Pharaoh took Moses from the river, sparing his life out of compassion (Exodus 2).
- In the Koran, the first miracle assigned to Jesus is the making of a clay bird and then breathing life into it so it became a living bird (Koran 3:49). In the Bible, the first miracle of Jesus is turning water into wine at the marriage feast in Cana (John 2:11).
- In the Koran, Zechariah is speechless for three nights (Koran 3:38-41; 19:16-34). In the Bible, Zechariah is mute from the time the angel speaks to him until after John the Baptist is born (Luke 1).
- In the Koran, Jesus was not crucified; instead, it was only made to seem to the witnesses that he was crucified (Koran 4:157). In the Bible, Jesus was crucified, died, and was buried (Matthew 17; Mark 15; Luke 23; John 19).
- The Koran says of Jesus: "Christ, the son of Mary, was no more than a messenger" (Koran 5:75). The Bible presents Jesus this way: "In the past God spoke to our forefathers through the prophets at many times and in various ways, but in these last days he has spoken to us by his Son, whom he appointed

heir of all things, and through whom he made the universe. The Son is the radiance of God's glory and the exact representation of his being, sustaining all things by his powerful word. After he had provided purification for sins, he sat down at the right hand of the Majesty in heaven." (Hebrews 1:1-3).

- The Koran says that "Allah loveth not those who reject Faith" and "Allah loveth not those who do wrong" (Koran 3:32, 57). The Bible says that God "so loved the world that he gave his one and only Son, that whoever believes in him shall not perish but have eternal life" (John 3:16) and that "while we were still sinners, Christ died for us" (Romans 5:8).

- The Koran says to men that they are to be the "protectors and maintainers of women" but also gives men these rights if they fear their wives are disloyal or show ill conduct: "admonish them [first], [next] refuse to share their beds, [and last] beat them lightly" (Koran 4:34). The Koran also says to husbands, "Your wives are as a tilth [a piece of farmland, a place of sowing seed] unto you so approach your tilth when or how you will" (Koran 2:223). The Bible says, "Husbands, love your wives, just as Christ loved the church and gave himself up for her" (Ephesians 5:25-28) and "Husbands, in the same way be considerate as you live with your wives, and treat them with respect as the weaker partner and as heirs with you of the gracious gift of life" (1 Peter 3:7).

- The Koran says about man's relationship to God: "(Both) the Jews and the Christians say: 'We are sons of Allah, and His beloved.' Say: 'Why then doth He punish you for your sins? Nay, ye are but men—of the men He hath created: He forgiveth whom He pleaseth, and he punisheth whom He pleaseth: and to Allah belongeth the dominion of the heavens and the earth, and all that is between: and unto Him is the final goal [of all]" (Koran 5:18). The Bible says this about Christians' relationship to God: "We are children of God, and what we will be has not yet been made known. But we know that when he appears, we shall be like him, for we shall see him as he is" (1 John 3:2).

A BOOK LARGELY UNREAD

Few Muslims have actually read their own holy book for themselves. Reza F. Safa, a former radical Shiite Muslim who converted to Christianity, has written, "I have more knowledge of the Koran now as a Christian than I ever had as a fanatical Muslim. Of all the Muslims I knew, only a handful had some knowledge of the Koran. Even today when I confront many fanatical Muslims with strange revelations of Muhammad in the Koran, they are unaware these verses are in the book."[5] There are several reasons Muslims have not and do not read the Koran.

First, the rate of illiteracy among Muslims is very high. In some Muslim nations in Asia and Africa, 75 to 85 percent of the people cannot read or write.

Second, many Muslims are too poor to own a copy of the Koran. The book has not been widely published or circulated to the poor, in part because the reading of the Koran is not emphasized as a spiritual discipline. Note that knowledge of the Koran is *not* one of the Five Pillars of Islam (we will explore the Five Pillars in Chapter 5).

Third, Muslims believe that the Koran must be read in Arabic, which is spoken only by Arab Muslims. In fact, translations in non-Arabic languages are not considered the genuine Koran, but a mere interpretation of the Koran.

Only 280 million Muslims live in the twenty-two Arab-speaking nations of the world—roughly 20 percent of the world's Muslim population. Of the more than 1 billion people who call themselves Muslims, some 800 million of them cannot read, write, or speak Arabic. Even those who can read Arabic rarely read the Koran. Many consider the language too "poetic" or difficult to understand.

If Muslims do not read the Koran, how do they know what the Koran teaches? They know only the interpretation of the Koran that has been given to them by their religious leaders. Many Muslims know little beyond the Five Pillars of Islam and the traditions and customs for obeying the Koran in their own culture. Most Muslims have not been challenged to read the Koran and they feel no need to read it.

HAS THE BIBLE BEEN CORRUPTED?

There is little to be gained from arguing the accuracy of the Bible versus the Koran with a Muslim because Muslims almost universally believe that the Bible has been corrupted or altered. This argument is routinely taught in Islam and is based, in part, on the fact that Jesus did not write or dictate the Gospels personally.

Many Muslims believe the Gospel accounts have been "elaborated upon" or "edited" in the last two thousand years. For example, Muslims teach that when Jesus spoke of sending another "Comforter" to the people after he left the earth, Jesus meant Muhammad, not the Holy Spirit. Some have gone so far as to claim that the Bible was edited to insert references to the Holy Spirit—even though this would have required the universal and simultaneous editing of more than 200,000 handwritten manuscripts that were already being circulated around the known world by the time of Muhammad.

Ironically, while modern-day Islam rejects the Gospel accounts as corrupt, the Koran itself commands Muslims to read the Injeil—that is, the Gospel accounts of the life of Jesus. Few Muslims are aware of this command, and are equally unaware of these statements in the Koran:

- "Say ye: 'We believe in God, and the revelation given to us, and to Abraham, Ishmael, Isaac, Jacob, and the Tribes, and in that given to Moses and to Jesus, and that given to all the prophets from their Lord. We make no distinctions between one and another of them" (Koran 2:136).
- "If thou wert in doubt as to what we have revealed to thee, then ask those who were reading the Book [that is, the Bible] from before thee" (Koran 10:94).
- In the Koran, Jesus is called Muhammad's "Lord" (Koran 89:22) and the Truth (Koran 2:91). The Koran also describes Jesus as the "Word of God" (Koran 3:45, 4:171) and a "Spirit Proceeding forth from God" (Koran 4:171).

ISLAMIC CULTURE IS INSEPARABLE FROM ARAB CULTURE

Muhammad did not merely espouse a new religious doctrine; he formed a new religious society. Islam is far more than a religion. It is a total, all-encompassing way of thinking, feeling, and responding to all of life. It is a culture and a system of government.

To ensure his political preeminence, Muhammad spoke about rewards—economic and spiritual—that would go to those who embraced his doctrines and moral code. He declared, "Paradise is the reward for those who die in the way of God and the booty is the reward of those who survive the war." Presumably this war is the war against non-Muslims.

Throughout the Koran, Muhammad developed a form of theocratic government that pertains to all aspects of life. He began with the conduct of dissidents, the treatment of allies, the formation of treaties, and other political matters. Later, elements of a code of conduct and moral law were introduced.

The *Hadith* stands next to the Koran in the writings of Islam. It is a collection of Islamic traditions, including sayings and deeds of Muhammad as heard by his contemporaries or related in a second- or third-hand way. Many of the sayings elaborate on the teachings of the Koran. A great many Muslims are unable to differentiate *Hadith* from Koran—they do not know what Muhammad "recited" and what others say he said or did.

Toward the end of his life, Muhammad began to clarify his aspirations for the future of Islam. He made a silver seal engraved with the words "Muhammad the apostle of God" and sent four simultaneous messages bearing this stamp to the rulers of Egypt, Abyssinia, Syria, and Persia. He urged them to forsake their idols and to believe in the universal faith of God's message given through him, God's messenger.

In launching this appeal to the nations, Muhammad sought to export not only the religion of Islam, but the culture of Islam—a culture that is distinctly Arabic in nature. Throughout the Muslim world, Arab culture is considered the ideal expression of Islam. The vast majority of OPEC members are Muslim nations—Venezuela and Nigeria are the only notable exceptions—and the vast majority of Muslim nations are Arabic in culture. Algeria's first president, Ahmed Ben Bella, once said, "I cannot see Arab culture separate from Islamic culture. I honestly would not understand the meaning of Arab culture if it were not first and foremost Islamic."

This alignment between the Arab culture and Islam runs deep in the hearts and minds of the Arab people. It is one of the foremost reasons that fanatical Muslims are deeply angered when their Arab countrymen adopt Western cultural behaviors, such as a preference for Western dress or Western styles of entertainment. To the Arab Islamic mind, the Western lifestyle is inherently anti-Islamic, and thus anathema to Arabs.

People sometimes ask why Muslims are so adamant about head coverings, such as the burkah and chador for women, or the turban-style coverings for men. The answer: These head coverings were popular in the Arabic culture for thousands of years, largely as protection against the blowing desert sands. When Islam became the religion of Arabia, the dress of Arabia became an expression of Islam. Whether a person lives in the cold mountains of Afghanistan or the jungles of Indonesia, to be a Muslim means to dress like Arabs.

THE DEATH OF THE PROPHET

When Muhammad was sixty-three, and Islam was only twenty years old, the self-proclaimed "apostle of God" fell ill with a sudden fever and died. As the news of his death spread, many recently converted Muslims were seized with panic and confusion. Abu Bakr, Muhammad's close friend and later the first Islamic caliph (ruler of the Islamic *Ummah* or community), declared to Muhammad's distraught followers, "Whichever of you worships Muhammad, know that Muhammad is dead. But which of you worships God, know that God is alive and does not die." He then quoted a verse from the Koran that gains even greater significance with the hindsight of history: "Muhammad is a Prophet only; there have been Prophets before him. If he dies or is slain, will ye turn back?"

Muhammad's goal was to create a society in which religion encompassed all aspects of the culture—from dress to entertainment to education to government. The goal of Islamic leaders today is still a complete blend of the Islamic religion and Arab culture with a goal of dominating the world.

4

ARE ALLAH AND JEHOVAH THE SAME GOD?

"There is no god but Allah," says the *Shahada*, "and Muhammad is the Messenger of God." This one line sums up the central belief of all the world's Muslims. It also establishes what appears to be common ground between Islam and the other religions that proclaim the existence of one sovereign God. Like Judaism and Christianity, Islam is monotheistic. It is also a "revealed" religion in which the adherents believe that its tenets came by direct revelation from God.

But is Allah the same God as Jehovah, the God of Judaism and Christianity? Do Christians, Jews, and Muslims worship the same God? What do Muslims believe about the nature of God and the nature of humanity? What do they believe about how God and human beings are to relate to one another? These are vitally important questions to ask—and most Westerners, unfortunately, do not know the answers to these questions.

ALLAH AND JEHOVAH—COMPARE AND CONTRAST

Monotheism is central to Islamic doctrine. The Koran does not attempt to prove or argue the existence of Allah. It simply proclaims his existence as a matter of fact.

The Koran gives ninety-nine attributes of Allah. These are called the "most Beautiful Names." Many are names which Christians attribute to the God of the Bible: all-powerful, Creator, the Merciful, the Compassionate. The essence of Allah, however, is power. His power overrides all of his other attributes.

You may have heard some Muslim apologists make the claim that Islam is "the religion of peace," suggesting that the very word *Islam* comes from the Arabic word *salam*, which means "peace." But anyone with even the most elementary knowledge of Arabic knows this is not true. Islam actually means "total surrender" or "total submission to God." The image the word suggests is that of a vanquished army on its knees in surrender before a victorious conqueror. The very word *Islam* suggests the power of Allah to vanquish all opponents. In a religious context, Islam is a call for human beings to abjectly surrender themselves to the all-powerful Allah.

The name *Allah* comes down from pre-Islamic times. It corresponds to the Babylonian name Bel or Baal.[1] According to Middle East scholar E. M. Wherry, pre-Islamic Arabs worshipped gods they called Allah. Both pre-Islamic Allah-worship and Baal-worship involved worship of the sun, the moon, and the stars, which is why they are called "astral" religions. The crescent moon, which was the symbol of pagan moon worship, is also the symbol of Islam. It is printed on the flags of many Islamic countries and placed on top of minarets and mosques.[2]

What is Allah's character like? He is remote, aloof, and distant. Islam describes Allah as being neither wholly a spirit nor a physical entity, but an entirely separate form of being. By contrast, Jehovah—the God of Judaism and Christianity—has always been portrayed in both the Old and New Testaments as continually seeking a relationship with humankind. He walked and talked with Adam and Eve in the Garden of Eden. He told the people of Israel, "You will be My people and I will be Your God" (Jeremiah 30:22; see also Genesis 17:7-8; Exodus 6:7).

The Koran presents Allah as "far," a transcendent and distant God. As a Muslim theologian has stated, "He remains hidden forever." The Bible presents Jehovah as "drawing near," "coming down," and "seeking after" humanity. The first question we find in the Bible is God calling to Adam and Eve, "Where are you?" (Genesis 3:9). In the Koran, Allah hides from humanity. In the Bible, humanity hides from God.

Although Allah is considered supremely powerful, Islam requires that human beings take revenge on behalf of Allah whenever Allah is insulted. Islam also requires that faithful Muslims demand that others submit themselves to Allah. Jehovah—the God of the Bible—does not make such demands. In the Judeo-Christian worldview, we don't avenge God—He avenges us! While Muslims are commanded to fight for Allah, Jews and Christians are told to ask God to fight on their behalf.

Jesus taught us that instead of fighting, slaying, and beheading our enemies, we are to pray for our enemies, do good to them, and "turn the other cheek" when they mistreat us. We do not demand that unbelievers convert to Christ at the point of a sword. We appeal to unbelievers to accept God's mercy and forgiveness through Christ. If they reject our Gospel, we don't slay them—we continue to pray for them and show them the love of God.

THE ISLAMIC VIEW OF TRUTH AND SIN

Islam teaches that the angel Gabriel revealed Allah's will to Muhammad. In other words, Gabriel gave the human race, through Muhammad, a set of instructions. Gabriel did *not* give Muhammad any insight into the nature, character, or personality of Allah. That is why the Allah of the Koran remains hidden and mysterious, whereas the God of the Bible is personal and knowable. Jehovah God revealed Himself to Abraham, whom He called "friend." God conversed with Moses, revealing his name to Moses ("I AM"), and showing himself to Moses (though not face to face).

We read repeatedly in the Bible, "Thus saith the Lord." And God does not send an angel to one prophet with his revealed message. Instead, God speaks directly to the prophets. The God of the Bible reveals himself to humanity by telling us his names—names that describe his character and attributes. Here are just a few of God's names, as revealed in the Bible and the attributes those names describe for us:

Adonai (Lord, Master)
El Shaddai (Lord God Almighty)
El Elyon (The Most High God)
El Olam (The Everlasting God)
Jehova Gmolah (The Lord Who Recompenses/Rewards in Full)
Jehovah Jireh (The Lord My Provider)
Jehovah Mekoddishkem (The Lord Our Sanctifier)
Jehovah Nissi (The Lord My Banner)
Jehovah Raah (The Lord My Shepherd)
Jehovah Rapha (The Lord Who Heals)
Jehovah Sabaoth (The Lord of Hosts)
Jehovah Shalom (The Lord is Peace)
Jehovah Shammah (The Lord is Present)
Jehovah Tsidkenu (The Lord Our Righteousness)

Islam and Christianity present very different pictures of how humanity should relate to Allah or God. Both Islam and Christianity call for people to accept "by faith" what has been revealed by God. There is no disagreement about the need for faith. There is vast disagreement, however, when it comes to what has been revealed. Islamic and Christian claims to divine truth contradict each other.

Islam contends that the ultimate truth was revealed by Allah to Muhammad through the angel Gabriel. Muslims contend that the Bible in its present form is corrupt and that only the Koran contains the true divine message.

Christians contend that the ultimate truth was evident in the life of Jesus Christ, who said, "I am the way and the truth and the life. No one comes to the Father except through me" (John 14:6). Jesus revealed God's truth by his life as the incarnate Son of God. As the Son, Jesus is the *Logos*, the Word of God, the full expression of God's character, truth, and love toward humanity (John 1:1-3, 14).

Many Christians are surprised to learn that Muslims view the issue of sin very differently from Christians and Jews. At first glance, we see that much of what the Koran says about sin sounds much like what the Bible says. The Koran uses several words for sin, all of which suggest the idea of failing to meet the standards set by God.

Islam states that human beings were created for the service of Allah. That service includes absolute obedience to what Allah commands. Therefore, says Islam, the root of sin lies in humanity's prideful opposition to God's will. Humanity is prone to wrong actions because human beings are morally weak. Therefore, it is up to human beings to choose to be strong and to do good works. If they obey Allah, their good works will counterbalance and cancel out their evil works. The Koran teaches, "Surely good deeds take away evil deeds" (Koran 11:14).

Muslims believe Allah has given to all people the ability to obey. Therefore, human beings only need to be guided into obedience. The actions of an obedient will are the expression of faith, according to Islam.

The Koran does not consider the original sin of Adam and Eve to have totally depraved mankind. As a result, Islam has no doctrine of a "sin nature," as Christianity has. The Koran reveals that Muhammad himself had no deep conviction concerning sin, and he did not demand that believers experience any such conviction. Rather, Islam puts forth ideas about specific wrongdoing—classifying various misdeeds as being great or small for the purpose of determining the degree of punishment those misdeeds deserve.

"Little sins"—*saghira*—include lying, deception, anger, and lust. Sins of this class are easily forgiven if the greater sins are avoided, and if some compensatory good works are performed. In fact, a lie may actually be a good deed if it helps someone.

"Great sins"—*kabira*—include acts such as murder, adultery, disobeying God, disobeying one's parents, drinking to excess, practicing usury, neglecting Friday prayers, not keeping the fast of Ramadan, forgetting the Koran after reading it, swearing falsely or by any name than Allah's, performing magic, gambling, dancing, or shaving the beard. Such sins can be forgiven only after repentant deeds.

Acts which the Christian Bible recognizes as sexual sins—adultery and fornication—are often labeled in the Koran as acts of a "temporary marriage" rather than sin (Koran 4:3-34). Temporary marriage (*nikah mut'ah*) is an arrangement by which a man and a woman can be married for a fixed, temporary period of time. Students or workers who are away from home may marry for a period of days, weeks, or months so that their needs for companionship and sex may be met—then, when that period of time is over, the marriage is dissolved without divorce. The man often makes a payment to the woman called a *mahr* (or dower).

Sometimes the temporary marriage can be as brief as a half-hour in duration, in which case it serves as a fig leaf for legalized prostitution—but it is not considered a sin.

The sin that surpasses all others in Islam is *shirk*, the association of other deities with Allah. The sin of *shirk* is unpardonable. According to tradition, Muhammad was asked to identify the greatest sin and he said it was polytheism, the worship of more than one deity. Muslims believe that Christians are guilty of polytheism and *shirk* because they view Christians as believing in three gods (the Trinity) rather than one God. This belief is all the justification Muslims need to justify a holy war against Christians—and to attempt to convert, conquer, or eliminate Christians because they are unbelievers who have corrupted the true faith of Allah.

The Muslim view of Allah is that of an elderly, grandfatherly Arab gentleman who is always happy when people obey him—and who is quickly infuriated when people disobey. Allah rewards or punishes his people according to his mood—that is, according to his feelings of either happiness or anger. To the faithful, Allah is the Lord of blessing and bounty—but like a benevolent dictator, he insists on total compliance with his laws.

That is why democracy is rare in the Islamic world. Except for Iraq and Afghanistan, where democracy has been largely imposed by the United States, there was only one Islamic democracy in the world—Turkey—and that is because they embraced secularism after the collapse of the Ottoman Empire. Islamic governments tend to be dictatorial and authoritarian. The Muslim view of Allah is intertwined with the Arab view of leadership, which holds that a ruler must be a monarch or a strongman dictator. A "ruler" whose powers are constitutionally limited by checks and balances would not fit the Islamic view of power. In Islam, a ruler must rule, rewarding those who please him and punishing those who disobey.

Yet Muslims also believe that Allah can be merciful if he chooses. He accepts repentance and forgives faults and shortcomings. Every chapter of the Koran but one opens with the words, "In the name of Allah, the merciful." Muslims believe that every word and accent in the Koran reveals the mercies of Allah.

The Koran teaches that human beings must seek forgiveness from Allah because he is all-knowing. Here we see another similarity to the God of the Bible. Allah sees the secrets of the heart—nothing escapes his notice. It is Allah's *maghfera* ("forgiveness") that preserves and protects a person from Allah's wrath and punishment. The Koran proclaims repeatedly that Allah forgives sins, but here we see an important distinction between Islam and Christianity: Muslims believe that forgiveness is purely the prerogative of Allah—and the mind of Allah is unknowable. In Islam, there is no means by which a human being can be certain that his sins are forgiven. There is no promise of grace and forgiveness in the Koran as there is in the Bible. The only inference of forgiveness a Muslim can make is that if nothing bad happens to him, then Allah must have forgiven him.

Islam provides no means for atoning for the sins of humanity. There are no sacrifices, as are found in Judaism. There is no atoning blood of Christ to cover the sins of a believer once and for all. There is no assurance of forgiveness and salvation in Islam as there is in the Christian Gospel. Even though Allah is addressed as "merciful," he remains a stern, unbending figure who may dispense mercy or judgment, depending on his whim at the moment.

In summary, Allah offers no means for humanity to be cleansed of sin, because Islam does not recognize that human beings need such cleansing. Judaism and Christianity disagree sharply with the Islamic view. Both teach that human beings have a sin nature from birth, and that sin must be cleansed. For the Jews, Jehovah provided a means of atonement through the blood sacrifices of the Mosaic Law. For Christians, the ultimate atoning sacrifice was the death of Jesus on the cross, which was foreshadowed in the Mosaic sacrifices.

A DIFFERENT VIEW OF JESUS

The incarnation of Christ is a major stumbling block for Muslims. Christians believe that Jesus is God's Son, that he is "God in the flesh." Muslims reject the idea that God has taken human form in order to dwell among us and experience the human condition.

Muhammad, influenced by the polytheistic environment of pre-Islamic Arabia, mistakenly thought that Christians believed God had "married" a human woman and produced a son by her. Such stories, in fact, are common in polytheistic religions. The gods have sexual relations with human beings and produce human offspring who possess supernatural powers. Muhammad rightly rejected these crude pagan beliefs.

However, Muhammad—because of his illiteracy and his limited contact with Christian theology and Christian Scripture—mistakenly thought that Christians believed the Trinity was composed of Jesus, God, and Mary! Muhammad's confusion is understandable. There were many heresies in Muhammad's time which involved the worship of Mary, so it's not hard to imagine how Muhammad came to the conclusion that Christians worshiped more than one god.

Islam contends that Jesus (called Isa in the Koran) was a prophet of God. The Islamic religion accepts Jesus' miracles. Christians have a special status in Islam as "People of the Book." But Muslims do not believe Jesus was God in human flesh. Islam not only denies that Jesus is the Son of God, but it pronounces a curse on all who confess Jesus to be the Christ, the Son of God, and the Lord of All. The Koran says: "The Jews call 'Uzayr [a person of unknown identity] a son of God,' and the Christians call 'Christ the Son of God.' That is a saying from their mouth; [in this] they but imitate what the Unbelievers of the old used to say. Allah's curse be on them: how they are deluded away from the Truth" (Koran 9:30). A "curse" in Islam is tantamount to a death sentence.

One of the hardest aspects of Christianity for Muslims to grasp is the cross of Christ. The purpose of the cross eludes Muslims because they see no need for a sacrifice for sin. Moreover, the idea of substitutionary atonement for sin is, to their minds, a primitive idea. Though Muslims do not abhor the shedding of blood, they vehemently reject the notion that there is virtue in dying for someone else. Muslims will die in order to advance Islam, but they would not die for the sake of fellow Muslims. A Muslim cannot comprehend what Christians regard as the highest expression of love—a love that takes the penalty of sin upon oneself and finds meaning in forgiveness and redemption.

Moreover, Islamic teaching about Jesus has rendered his substitutionary death on the cross a moot point. Muslims don't believe Jesus died on the cross. They believe that when the Roman soldiers came to Jesus by night in the Garden of Gethsemane, God took Jesus up into heaven before the soldiers even laid hands on him. Therefore, Jesus was never crucified, did not shed blood, and did not die. He ascended directly to heaven.

Islamic scholars offer different theories as to who was actually crucified. Some say that Judas Iscariot was crucified in Jesus' place, and others suggest Simon of Cyrene, the man who carried the cross of Jesus for a while. Another theory is that one of the disciples volunteered to be crucified in Jesus' place. Each theory involves the idea that the likeness of Jesus was supernaturally transferred to the man who died in Jesus' place.

The Bible teaches that Jesus voluntarily humbled himself and submitted himself to death on the cross out of love for us. In Islam, by contrast, that kind of self-sacrificing love is seen as a sign of weakness. To love is to be vulnerable. Far be it from Allah, the all-powerful, to be vulnerable. Muslims fail to recognize that love also produces confidence and hope, and it teaches those who are loved to love others. Islam has no concept of the strength of love. It holds no belief that love is a God-like and desirable character quality.

In Islam, God and man are wary of each other, whereas in Christianity, God and man are in love with each other. This difference is of great importance because it lies at the heart of the tension Muslims feel toward Christians.

How we relate to God is generally how we relate to others. Muslims are taught to view the giving of alms (charitable donations) as a religious duty. Muslims are also taught to judge, condemn, reject, and even eliminate those who fail to measure up to the highest standards of faith and religious practice. Why? Because that is how they expect Allah to deal with them if they disobey his commands.

Muslims go to great lengths to express their homage to Allah's power out of their belief that Allah is primarily concerned with exacting tribute from an error-prone humanity. In this regard, Islam is curiously similar to the pre-Islamic tribal religions that Muhammad rejected. Islam is focused on an outward show of obedience to Allah, not an inward attitude of gratitude.

The tragedy of Islam is its failure to recognize God's real concern for reestablishing a relationship of love with humanity. In an effort to give Allah honor, Islam underestimates the real power of God. Muslims cannot comprehend the tremendous power of divine love—a love that compelled God to take human form and live humbly as a man among men so that all might know who God is and what God is like.

A DIFFERENT MEANS OF RELATING TO GOD

Muslims reject the doctrine of "the Word made flesh," God in human form, the claim that Jesus himself made in John 14:6. As a result, they also reject the concept of the restored relationship between God and man that is at the heart of the Christian faith. Muslims reject the notion that God would enter into human history to re-establish a personal relationship with humanity after the Fall. Moreover, they reject the very idea that God has any interest in having a personal relationship of love and friendship with human beings.

Jesus himself spoke of this new relationship between God and humanity, and his followers affirm this new relationship as the reason for the life, death, and resurrection of Jesus. As Jesus told his disciples, "I no longer call you servants, because a servant does not know his master's business. Instead, I have called you friends, for everything that I learned from my Father I have made known to you" (John 15:15). The Christian Gospel emphasizes God's offer of intimate friendship and loving communion between God and his people.

Islam, in sharp contrast, regards divinity and humanity as being mutually exclusive entities. Muslims believe that God could not have entered into human life and remained God. Therefore, the relationship between God and Christians seems impossible to Muslim thinking. Fellowship with God—which is the deepest of all religious experiences for the Christian—is unimaginable to Muslims. In fact, they consider the Christian assertion that we were created in God's image to be blasphemous (which, of course, constitutes a rejection of the creation story of Genesis).

Muslims regard the creation of humanity as an act of Allah's absolute power, and an expression of his might as the Lord who reigns over all worlds and kingdoms. God's eternal power is clearly demonstrated through the creation of the universe, as the Koran states: "See they not the clouds, how they are created? And the heaven, how it is raised high and the mountains, how they are fixed and the earth, how it is spread out?" (Koran 88:17-20).

Man's role, according to Islam, is as a servant to a master. Allah decrees all that happens, and man has no real choice but to submit to the divine will. Allah's power, of itself, qualifies him to act as arbitrarily as he pleases. According to the Koran, "He leads and misleads whom he will" (Koran 74:34). This concept of God "misleading" man, of course, is totally opposite to both the Jewish and Christian concepts of Jehovah. God does not mislead—He cannot do so because He is entirely righteous.

The Koran also states that human beings have little choice in determining the purpose of their lives: "Man does not enter the world or leave it as he desires. He is a creature; and the Creator, who has brought him into existence and bestowed upon him higher and more excellent faculties than upon other animals, has also assigned an object to his existence" (Koran 15:29).

This statement may sound similar to the teaching of the Bible, but in the Koran the image of a sovereign God is not tempered by an image of a loving and compassionate God. Instead, Allah in the Koran is stern, remote, and unknowable. Adherents to Islam are not invited into a relationship with God. Instead, Muslims are commanded to devote all of their faculties to the practice of religious rites and duties: "Therefore stand firm in your devotion to the true faith, which Allah himself has made and for which he has made men" (Koran 30:30). Sadly, the motivation for such devotion is not a love relationship with the Creator, but the fear of punishment and rejection by the Creator.

The Koran tells us how God created Adam, the first man: "He formed and fashioned the body of Adam from the dry clay and then he breathed into the body of his own spirit; and man, an embodied soul, came into being" (Koran 15:28-29). On the surface, this account seems to parallel the biblical account of creation. But there is a subtle difference. In the Koran's account, Allah creates man to be his servant, carrying out Allah's will on the earth. In the Bible's account, God creates man to be a friend. God and Adam walk and talk together in the Garden, and the bond of God breathing his breath into Adam speaks of a spiritual relationship between God and humanity.

The Koran does not attach any particular significance to the story of Adam and Eve and their sin in the Garden of Eden—the story of humanity's fall from communion and fellowship with God. There are two reasons for this: First, Muslims do not believe in man's original communion with God as the purpose for which man was created. Second, Muslims do not believe in original sin.

The Koran's view of man's nature can be summed up this way: Man was created in a state of moral goodness. In fact, man's nature is superior to the nature of the angelic hosts, who were commanded to bow down before mankind at his creation. But being mortal, man is inconstant when tested by temptation. He fell through the temptation of Satan, and lost paradise, but he is not radically estranged from God. Man is prone to sin, but his basic nature is not sinful.

In sharp contrast, Christians believe that the Fall radically damaged human nature. Human beings became totally sinful and alienated from God. Human beings became incapable of pleasing God and reconciling with him through their own effort and good works. Christians also believe that the whole purpose of our existence is to live in fellowship with our loving God. This is the relationship for which we were originally created, but which sin destroyed. In order to restore the relationship that was broken by sin, we had to experience salvation and redemption.

Through his death upon the cross, Jesus Christ saved us, redeemed us from enslavement to sin, and fulfilled our longing to live a meaningful, purposeful life. We have a reason for living because Christ died for us and saved us from the curse of sin.

The Bible teaches that we were initially created in God's image and had fellowship with God (see Genesis 1:26-27) and that humanity acquired a sin nature and lost fellowship with God through the initial sin committed by Adam and Eve (see Romans 5:12, 18-19). Jesus Christ came to take our sin upon himself through death upon the cross, and to suffer the consequences of sin that we deserved. By dying in our place, Jesus reclaimed for us the opportunity to enter into fellowship with God and reflect God's image on this earth.

Muslims reject this entire notion. They do not see man as totally sinful and incapable of saving himself. They envision a life of serving and obeying God, not a life of fellowship with him. The best any Muslim can hope for in this life is to avoid incurring the wrath of Allah.

A DIFFERENT CONCEPT OF DEATH AND JUDGMENT

Muslims believe that Allah decrees everything that happens, including one's entrance into this world and one's death, which leads to the next world. Birth and death are merely two aspects of the phenomenon of life that Allah owns and controls. The Koran teaches that man's hour of death is ordained: "When their doom comes, they are not able to delay it an hour, nor can they advance it" (Koran 16:61).

The irrevocable finality of death is also spelled out in the Koran. If a man begs Allah to return him to earth, the answer comes: "By no means! It is but a word that he speaks and before them is a barrier, until the day they are raised" (Koran 23:100).

Only Allah knows exactly when the Last Judgment will come: "They ask then about the hour when will it come to pass? Say: The knowledge thereof is with my Lord only" (Koran 7:187).

Islamic belief divides the afterlife into heaven and hell—a division that is superficially similar to Christian belief. In heaven, according to Islam, believers will experience God's favor and benevolence. In hell, unbelievers will experience God's judgment and wrath. Both destinations are vividly described in the Koran.

Heaven is an oasis-like paradise filled with "gardens watered by running streams," rivers of milk, wine, clarified honey, and shade trees bearing all kinds of fruits. In hell, sufferers will be made to drink boiling water, molten metal, and decaying filth. The Koran says, "Then as for those who are unhappy, they will be in the fire; for them there will be sighing and groaning" (Koran 11:106). The Islamic hell has seven divisions, each with its particular purpose and terrors. There is a Muslim purgatory, a special division of hell for Christians, a division for Jews, and a bottomless pit for hypocrites. Many details of the Islamic version of hell stand in stark contrast with the teachings of the Bible.

The Day of Judgment is a central theme in Islam, second in importance only to Allah himself. Muslims accept the reality of this Day of Judgment to the same degree that they accept the reality of Allah's existence. Some of the most striking language in the Koran is used to describe "the event which will overwhelm mankind," the Day when earth and human society will be destroyed, the dead will be resurrected, and every soul will stand before God to be judged and assigned an eternal place in heaven or hell.

The Koran says: "We molded man into a most noble image and in the end we shall reduce him to the lowest of the low, except the believers who do good works, for theirs shall be a boundless recompense. What, then can after this make you deny the Last Judgment? Is Allah not the best of judges?" (Koran 95:4-8).

Allah is not only the benevolent Creator who lavishes all earthly blessings on humanity, but he is also the vengeful Judge who, having demanded absolute submission to his divine will, mercilessly imposes inevitable and terrible punishment on those who reject him and transgress his laws. This belief stands in stark contrast to Christianity's loving God, who, even as He judges in righteousness, is "patient with you, not wanting anyone to perish" (2 Peter 3:9).

As for the last Judgment itself, the clearest and most concise description of the Muslim's view is found in L. Bevan Jones' book, *The People or the Mosque* (Calcutta: Associated Press, YMCA, 1932). Jones states that, according to Islamic doctrine, the Last Day will not come until there is no one found who calls on God. Then the sounding trumpet will signal the arrival of the Day of Judgment. The Last Day and subsequent Judgment unfold in a precise sequence:

1. At the first blast of the trumpet, everyone in heaven and earth will die except those whom God saves.
2. At the second trumpet blast, the dead will be resurrected.
3. After the resurrection, there is a forty-year period when people will wander about the earth naked, confused, and sorrowful. They must await "the descent of the books" that have been kept by the recording angels. Each book will be given to its owner, delivered into the right hand of the righteous and into the left hand of the wicked.
4. Everyone's deeds will be weighed on Allah's scales of justice (Koran 21:47). The scales weigh each one's good deeds and bad deeds, and the fate of each individual is determined. Good deeds are heavy; bad deeds are light; those whose balance is light will lose their souls and go into hell (Koran 23:102-103; 101:6-11). Prophets and angels are exempt from this trial and (according to some Islamic authorities) so are believers.
5. After one's deeds are weighed, the next stop is to cross the bridge—a narrow pathway that is described as "sharper than the edge of a sword, finer than a hair, suspended over hell" (Koran 36:66). The righteous who are to be saved pass over it quickly and easily, but the condemned fall into hell and remain there forever.

A popular belief among Muslims is that Jesus will return to earth as the Last Day approaches and declare himself to be a Muslim. He will call the entire world to Islam, and then he will die a normal death.

In Islam, the promise of eternal life is always linked to good works—and to a predominance of good works over bad deeds. The Koran records twenty-four times that Allah does not love sinners (Koran 2:190 and following), and that he loves only those who fear him (Koran 3:76). The concept of salvation for sinners does not exist in Islam.

To be a Muslim is to believe in Allah, his messenger Muhammad, and the Last

Judgment. And since Muslims believe in very precise rules of conduct, a person who fails to live as the Koran instructs has practically guaranteed that he will be damned to everlasting torment. So in Islam, the underlying motivation for faith is fear.

WHERE DO THESE DIFFERENCES LEAD?

As we read through these comparisons between Islam and Christianity, two observations become clear:

- Islam has adopted only bits and pieces of the teaching of the Old and New Testaments, and it has presented them in a distorted form.
- Despite a few superficial similarities, Islam and Christianity differ radically in how they portray the nature of God, the nature of humanity, and the way in which God and man relate to each other.

What do these differences mean? Where do these differences lead? They lead to completely opposite prescriptions for living. The Christian Gospel leads to a personal relationship with God through Jesus Christ. A Christian is motivated by gratitude to God to live a life of submission, obedience, and good works. The Christian faith leads to a life of obedience to God's commandments through reliance on the power of the Holy Spirit to express Christlike character in us—the fruit of the Spirit that results in moral, ethical, humble living (see Galatians 5:22-23). In Christianity, *we know and we have the assurance* that we have been made acceptable to God by faith in the shed blood of Jesus Christ.

In Islam, there is no personal relationship with God. For the Muslim, good works are motivated by fear of being punished and rejected by a remote and impersonal God. The Muslim *hopes* to be made acceptable for God by his deeds—but he *never has the assurance* that he has done enough.

The difference between Islam and Christianity is profound, and it has a direct bearing on the ultimate expression of extreme fundamentalist Islam—an expression called terrorism.

A SIDE-BY-SIDE COMPARISON OF ISLAM AND CHRISTIANITY

	ISLAM	CHRISTIANITY
1. Allah/God	Distant (unknowable). Does not reveal himself; reveals only his will. Merciful (depending on his mood). Capricious (he leads and misleads). Vengeful. Almighty (emphasis on power).	Personal (knowable). Reveals himself through the incarnation of Jesus Christ. Loving (his love is unchanging). Truthful. Just and loving. Almighty (power balanced by love).
2. Christ	A prophet. Denial of the Incarnation.	God's Son. The Word made flesh.
3. Bible	Revealed by God. Changed and corrupted by unfaithful Jews and Christians.	Revealed by God. Authoritative Word of God.
4. Trinity	God, Jesus, and Mary (Islam's distorted version).	Father, Son, and Holy Spirit. One God in Three Persons.
5. Faith	Intellectual agreement that Allah is One and Muhammad is his Prophet.	Recognition that we are sinners and unable to save ourselves; we trust in Christ's substitutionary payment (atonement) for our sins.
6. Sin	Rebellion against God. Result: shame, embarrassment. Dishonor to family. People are inherently good. We are absolved by good works.	Rebellion against God (primarily). Result: Guilt. Requires God's forgiveness. People are inherently fallen. The penalty of sin is death; Jesus paid the penalty for our sin.

	ISLAM	CHRISTIANITY
7. Salvation	God saves those whom he chooses. Faith and works are required. We cannot be assured of salvation.	Salvation is available to all who believe. Our works cannot save us. All who believe in Jesus will be saved.
8. Sanctification	Based on rituals and obedience to the Koran. Keep the Five Pillars of Islam. External and ceremonial.	Based on our growth toward Christlikeness through the work of the Holy Spirit. Inward, spiritual, based on a living relationship with God.
9. Love	Islam recognizes erotic love and family love. Self-sacrificing love is seen as weakness.	Highest form of love is Christlike, self-sacrificing *agape* love. Family love, friendship love, and erotic love have their place, but secondary to *agape* love.
10. Belief in the Supernatural	Belief in unseen world. Angels (good and evil). Satan is a force of hate and power. Islamic belief is fatalistic; all events are foreordained by Allah.	Belief in spiritual realm (Ephesians 6:12). Belief in angels and demons as described in the Bible. Satan is the rebellious archenemy of God, completely evil, but his power is no match for God's power. Human beings can overcome evil only through the power of God that is supplied by the Holy Spirit.

5

TWO DIFFERENT PRESCRIPTIONS FOR LIVING

American inventor and entrepreneur Steve Jobs was one of the most brilliant men of our age, and was often compared to Thomas Edison and Walt Disney. But in October 2003, Steve Jobs made an error in judgment that probably shortened his life by many years. When his doctors told him he had pancreatic cancer and needed an immediate operation to remove the tumor, Jobs refused. For the next nine months, he ignored the pleas of his doctors, family, and friends, and he tried to cure his cancer with a self-prescribed combination of fruit juices, acupuncture, visits to New Age spiritualists, and various other "magical" treatments he found by Googling on the Internet.

Finally—belatedly—Jobs realized he was following the wrong prescription. He agreed to undergo surgery and employ the most advanced cancer-fighting therapies available. Those therapies managed to extend his life for another eight years beyond the original diagnosis. His doctors still believe that Steve Jobs might have beaten the cancer completely if he had allowed them to remove the tumor when it was first discovered, before the cancer spread from his pancreas to the surrounding tissues.

Why did such a brilliant man reject scientifically proven cancer treatments in favor of out-and-out quackery and voodoo medicine? Jobs' biographer, Walter Isaacson, explained that Jobs felt that "if you ignore something you don't want to exist, you can have [what you desire through] magical thinking. . . . He would regret it."[1]

In every arena of life, it is important to follow the right prescription. In the medical realm, the wrong prescription can cost you your life. In the spiritual realm, the wrong prescription can cost you all of eternity.

Christianity and Islam are two very different prescriptions for living. They are as different as surgery and acupuncture, or chemotherapy and fruit juice. If you want to know God, if you want to experience God's peace and joy and power in your life, if you don't want to suffer the everlasting regret of an eternity apart from God, then you must choose the right prescription for living.

The Christian prescription is a faith that is rooted in love, forgiveness, and new life. It's a faith that brings you into a personal relationship with the God of the universe. The Christian faith sets you free from guilt, shame, and bondage to sin. Genuine biblical Christianity does not impose itself on unwilling people. It does not force anyone to become a Christian at the point of the sword. If you choose to reject Jesus, you're perfectly free to do so. As the apostle Paul writes, "Now the Lord is the Spirit, and where the Spirit of the Lord is, there is freedom" (2 Corinthians 3:17).

The reason we have freedom of religion written into the First Amendment to the Constitution is that the American government was designed by people who believed in God. They came from many Christian faith traditions. They were Congregationalists, Presbyterians, Episcopalians, Roman Catholics, Deists, and more—and they believed in freedom of worship, both their own freedom and the freedom of their neighbors.

Islam, by contrast, is a religion of law, submission, and punishment. The ideal world, according to Islam, is a world that strictly obeys every tenet of Islam, with no separation between religion and state. The ideal political leader, to the Islamic mind, is the religious leader. The edicts of religion, the Muslim believes, should be enforced with the power of the state, the power of the sword. There should be no tolerance given to other religions. The religious body and the state should be one and the same, and should impose complete autocracy and absolute theocracy. That is why some fundamentalist Islamists say what is vile and abhorrent to you and me: "Freedom can go to hell."

The Islamic faith offers no loving God, no forgiveness, no power over sin, no newness of life, no personal relationship with Allah, no freedom from guilt, no freedom of any kind. Where the Spirit of the Lord is, there is freedom, but where Islam reigns, there is punishment and fear.

Islam and Christianity offer totally different prescriptions for living. And the wrong prescription, as we well know, can be deadly.

THE CHRISTIAN PRESCRIPTION

The most basic prescription for Christian living is summed up in two simple commandments, voiced first in Judaism and then by Jesus: "'Love the Lord your God with all your heart and with all your soul and with all your mind.' This is the first and greatest commandment. And the second is like it: 'Love your neighbor as yourself.' All the Law and the Prophets hang on these two commandments." (Matthew 22:37-40; see also Deuteronomy 6:5).

Do Christians universally obey these simple commandments? Tragically, no. All too many professing Christians display unloving behavior—unloving toward God, and unloving toward their neighbors. Christians are not immune to self-righteousness, prejudice, hatred, anger, and bitterness. But there is nothing in Christianity that condones, much less endorses, an unloving attitude or behavior. To the contrary, an authentic Christian will constantly strive, with the help of God, to weed out any habits or behaviors that hinder the expression of God's love in his or her life. The clear command of Jesus to His followers is still, "Love each other as I have loved you" (John 15:12).

Christians always fall short of Christ's example. The history of Christianity is filled with spectacular examples of such failures: the Crusades, the Spanish Inquisition of the Middle Ages, and the vicious extremism of contemporary Northern Ireland. Genuine Christians regard these historical periods with shame and tend to blame them on misguided zeal. We acknowledge our own weakness and failure, and our tendency to excuse ourselves and accuse our neighbors. But the overriding belief of orthodox Christians down through the ages has been that genuine Christians are known by their love. John wrote eloquently about this love in his letters:

- "This is the message you heard from the beginning: We should love one another. Do not be like Cain, who belonged to the evil one and murdered his brother" (1 John 3:11).
- "Anyone who hates his brother is a murderer, and you know that no murderer has eternal life in him" (1 John 3:15).
- "This is how we know what love is: Jesus Christ laid down his life for us. And we ought to lay down our lives for our brothers . . . . Dear children, let us not love with words or tongue but with actions and in truth" (1 John 3:16, 18).
- "This is his command: to believe in the name of his Son, Jesus Christ, and to love one another as he commanded us" (1 John 3:23).

The message of God's love toward us rings loud and clear throughout the Gospels. Jesus said, "For God so loved the world that he gave his one and only Son, that whoever believes in him shall not perish but have eternal life. For God did not send his Son into the world to condemn the world, but to save the world through him" (John 3:16-17).

The call to love one another is equally pervasive in the Gospels. Jesus said, "Love your enemies, do good to those who hate you, bless those who curse you, pray for those who mistreat you. . . . Love your enemies, do good to them, and lend to them without expecting to get anything back. Then your reward will be great, and you will be sons of the Most High, because he is kind to the ungrateful and wicked. Be merciful, just as your Father is merciful" (Luke 6:27-28, 35-36).

The ancient Greeks had four different words for four distinctly different kinds of love. There was *philia* or friendship love; *storge* or family love; *eros*, which is romantic love or the love of beauty; and finally there is *agape*, the highest love of all—a Christlike, self-sacrificing love that is rooted not in the emotions, but in the will. *Agape* love is the decision to keep loving and seeking the best for someone even when we don't feel like it, even when that person is mistreating us, abusing us, or sinning against us. When Jesus tells us, "Love your enemies," he is speaking of *agape* love. You can't have loving *feelings* toward people who are trying to hurt you—but you can *choose* to love your enemies through a deliberate act of your *will*. That's the kind of love God has shown to you and me, and that's the kind of love Jesus commands us to demonstrate to one another.

THE PRESCRIPTION OF CONFESSION AND FORGIVENESS

One way we live out Christlike *agape* love toward one another is by *forgiving* one another. Jesus said, "Do not judge, and you will not be judged. Do not condemn, and you will not be condemned. Forgive, and you will be forgiven" (Luke 6:37). The Christian faith calls us to confess our faults to one another, to forgive freely, and to make amends for the wrongs we have done.

Muslims frequently point to the Crusades and the Inquisition as two great indelible stains on Christian history, and they are justified in doing so. After taking Jerusalem in 1099, the Crusaders slaughtered innocent men, women, and children—Muslims, Jews, and even other Christians. Islamic historians have exaggerated the death toll, but there can be no justification for what the Crusaders did in the name of Christ. Most Christians today are appalled at what the Crusaders did.

On the one-thousandth anniversary of the fall of Jerusalem, Pope John Paul II issued an apology for the actions of the Crusaders and called the atrocities committed by them in the Holy Land "departures" from the Spirit of Christ and His Gospel. It was right for him to do so.

Will Muslims ever issue a similar apology for the historical actions of Muslim armies against Christians and Jews? No. The truth is that the spread of Islam throughout the Arab world and beyond took place largely through military conquest, not voluntary conversions. The history of Islam is a history of massacres, enslavement, torture, and brutality far exceeding the crimes committed by Crusaders.

As Christians, we have a duty to own up to our own failures. The Gospel of Jesus Christ challenges us to confess our faults, to seek and give forgiveness, and to love our neighbors and our enemies. There is no equivalent to these Christian duties in Islam. The Koran commands Muslims to wage war on the unbelievers, to conquer them, and if need be, to annihilate them.

Christians are to win their enemies over through love, compassion, and Christlike acts of charity. The prescription of confession and forgiveness is central to the Christian life. It is unknown and unheard of in Islamic life.

THE PRESCRIPTION OF ISLAM

In contrast to Christianity, Islam is a religion of law, blind submission, fear, and punishment. Under theocratic-Islamic rule, submitting to the ruler is equal with submitting to Allah. Islam doesn't simply require *belief* in Allah, the Koran, Muhammad as the prophet, and the Day of Judgment. Islam demands surrender and submission.

A bedouin tribe in seventh century Arabia professed faith to Muhammad, saying, "We believe in Allah!" Muhammad is said to have replied, "You have not believed until you say, 'We have submitted ourselves!'" (Koran 49:14).

A Muslim's fundamental religious duties and beliefs are summed up in the Five Pillars of Islam:

1. *Confession* (*Shahada*). This means reciting the statement, "There is no god but Allah, and Muhammad is the Messenger of God."
2. *Prayer*. Formal prayers must be recited five times a day: before sunrise, after midday, at mid-afternoon, shortly after sunset, and in the fullness of night. Prayer involves kneeling and prostrating oneself in the direction of Mecca.
3. *Paying the Alms Tax* (*Zakat*). The legal *zakat* or "purification tax" is levied on property. All Muslims pay this religious tax for the benefit of the poor (which may include one's own family members, the needy, and at times, the poor stranger who is passing through the area). The amount of the *zakat* is predetermined—usually about two and a half percent of one's wealth. In some circumstances, the percentage may be higher.
4. *Fasting and Prayers at Ramadan*. Fasting is generally limited to the holy month of Ramadan, the month in which Muslims believe the first verses of the Koran were revealed to Muhammad in 610 A.D. Between sunrise and sunset, adult Muslims do not smoke, eat, drink, or engage in sexual intercourse. Some Muslims read the Koran from beginning to end during the month. They may eat and drink only between sunset and sunrise. Ramadan is both the name of the ninth month on the Islamic calendar (a lunar calendar), and the name of the period of religious observance marked

by fasting. The three days that follow Ramadan are a feasting period, a time for almsgiving and exchanging gifts.

5. *Pilgrimage.* Every Muslim of sound mind and body who can afford the journey is expected to make a pilgrimage, called *Hajj*, to Mecca at least once in his or her lifetime. Those who make the pilgrimage may add *al-Hajj* to their names.

These five duties are regarded as the minimal obligations of every good Muslim. Observing the Five Pillars is not adequate to ensure that one is living a virtuous and acceptable life, but they are the absolute prerequisites of virtue.

In addition to the Five Pillars, Muslims are expected to "commend good and reprimand evil" and they are forbidden to gamble, charge interest on loans made to fellow Muslims, and consume alcohol or pork.

All Muslims are strictly commanded to keep the Five Pillars—but what these Pillars mean to the individual may vary from one Muslim to the next. Orthodox Muslims—sometimes called believers in "high Islam"—are those who tend to be trained in the Koran, more educated, and of higher cultural status. Hundreds of millions of Muslims, however, are considered to be "low" Muslims—less formal in their understanding, less educated in the Koran, more "superstitious," and more likely to interpret Islam according to cultural folklore and customs. The differences play out in these very basic ways:

	"HIGH" ISLAM	"LOW" ISLAM
Confession	Proves one is a true Muslim.	Words are used to drive away evil.
Prayer Ritual	Bodily washing results in purification.	Demonic pollution is removed.
The Alms Tax	Responsibility to fellow Muslims.	Precaution against "evil eye" (a look that causes bad luck).
Fasting	Sign of commitment to Islam.	Ritual observance to ward off evil and sickness.
Pilgrimage to Mecca	Visit the fountainhead of Islamic faith and history.	Ritual observance to ward off evil and sickness.

The most intensely devoted adherents to Islam are the Sufis, the ascetics and mystics of Islam. Sufis seek to be completely reliant upon God (*tawakkul*) and to keep Allah in perpetual remembrance (*dhikr*), usually through a discipline of repeating the names of Allah. The Sufi movement developed within orthodox

Islamic practice, but many in Islam regard the Sufis as heretical because they seek direct contact with the Divine.

AN OUTWARD EMPHASIS

The main emphasis in Islam is on external behavior, not the inward transformation of the heart, mind, and will. Islam is a religion of rituals and external acts—overt behavior that one must engage in with the hope of receiving Allah's favor.

There is no such thing as unconditional *agape* love in Islam, only a system of rewards and punishment. Nowhere does Islam state that Allah loves us simply because of who we are as people he has created. Instead, Islam teaches that Allah may or may not show favor to those who obey his commands. Observing the Five Pillars is a *minimum* requirement for Allah to even *consider* showing favor to a believer. Even the most devout and pious Muslim has no assurance of winning Allah's favor and entering paradise. A Muslim could conceivably observe all the tenets of Islam throughout his or her life and still be rejected by Allah in the end. There is no assurance of salvation in Islam.

Christians may be tempted to regard Islamic belief as "salvation by works." Salvation, however, is not a concept Islam accepts. Because Islam does not view humanity as having a sinful nature, human nature does not need to be transformed. Even so, Muslims live their lives in fear of offending Allah and suffering an eternity in hell. The Muslim experience is an experience of continual spiritual anxiety, because a Muslim can never be assured of having done enough good deeds and religious rituals to have earned acquittal before the eternal Judge.

Just as sin is not part of humanity's essential nature, according to Islam, forgiveness is not an essential part of Allah's nature. Unlike the God of the Bible, Allah has not bound himself by his own nature to offer forgiveness to human beings. Allah will generally behave in a consistent manner, and he is called "merciful," but there is no assurance that he will show mercy and forgiveness toward any given believer.

When Muslims pray to Allah, they employ a certain amount of cajoling and begging. Five times a day, they bow before a deity who is unwilling to give any assurance of grace and forgiveness. So a continual sense of insecurity and fear, bordering on terror, is integral to Islam. This fear affects a Muslim's relationships with other people: If a Muslim cannot know with certainty that he is forgiven, what is his motivation to forgive others? In Islam, there is no Parable of the Unmerciful Servant (see Matthew 18:21-35), no statement of "Forgive, and you will be forgiven" (Luke 6:37), no forgive-us-as-we-forgive-others principle as in the Lord's Prayer

(Luke 11:4). In Islam, Muslims see Allah as unyielding in demanding subjection to his will—and the result is that Muslims tend to respond to others in a judgmental, unyielding, unforgiving way.

The prescription of Islam focuses on outward rituals, outward observances, and outward appearances. The prescription of Christianity is focused on the inward reality of the believer's heart.

WHAT ABOUT THOSE WHO DON'T BELIEVE?

Christianity regards those who don't believe in Christ as "unconverted." Jesus commissioned his followers to preach his Gospel throughout the world and give every person an opportunity to accept him as Lord and Savior. That is the essence of Christian evangelism. The act of acceptance is an act of free will—never an act of force or duress.

By contrast, Islam considers those who do not adhere to Islam as "infidels." The word *infidel* comes from the same root as *infidelity*, the act or condition of being unfaithful or even treacherous and treasonous. That is how Islam views infidels. They are not merely people who do not believe. They are faithless and even treacherous. Islam does not seek to evangelize or persuade infidels. An infidel simply needs to be brought into subjection to the will of Allah. Subjection does not require free will. A person can be forced to surrender to the will of Allah even against his will.

This is a critical distinction to understand. It lies at the heart of the terrorism we have witnessed, and which Muslim zealots will likely continue to inflict against "infidels" in America and throughout the Western world. Many Westerners have asked me through the years, "Why are Muslims so fanatical about their religion? Why is it that the more devout a Muslim is, the more intolerant he tends to be toward other religions?"

From the viewpoint of Islam, Muslims believe they alone have been given "the final revelation" of God in the Koran. Note that word *final*. Muslims respect the Torah (the five books of Moses) and the Injeil (their version of the Gospel). But their sacred book, the Koran, teaches that they are called to enforce God's will. The Koran challenges all Islamic followers—moderate or zealot, young or old, religious or secular—to *convert or conquer* unbelievers. Muslims are not instructed to merely preach the Islamic message and give people the opportunity to convert to Islam. For the extreme Islamist who truly takes the Koran literally and seriously, there is no room for moderation or tolerance.

The oil wealth and growing political power of Islamic leaders in many nations has allowed an uncompromising and intolerant form of Islamic fundamentalism to manifest itself on a grand scale. Extreme Islamists are pursuing a goal of bringing all people throughout the world under Islamic control. According to the Koran, this is the fulfillment of Allah's will for all people throughout the world.

Look at the militarism of Iran under the ayatollahs, the repression of Afghanistan under the Taliban, the terror bombings sponsored by Libya's Muammar Gaddafi, the stealth propagandizing of the Muslim Brotherhood, the Saudi-financed Wahhabi madrassas (extremist Islamic religious schools) around the world, the bellicose words and deadly actions of Osama bin Laden and the Al-Qaeda leadership, the occupation of Lebanon by Syria, the Palestinian rocket attacks and terror attacks in Israel, the Islamic militias in Indonesia, the Philippines, Sudan, and elsewhere. These actions are rooted in the concept of imposing and enforcing Allah's will upon the entire world, including the so-called "infidels." The goal of all these actions is to subjugate all nations, including the United States, and bring these nations under the domination of the Islamic religion.

ISLAMIC LAW

Islamic law is at the core of Islamic thought. Islamic scholars may disagree on how various laws should be implemented, but there is little disagreement about one central idea: Non-Muslims do not belong to the House of Islam (*Dar al-Islam*); therefore, they belong to the House of War (*Dar al-Harb*). In simple language, if you aren't with us, you are against us. Infidels—those who do not believe in Islam—are to be humiliated, oppressed, denied due process of law, and ultimately coerced into conversion or killed.

The Koran says clearly and forthrightly, "Fight against such as those who have been given the Scripture [the Koran] as believe not in Allah nor the Last Day" (Koran 9:29). No genuine Christian would ever pursue such a warlike strategy—it goes against all the teachings of Jesus and Christian doctrine. But a commitment to such a strategy is precisely what makes a Muslim true to Muslim doctrine. Using this verse as justification, Muslim zealots consider moderate Muslims—those who do not follow these warlike teachings—to be infidels and deserving to be treated as non-Muslims.

There are only three alternatives for dealing with non-Muslims under Islamic law: They must be converted, or they must be subjugated and humiliated, or they must be eliminated (except women, children, and slaves). Islamic law distinguishes between types of non-Muslims; Christians and Jews are in different categories from other non-Muslims.

Some Islamic governments permit an "infidel" to enter a formal agreement or treaty that spares the unbeliever's life and property. Such non-Muslims are classified as *dhimmi* (which means "people of the *dhimma*" or "people of the contract"). A *dhimmi* is granted limited rights and responsibilities under Sharia law, and is subjugated by the Islamic state. A *dhimmi* must wear identifiable clothing and live in a clearly marked house. He must not ride a horse or bear arms. He must always yield the right-of-way to Muslims. A *dhimmi* cannot be a witness in a legal court except in matters relating to other *dhimmis*. He cannot be the guardian of a Muslim child, owner of a Muslim slave, or a judge in a Muslim court.[2]

The concept of *dhimmi* is of great significance because Islamic fundamentalists—those who interpret the Koran and Islamic law in the narrowest, most literal sense—often take minor concepts and establish major policies that affect Islamic society, political systems, and economic practice. Three categories of *dhimmi* are identified in Islam: *Hudna*, *Musta'min*, and *Zimmi*.

Hudna ("truce") are those who sign a peace treaty with Muslims after being defeated in war. They may continue to reside on their own land, yet are subject to the laws of Islam.

Musta'min ("protected ones") are those who come to an Islamic nation as messengers, merchants, visitors, or students wanting to learn about Islam. They are obliged to pay *jizya* (tribute, a "protection tax") and must not engage in war against Muslims. If they do not accept Islam, they are allowed to return safely to their own country. Once in their homeland, they are treated as belonging to the Household of War,

Zimmis (literally "those in custody") are non-Muslims who live in Muslim countries and agree to pay the *jizya* in exchange for protection and safety. They also agree to be subject to Islamic law. The imposition of the protection tax is intended to be a sign of humiliation and subjugation. Zimmis are not allowed to build new churches, temples, or synagogues. They may renovate "old churches," those which were in existence prior to the Islamic conquest. No *church*, temple, or synagogue may be built in Saudi Arabia (or the entire Arabian Peninsula). That land is considered "sacred" since it was the land of Muhammad.

"Infidels" classed as Zimmis are subject to severe religious restrictions. They are not allowed to pray aloud or read their sacred books aloud, not even at home or in church, because a Muslim passing by might hear and be offended. Zimmis are not allowed to print their religious books or sell them in public places and markets. They are not allowed to display the cross on their houses or churches. They are not allowed to broadcast or display ceremonial religious rituals on radio or television, or to use any form of media to publish pictures related to their religious ceremonies. They are not allowed to congregate in the streets during their religious festivals or join the army (unless there is an indispensable need for them, in which case they may be conscripted for service but not hold leadership positions).

Muslims are not allowed to emulate the Zimmis in their dress or behavior, to attend Zimmi festivals or support them in any way. They are not to lease their houses or sell land for the construction of a church, temple, liquor store, or anything that may benefit the Zimmi faith. They may not work for Zimmis in any job that might promote their faith (such as constructing a church), make any financial gift to a church or temple, or address Zimmis with any title such as "my master" or "my lord."

Muslims may console Zimmis in an illness or the loss of a loved one. They may escort a Zimmi funeral procession to the cemetery, but they are to walk in front of the coffin, not behind it, and they must depart before the deceased is buried. Muslims may congratulate Zimmis for a wedding, birth of a child, return from a long trip, or recovery from illness. But they are not to utter any word that may suggest approval of the Zimmis' faith, such as "May Allah exalt you," or "May Allah give your religion victory."

What does all this mean to us in the West? *Dhimmi*—and in particular, Zimmi, is the classification given to Christians in most Muslim countries. These are the restrictions under which Christians must live and work. In fact, this is how the Saudi government treated our soldiers when they went to defend Saudi Arabia from Saddam Hussein during the Gulf War. If you understand how Christians are required to live in Islamic nations, you'll understand better how to pray for your Christian brothers and sisters who are living in Muslim nations.

Most non-Muslims are not regarded as citizens by any Islamic state, even if they are original natives of the land. That is why Muslim extremists in such countries as Egypt, Syria, Lebanon, and even Iraq, where Christians are somewhat tolerated, want to topple these regimes. They do not consider these nations to be full-fledged Islamic states unless non-Muslims are given second-class status.

When a nation declares itself to be an Islamic state by law, its native non-Muslim people suddenly become second-class citizens. The history of Egypt gives us an excellent example of how this works:

The Islamic religion first came to Egypt in the middle 600s A.D. The onslaught of Islam was strongly resisted by the Coptic Church, which had been founded in A.D. 42 by Mark the Evangelist, the author of the second Gospel. The Coptic Church had six centuries in which to become established and strong before Muslims from Arabia overran Egypt. The price of resisting Islam and refusing to convert was often death. Those who were not martyred were taxed heavily.

Today in Egypt, the Copts have retained much of their original heritage. Estimates vary from 8 to 15 million Coptic Christians that comprise between 10 and 15 percent of Egypt's 85 million people. Life has always been difficult and precarious for the Copts. If the Muslim Brotherhood and other Islamist groups in Egypt get their way in the post-Mubarak government, the government will likely come under Sharia law and return to the concept of *dhimmi*, which would turn the Copts into second-class citizens in the land where they have lived for almost two thousand years.

For decades, the Muslim Brotherhood has targeted Egyptian Copts for violence. The Egyptian Christians have had their property confiscated or destroyed. Their people have been beaten, maimed, and killed. From time to time, waves of violence pass through the land like a paroxysm of religious hate, targeting Christian shops, restaurants, homes, and churches.

Westerners, steeped in the tradition of separation of church and state, find it difficult to imagine what life is like for Coptic Christians in Egypt. For their part, most Muslims are unable to even conceive of separation of religion and state. In the Muslim mind, the state is viewed as an extension of the religion. They see religion and government as intertwined, not only in their own culture but in other cultures, including America. So when America gets involved in events in the Middle East, Muslims do not see America as a secular government, but as a "Crusader" nation. To the Islamic mind, it's as if the Crusades are still going on.

That's why Osama bin Laden in his 1996 fatwa, "Declaration of War against the Americans Occupying the Land of the Two Holy Places," refers more than twenty times to "the American Crusader forces" (the American military) or "the Zionist-Crusader alliance" (Israel and America).[3] Bin Laden seems oblivious to the fact that "the American Crusader forces" have actually been engaged in the defense of Muslims—aiding the Muslim Mujahideen in Afghanistan against the Soviets, defending Muslim Bosnians and Kosovars against the Serbs, defending Kuwait and Saudi Arabia against the Iraqis, and on and on. What kind of "Crusader" nation would expend its own blood and treasure to protect Muslims?

Muslims overseas cannot differentiate between the Western way of life and the Judeo-Christian ethical system. They assume that all Americans are Jews or Christians since our values are rooted in the Judeo-Christian ethical system. They see their fellow Muslims who live in America as "strangers in a strange land." Muslims are expected to keep themselves separate from the culture as a whole. They are to pledge their allegiance to Islam, not America.

Those who oppose Islam—or who are perceived to be standing in the way of the advancement of Islam—are considered infidels of the worst kind. They deserve only to be killed in the process of subjugation. Fundamentalist Islamists believe those who oppose Islam should be killed as a matter of obedience to Allah.

The subjugation of non-Islamic people, and particularly those who oppose Islam, is at the heart of a concept called *jihad*. In the next chapter, we will explore the implications of this word.

6

JIHAD

The first word Palestinian school children learn in their reading primers is *jihad*. It is often the first word shouted as mobs of radical Muslims assault Coptic Christians and destroy their shops and homes in Cairo or Alexandria. It is the first word on the lips of those who plot terror attacks against the West.

The word *jihad*, often used to communicate the concept of "holy war," literally means "struggle." There are three types of jihad recognized by Muslim scholars. First, there is the jihad of one's self—the inner struggle of maintaining self-discipline and of battling evil in one's own mind and heart. Second, there is the jihad against Satan—the struggle against temptation and spiritual oppression that Christians would call "spiritual warfare." Third, there is the jihad against infidels and hypocrites—the fight against all who reject or oppose the advance of Islam. This is the form of jihad known as "holy war." Muslims often see themselves as dealing with all three forms of jihad at once—struggling for self-discipline, struggling against Satan, and struggling against infidels.

Muslims believe that forsaking jihad brings suffering to individual Muslims and to the Islamic community. They cite this statement in the Koran: "O ye who believe! What aileth you that when it is said unto you: Go forth in the way of Allah, ye are bowed down to the ground with heaviness. Take ye pleasure in the life of the world rather than in the Hereafter? The comfort of the life of the world is but little in comparison with that in the Hereafter. If ye go not forth he will afflict you with a painful doom, and will choose instead of you a folk other than you. Ye cannot harm him at all. Allah is able to do all things" (Koran 9:38-39).

Not every Muslim agrees that jihad requires spilling the blood of infidels. Some Muslims insist that the "struggle" refers only to an individual Muslim's personal struggle against evil. Nevertheless, the struggle for the victory of Islam is a factor in the life of every faithful Muslim. Even those who see jihad as a personal religious term must acknowledge that, down through the centuries, Muslims have regarded jihad as the struggle for Islam to gain preeminence over all other religious teachings. Muslim Brotherhood founder Hassan al-Banna explained the importance of jihad this way:

> *How wise was the man who said, "Force is the surest way of implementing the right, how beautiful it is that force and right should march side by side." This striving to broadcast the Islamic mission, quite apart from preserving the hallowed concepts of Islam, is another religious duty imposed by God on the Muslims, just as he imposed fasting, prayer, pilgrimage, alms, and the doing of good and abandonment of evil, upon them. He imposes it upon them and delegated them to do it. He did not excuse anyone possessing strength and capacity from performing it.*[1]

Jihad, according to Islamic law, must be waged until the Day of Judgment. There may be times when Muslim armies appear to be defeated, but even legal armistices can be broken when doing so is perceived (by Muslims) to be in the best interests of Islam. Islam allows no permanent peaceful coexistence and co-equality with infidels. Superiority is such a central aspect of Islamic thought that domination is the only worthy expression of Islam's greatness.

It's not strange, therefore, to read in the Koran that Allah exhorts Muslims not to befriend Jews or Christians: "Oh ye who believe! Take not the Jews and Christians for friends. They are friends one to another. He among you who taketh them for friends is one of them" (Koran 5:51).

Elsewhere, the Koran states: "Believers, do not make friends with anyone other than your own people. They desire nothing but ruin. Their hatred is clear from what they say, but more violent is the hatred that their breasts conceal" (Koran 3:118).

Extremists, of course, take quotes such as these as proof that they are to enforce intolerance of non-Muslims. The result is an array of laws and rules that prohibit interaction between Muslims and those who are not of their own "brotherhood." Extremists also exhort the "faithful" to engage in a holy war against Jews, Christians, and other non-Muslims.

Those who are not extremists sometimes state that they believe these texts were only for certain historical periods, and that they are not binding upon Muslims today. Those voices of moderation tend to be muted. The dominant sentiment throughout the Muslim world is that hatred, holy war, and world domination are an integral part of Islam today, just as in times past.

The doctrine of Islamic superiority reaches its apex in Koran 5:33. In this statement, Muslims are commanded to *fight* non-Muslims and anyone who rejects

Allah and his apostle (Muhammad). How are they to deal with the enemies of Islam? By crucifying them, cutting off their hands and feet on alternate sides, or banishing them from the country.

Many scoff when jihad is declared by a small group of extremists from a tiny Islamic nation about which little is known. The imperative to subjugate non-Muslims, however, runs deep among Muslims around the world—not just in the hills and caves of Afghanistan or the remote sands of Yemen. Jihad is an essential ingredient of Islamic philosophy, and all who truly love the Koranic faith are devoted to jihad. The concept of jihad is the nail on which hang all rationales for the use of political power, military force, and terrorist violence to advance the Islamic cause.

Muslims have been left to define for themselves the means of waging jihad against infidels. Islamic scholars generally endorse any means of achieving victory, so long as it will reduce the loss of Muslim lives to a minimum. That was the jihadist thinking that produced the 9/11 attacks in which nineteen Muslim men sacrificed their lives in order to kill three thousand Westerners, destroy the symbols of American economic and military might, and inflict a massive wound to the American psyche.

From the Islamist's and jihadist's point of view, the 9/11 attacks succeeded beyond Al-Qaeda's wildest dreams.

NO MERCY FROM ISLAMIC FUNDAMENTALISTS

Though the concept of mercy does appear here and there throughout the Koran, the Islamic view of mercy is a highly restricted concept. There is no room in Islam for mercy toward those who oppose the advance of Islam. While passages of the Koran decry the murder of innocents and urge mercy and tolerance toward life in general, mercy is not extended to those who stand in the path of Islam's quest to dominate the world.

The Koran states: "When the sacred months are past, kill those who join other gods wherever you find them, and seize them, beleaguer them, and lie in wait for them with every kind of ambush; but if they convert and observe prayer and pay the obligatory alms, let them go their way" (Koran 9:5). And, "Strive hard against the unbelievers and the hypocrites, and be firm against them. Their abode is Hell, an evil refuge indeed" (Koran 9:73).

The terms "militant" and "fundamentalist" have come to mean the same thing in certain circles—whether the terms are applied to Muslims, Christians, or Jews. Fundamentalists are perceived to be fanatics who have withdrawn from mainstream society to form enclaves of intense, single-minded devotion to their beliefs. Fundamentalists interpret their scriptures in the most literal sense, and they see themselves as defenders of the pure faith against those who would water down and compromise that faith.

In its original sense, the word *fundamentalist* referred to someone who upheld the "fundamentals" or "essentials" of the faith. A fundamentalist recognized that there was a set of irreducible beliefs, and if one were to stray from those "fundamentals," it would constitute compromise, heresy, and apostasy.

Not all fundamentalists are militant. In fact, the vast majority of those Christians who believe strongly in the Bible's commandments are not militaristic, separatist, countercultural, or on the offensive.

But Islamic fundamentalism is *always* militant. Those who believe strongly in the fundamentals of Islam are nearly always militaristic, because Islam is presented as a militant and militaristic faith in the Koran.

Norman Geisler is the co-author (with Abdul Saleeb) of *Answering Islam* (Baker Book House, 1994). He said, "What Islam engages in is consistent with the teachings of the [Koran] and Muhammad, while what some Christians did in the Crusades is contrary to the teachings of the Bible and Jesus Christ." He also said, "Violence is the logical outworking of Islam and the illogical outworking of Christianity."[2]

Within the Muslim world, a power struggle rages between radical, militant Muslims and moderate Muslims. Radical Islam can never coexist peacefully with the voices of moderation. The goal of fundamentalist Islam is total fidelity to the most extreme and militant passages of the Koran—and those passages demand domination of the world and subjugation of all non-Muslims. Moderates, in the eyes of the radicals, are only one step removed from being non-Muslims, because they stand in the way of Islam's advancement and absolute supremacy.

The shout of the radical always drowns out the voice of reason and moderation.

WASHING BLOOD WITH BLOOD

An ancient Middle Eastern saying states, "Wash blood with blood." In other words, when your enemy draws blood, be prepared to spill more blood, his and yours. We hear the command to wash blood with blood in these statements by prominent Islamic leaders:

- Just one week after the United States Marine battalion headquarters in Lebanon were bombed, Sheikh Muhammad Yazbeck said, "Let America, Israel, and the world know that we have a lust for martyrdom and our motto is being translated into reality."[3]

- Hussein Musawi, leader of the Islamic Amal movement, said, "This path is the path of blood, the path of martyrdom. For us, death is easier than smoking a cigarette if it comes while fighting for the cause of God and while defending the oppressed."[4]
- Hasan Al-Banna, the founder of the Muslim Brotherhood of Egypt, told his followers, "You are not a benevolent organization, nor a political party, nor a local association with limited aims. Rather, you are a new spirit making its way into the heart of this nation, and reviving it through the Koran; a new light dawning and scattering the darkness of materialism through the knowledge of God; a resounding voice rising and echoing the message of the Apostle."[5]
- Shukri Ahmed Mustafa, a leader of the Muslim Brotherhood offshoot group Jama'at al-Muslimin (Society of Muslims), which was accused of killing an Egyptian government official, said his movement's philosophy was based on "sacred hatred" of Islamic nations he believes have departed from the true faith. Mustafa told a reporter before he was hanged in 1978, "Spilling the blood of heretics is the sacred duty of all Muslims." Mustafa saw the assassination as part of a pattern of assassinations, including the assassination of Anwar Sadat, as a means of prodding the masses into Islamic revolution. The goal was to spur Egypt to becoming the "Islamic Republic of Egypt"—a first step toward Islamic rule over the world.

It is important to note that the Islamic Jihad organization of Egypt did not come to the world's attention until the assassination of Anwar Sadat—much as Al-Qaeda did not become a household word until September 11, 2001. Both organizations, however, existed long before the tragic events that catapulted them to notoriety. Those who have followed the history of these groups know that the Egyptian Islamic Jihad merged with Al-Qaeda in mid-2001, shortly before the 9/11 attacks.

The Muslim Brotherhood, which fathered all of these groups, was founded in 1928 and initially consisted of just seven people. By the 1950s, however, the Brotherhood had become one of the most powerful and popular organizations in Egypt. Today its reach extends around the world, and the Brotherhood has a strong (though largely hidden) presence in the United States.

Some Americans believe that by rounding up hundreds or thousands of Al-Qaeda leaders and fighters, we can end Islamic terrorism. But this would be like washing blood with blood. No matter how many terrorists you kill, there are always more lining up to take their place. Though the War on Terror is critically important to restraining the jihadist onslaught, war alone is not the answer. We must also fight for the hearts and minds of those who would do us harm.

THE BLOODY EXAMPLE OF KHOMEINI'S IRAN

After the Ayatollah Khomeini assumed power in Iran, he came down hard on everything that was not according to his interpretation of Islamic law and tradition. As a result, Iran suffered a torrent of executions, bombings, assassinations, and other atrocities. Khomeini did not only target officials of the former regime of the shah. He also targeted members of the Mojahedin-e Khalq (The Holy Warriors of the Iranian People), an Islamic fundamentalist organization with a leftist ideology that had fought a guerrilla war against the shah.

Before Khomeini came to power, the Mojahedin-e Khalq had been allies and admirers of the ayatollah. One Mojahedin pamphlet said of him, "The person of the Ayatollah is the symbolic figure of the people's epic. . . . He is a famous hero and the symbol of the Iranian struggle."[6] After Khomeini came to power, he treated the Mojahedin as a threat to be neutralized. Within months, 2,500 Mojahedin followers were arrested and executed by hanging and firing squads.

The Mojahedin countered with its own brand of terror, killing hundreds of Khomeini supporters and officials with suicide bombing attacks. The majority of the suicide assassins were young, aged fifteen to twenty-five. The Mojahedin declaration of June 20, 1981—issued after the first wave of Khomeini-ordered executions—said in part:

> *Khordad 30th (June 20, 1981) is our Ashura. On that day we had to stand up and resist Khomeini's bloodthirsty and reactionary regime, even if it meant sacrificing our lives and the whole of our organization. We had to take this road to Karbala to keep alive our tawhidi ideology, follow the example set by Imam Hussein, fulfill our historic mission to the Iranian people, and fight the most bloodthirsty, most reactionary, and most savage regime in world history.*[7]

Khomeini responded in an equally defiant and ruthless tone: "Our nation is no longer ready to submit to humiliation and abjection; it prefers a bloody death to a life of shame. We are ready to be killed, and we have made a covenant with God to follow the path of our leader, the Lord of Martyrs."[8]

The bloodshed between the Islamic government of Khomeini and the Mojahedin continued for four years. In all, more than 12,250 political dissidents died, three-quarters of them Mojahedin members or sympathizers.

These killings went largely unreported in the West. Many Western leaders and media pundits viewed this bloodshed as a civil war in Iran. The Mojahedin specialized in using car bombs and suicide bombs to achieve mass killings. Terrorists in other parts of the world—especially the Palestinians who struggled against Israel—learned many lessons in mass slaughter from the Khomeini-Mojahedin conflict.

Khomeini Shiite forces justified their slaughter of the Mojahedin on the grounds that they were avenging the beheading in A.D. 680 of Hussein ibn Ali, a descendant of the prophet Muhammad and a revered martyr of the Shia. That's right, the slaughter of the Mojahedin was justified as revenge for *a thirteen hundred-year-old murder*. Muslim memories are long, and one never knows what ancient historic event might be used to justify vengeance and bloodshed today. There are thousands and thousands of scores to settle, and a blood-debt is never fully and finally repaid.

WHO DIES? THE YOUNG!

To a Muslim, dying and killing for the cause of Islam not only brings honor to oneself and one's family, it is a way of pleasing Allah. In fact, the only way Muslims can be certain of their admittance into paradise is by becoming a martyr for the cause of Islam. Death in the struggle against infidels is eagerly desired by fanatical Muslims.

In preparing to wage war against Iraq, Khomeini called for ten thousand volunteers to join the fight. Thousands of young boys stepped forward to become *basijis* ("the mobilized"). A *basiji* is not only prepared for the *possibility* of death—he is totally committed to dying for Islam. The *basijis* volunteered to clear the minefields with their bodies, and they did so. Military leaders sent out as many as five thousand boys at once to run through the fields and trip the mines.

Sometimes they asked the boys to clear high voltage border fences by throwing their bodies against the live wires. Thousands of young boys were electrocuted, many only twelve or thirteen years old. To them, Khomeini held out the same promise that is held out to suicide terrorists throughout the Muslim world today: certain entrance into paradise (*behesht*). Each boy received a key to hang around his neck—supposedly the key to open the gate of heaven.

One young Iranian soldier, Mohsen Naeemi, who died in the war with Iraq, left behind a note that read in part: "My wedding is at the front and my bride is martyrdom. The sermon will be uttered by the roar of guns. I shall attire myself in my blood for this ceremony. My bride, martyrdom, shall give birth to my son, freedom. I leave this son in your safekeeping. Keep him well."[9]

Many people in the West try to separate the blood-splattered acts of Khomeini and other Islamic extremists from the tenets of Islam. They claim that these acts are a perversion of Islam, which they call a "religion of peace." These idealistic but naïve apologists for Islam fail to recognize that violence and bloodshed are not exclusive to the Shiites, or to any one Islamic nation or region. Muslim violence throughout the world is marked by methods almost identical to those of the Islamic revolution in Iran.

This same death-cult mentality can be seen throughout the Islamic world. The Muslim Brotherhood in Egypt and Syria trained many of the Arab Palestinians to fight against Israel. The motto of the Brotherhood was, "The Koran is our constitution, the Prophet is our guide; death for the glory of Allah is our greatest ambition."[10] The former Egyptian Interior minister, Ahmed Mortade al Maraghi, once described how young militants were recruited by the Muslim Brotherhood:

> *A small room lit with candle light and smoky with incense is chosen. . . . Once the likely young man is selected, he is brought to this room . . . where he will find a sheikh repeating verses from the Koran. . . . The Sheikh with eyes like magnets stares at the young man who is paralyzed with awe. . . . They will then pray, and the sheikh will recite verses from the Koran about those fighting for the sake of Allah and are therefore promised to go to heaven. "Are you ready for martyrdom?" the young man is asked. "Yes, yes," he repeats. He is then given the oath on the Koran. These young men leave the meeting with one determination: to kill.*[11]

A number of terrorist groups have sprung from the Muslim Brotherhood, including Al Jihad ("The Jihad Organization") and Al Taqfir Wal Higrah ("Repentance and Migration"). Hamas, Hezbollah, Amal, and the Palestinian Liberation Organization (PLO) have all taken their cues from the Muslim Brotherhood. Islamic scholar Bernard Lewis observes:

> *"There is something in the religious culture of Islam which inspired, in even the humblest peasant or peddler, a dignity and a courtesy toward others never exceeded and rarely equaled in other civilizations. And yet, in moments of upheaval and disruption, when the deeper passions are stirred, this dignity and courtesy toward others can give way to an explosive mixture of rage and hatred which impels even the government of an ancient and civilized country—even the spokesman of a great spiritual and ethical religion—to espouse kidnapping and assassination, and try to find, in the life of their prophet, approval and indeed precedent for such actions.*[12]

It seems that the stirring of fanatical hatreds has a special appeal to the young. There seems to be no shortage of hot-blooded youths willing to blow themselves up in minefields or strap bomb vests to their bodies for the sake of Allah. What motivates Islamic youth to sacrifice their young lives on the altar of Islamic fanaticism?

REWARDS FOR THE MARTYRS

Those who die for the cause of Islam are heralded as martyrs. Their photographs are often enlarged to poster size and carried through the streets by chanting crowds or put on display in village squares. The photographs of suicide bombers are routinely shown to Islamic school children, beginning in kindergarten. The suicide bombers are called heroes and young boys are asked to imagine themselves attaining the glory of these heroes.

In addition to the rewards of honor and glory, there is also a monetary reward for martyrdom. Before he was deposed, Iraqi dictator Saddam Hussein would send his Iraqi-funded Arab Liberation Front to the door of a Palestinian suicide bomber's home with a check for $10,000. That's a lot of money to a poor Palestinian family—and hundreds of these checks have been issued. In fact, Saddam Hussein pledged almost a billion dollars to support the Intifada, the Palestinian uprising.

Suicide bombers are promised that they and their families will be exalted if they die in the cause of jihad. Although the families of these martyrs appear to mourn at a funeral, they privately celebrate the martyr's death as a wedding. Why? Because Islam teaches that when the martyr arrives in paradise, there are seventy-two virgins waiting for him, ready to fulfill his wildest sexual fantasies.

This notion has strong appeal for a young man with raging hormones—and the appeal is all the stronger if these young men have no chance for a decent education, a good job, or a prosperous home life with a wife and children. The majority of the world's Muslims today are under age twenty-five, and they live in the grip of a deadly ideology. The alternative to martyrdom for many of these young men is a life of gun-running or selling illegal drugs.

Young Islamic men are ripe for the message of Islamic extremism. They look beyond the violence of death to a paradise of endless sexual pleasure. Now, perhaps, it is easier to understand why there is no shortage of boys and young men who are willing to throw away their lives for an idea called *jihad*.

7

THE GOAL OF A WORLD EMPIRE

Few in the West are aware that, from the time it was founded, the goal of Islam has been a world empire.

Islam experienced a phenomenal expansion under Umar ibn al-Khattab, the second caliph (Umar succeeded the first caliph, Abu Bakr, who was the successor to Muhammad). Under Umar, Muslim armies defeated the armies of the Sassanian (Persian) and Byzantine Empires. Muslim forces swept through the area that is present-day Iraq and Iran to Central Asia (Bukhara and Samarkand) and the Punjab region of Pakistan and India. The Muslims conquered all the Asiatic territories of the Roman Empire except Anatolia (modern Turkey). Moving northward they conquered Syria, and Damascus became the capital of the Umayyad Caliphate (661–750). Muslim armies conquered Egypt and moved across North Africa and into Europe, ruling most of Spain.

Within a hundred years after Muhammad's death in 632, the Empire of Allah stretched, as someone once said, "from the Pyrenees to the Punjab, from the Sahara to Samarkand." This empire began to disintegrate in some areas by the end of the tenth century—then Islam experienced a resurgence from the fifteenth to the eighteenth centuries. Islam rose up in the form of three new and powerful empires—the Mughal in India, the Safavieh in Iran, and the Ottoman in Anatolia. Islam spread into many new regions in Africa, Asia, and the Middle East, and millions were converted to Islam, either voluntarily or at the point of a sword.

Of particular concern to Western civilization was the Ottoman Empire, the most aggressive of the three Islamic movements. By the end of the sixteenth century, the Ottomans had conquered several Byzantine provinces, including Greece and Bulgaria. Constantinople, long a bulwark of Christendom, fell in 1453 and became Istanbul, capital of the Ottoman Empire.

Under Suleiman the Magnificent (who reigned from 1520 to 1566) the Ottomans gained control of all the Balkan Peninsula except Montenegro, and a strip of the Dalmatian coast. The Ottoman Empire reached into Hungary, encircled the Black Sea, embraced Asia Minor, the Euphrates valley, Armenia, Georgia, Syria,

Palestine, Egypt, and the north coast of Africa as far as Morocco. The advance of the Ottomans was stopped at the gates of Vienna in 1529. Many once-Christian regions became predominantly Muslim. Christian communities survived, but forced conversion to Islam was commonplace. Sons of Christian parents were taken from their homes, reared as Muslims, and enrolled in the armies of Islam. Many churches became mosques.

Though these events seem like ancient history to us today, the troubles we have had to deal with in the former Yugoslavia, involving clashes and ethnic cleansing in Serbia, Croatia, Bosnia, and Herzegovina all have their roots in the Muslim invasion during the sixteenth century. As we have seen, many Islamists do not speak of "the West" or "Christians" or "Americans." They use the term "Crusaders" (*al-Salibia*), because what is "ancient history" to us is "yesterday's news" to the Muslim world.

CHRISTIANITY—ENEMY NUMBER ONE

Militant Islamists view Christianity as the foremost foe of Islam. Christianity blocks the advancement of Islam on virtually all geographic, historical, and ideological fronts. Islamists resent Christianity for four primary reasons:

First, Islamic militants see Christianity as the primary expression of infidel values and practices. Because the Islamists mistakenly assume that Christian values pervade Western civilization in the same way Islamic ideology pervades the Muslim world, they identify all of our culture's ills with Christianity. Though it seems amazing to you and me, Muslims see Hollywood vice and violence, the opulent and wasteful American lifestyle, and corporate greed and corruption as the result of *Christian* influence in our society!

Second, Islamic extremists see Christianity as the most potent ideology they face—far more potent than other religions, communism, or atheism. If Islam's most potent foe can be subjugated, then all other foes will be eliminated in a "mopping-up" action.

Third, though Muslims regard Christianity as a potent ideology, Islamic extremists tend to regard Christians themselves as weak, soft, passive targets—especially Christians in the democratic West. Muslims see our Western tolerance, our lax immigration rules, our "politically correct" willingness to give way whenever Muslims complain of discrimination or "Islamophobia"—and they interpret all this as a weakness they can exploit to subjugate us. America, following in the footsteps of Europe, has made a seemingly suicidal decision not to defend this nation and culture from being infiltrated and undermined by Islamic extremists, so the extremists are busily taking advantage of that fact.

Fourth, Islamic extremists see the Christian West, and especially the United States, as being responsible for many of the social ills people suffer in the Middle East—poverty, ignorance, unrest, and oppression. Above all, the Islamists blame the United States for the establishment and continued existence of the state of Israel. They also resent America for the establishment of U.S. military bases in Saudi Arabia and other Muslim nations. And they blame America for introducing some of the most anti-Islamic features of Western culture (our entertainment and our attire) into the Muslim world.

As a result of this growing resentment, Christians around the world have been targets of violence perpetrated by Muslim extremists. Some examples:

- Pakistan's Christian community (about 2 million strong in a nation of 140 million people) was targeted in the 1998 riots that followed United States military invasion of Afghanistan for attacks on U.S. embassies.

- Enraged Pakistani Muslims killed a pastor and fifteen parishioners of a church in Behawalpur. The attack came shortly after American military troops entered Afghanistan in October 2001. Though Pakistani Christians had nothing to do with American actions, to a Muslim extremist, a "Crusader" is a "Crusader" no matter where you find him.

- Radical Muslims in Indonesia reportedly killed about ten thousand Christians in 2000–2001. Many Christian homes and churches were burned.

- Christians in Iraq—a small minority—were denied food rations by the Iraqi government after the United States began military operations in Afghanistan in October 2001.

- Muslims have waged a twenty-year "holy war" against Christians in Sudan, resulting in more than 2 million deaths and 13 million refugees. Sudanese clerics have issued a *fatwa* stating, "America is the greatest enemy of Islam and it embraces blasphemy, guards the Jews, and protects their terrorism."[1]

- Since September 11, 2001, persecution against religious believers has intensified in Saudi Arabia, which has been classified by the United States as one of the worst violators of religious freedom in the world. The majority of the people arrested have been Christians from Africa and Asia—even though Saudi law states that non-Muslims from other nations are free to worship in private.

- At least two hundred people died during fighting between Muslim and Christian groups in Kano, Nigeria on October 13, 2001. The deaths came in a riot that followed the staging of an anti-American protest that included

Islamic religious slogans and pictures of Osama bin Laden. An eyewitness claimed Christians in Muslim-dominated areas were slaughtered outright.

Consider also these actions by militant Islamists against "the Crusader forces" of the United States:

- In 1979 a group of Muslim students seized the United States Embassy in Tehran and held fifty-two Americans hostages for 444 days.
- Also in 1979, the U.S. Embassy in Islamabad, Pakistan, was set ablaze by Muslim fundamentalists.
- In 1982, thirty-seven Americans and other Westerners were taken hostage by Hezbollah in Lebanon. Hezbollah freed the last American in 1991.
- In 1983 Hezbollah launched three suicide bomb attacks in Beirut, killing 350 people. The American Embassy, the United States military barracks, and the French military barracks were targeted. Among the dead were 241 United States Marines.
- In 1985, Hezbollah hijacked a TWA jetliner to Beirut, killing a United States Navy diver on board.
- In 1988, Islamic terrorists from Libya downed a Pan Am jetliner over Scotland, killing all 259 passengers.
- Throughout the 1980s, nearly a hundred foreigners were kidnapped in Lebanon by Hezbollah. At least eight hostages were killed, including three Americans.
- In 1993, a powerful bomb rocked the World Trade Center in New York City. Six people were killed and a thousand more injured. Sheik Omar Abdel Rahman and 14 of his followers were arrested and charged with the bombing. In the aftermath of their arrests, officials uncovered plots to blow up a federal building in Manhattan, the United Nations building, the Lincoln and Holland tunnels, and the George Washington Bridge.[2]

In recent years, we have witnessed the bombing of two U.S. embassies in Africa, the bombing of the destroyer USS *Cole*, the 9/11 attacks, and numerous other attempted and successful attacks, such as the mass killing of thirteen soldiers at Fort Hood, Texas, on November 5, 2009.

AMERICANS ON ISLAMIC HOLY GROUND

One of the greatest complaints of the Islamic extremists is their condemnation of U.S. military and civilian personnel in the Middle East. The Islamists especially object to Americans on the "holy ground" of the Arabian Peninsula and the Jewish and American presence in Palestine.

These anti-American feelings run deep. As far back as 1981, Iranian pilgrims bound for Mecca were stopped and deported by Saudi troops for carrying posters of the Ayatollah Khomeini and tracts calling for the overthrow of the Saudi regime. Why were the Iranians angry with the Saudi regime? Khomeini and his followers were convinced that the Saudis were too closely aligned with "the Great Satan," the United States. The onset of the Gulf War, which brought thousands of additional U.S. troops into the region in the early 1990s, only exacerbated these angry feelings.

You might wonder: If the animosity between Islam and Christianity is so great, why did Saudi Arabia allow the American military into its borders—not only during the Gulf War, but with an ongoing presence to this day? The answer: Islamic jurisprudence allows for a temporary agreement with infidels if Muslims are in a state of need. Once the need passes and the Muslims become self-sufficient, the treaty is no longer binding and the Muslims can break it.

We should not be surprised if, down the road, the Muslim government of Saudi Arabia decides to abruptly kick American forces off the Arabian Peninsula.

ISLAM AT WAR WITH ITSELF

One of the most surprising aspects of Islamic governance is the fact that Muslims are constantly fighting and killing other Muslims. For example, in 1981, a group of Shiite Muslims from several Arab states attempted to overthrow Bahrain's Sunni government. The attempt failed. This act of aggression was just one more incident in the centuries-long conflict between Sunni Muslims and Shiite Muslims. In fact, much of the instability in the governments of the Middle East grows out of the longstanding Sunni-Shiite schism—a split that goes back to the early years of Islamic history.

Following the death of Muhammad, his trusted friend Abu Bakr was named the first caliph. He was one of the first converts to Islam, and was Muhammad's close advisor in addition to being his father-in-law. The choice of Abu Bakr to lead the newly founded Islamic community—the *Ummah*—disappointed Ali ibn Abi Talib, Muhammad's cousin, son-in-law, and close friend. Ali considered himself to be Muhammad's legitimate heir and successor. Ali did not assume power, however, until after two more successors, Umar ibn al-Khattab (the second caliph) and Uthman ibn Affan (the third caliph) had died.

After Ali was named caliph, a power struggle ensued and Ali was assassinated by Abd-al-Rahman ibn Muljam, who attacked Ali during prayers, using a poisoned dagger. After Ali's death, his eldest son Hasan ibn Ali claimed that, as Muhammad's grandson, he was next in line as successor to the caliphate. The struggle that followed split the Muslim empire into two factions. One group was the *Shi-at Ali*—literally "the party of Ali," which supported the descendants of Ali as the rightful rulers of the Islamic world. These became known as the Shias or Shiites. The other group became the Sunnis, the "followers of the Prophet's Path," supporters of the Umayyads and later the Abbasids.

Hasan ibn Ali was later poisoned and his brother, Hussein ibn Ali, was beheaded at the Battle of Karbala. The Shiites still nurse a grudge against the Sunnis, feeling they were aggrieved by the death of Hussein, more than thirteen centuries ago. As James Cook observed:

> *They [the Shiites] became dissenters, subversives within the Arab empire, given to violence against authority. Shiite Islam was an extremely emotional sect and still is. Its adherents at times clothe themselves in black cloaks and black turbans, and once a year re-enact the passion of [Hussein], sometimes flagellating themselves as a means of atoning for [Hussein's] martyrdom.*[3]

Shiites believe that the descendants of Ali are the imams (leaders). Imams are considered to be sinless and virtually infallible leaders in all spheres of life, including politics. Shiites believe in a continuing revelation of Allah through the imams. Therefore, the imams are the only ones capable of properly interpreting the Koran.

The Twelver Shiite sect teaches that the infant Twelfth Imam went into hiding in the ninth century and will remain hidden until the end of time, when he will return to earth as the *Mahdi* (Messiah) to establish a millennium of perfect peace and fairness to all.

Twelver Shiites believe that until the Twelfth Imam returns, every true Muslim must put himself under the authority of an ayatollah (holy man). This belief has given rise to a strong clergy and a rigid religious hierarchy. Ayatollahs wield enormous power.

Early in the sixteenth century, Twelver Shia Islam became the official religion of Persia (now called Iran). The clergy became increasingly powerful and developed a tradition of opposing the political state, claiming that the state owed religious obedience to the clergy. In 1906 the Shiite clergy in Persia led a revolution that established a constitution and caused the fall of the two hundred-year-old Qajar dynasty. This gave rise to the first Pahlavi Shah, Reza Shah, and the fall of the second, Muhammad Shah.

In other Middle East nations, the Sunni religious authorities were more readily absorbed into political life. In Egypt, for example, Sunnis became part of the civil service.

In Iran, the Ayatollah Khomeini played on the Twelver Shiites' expectation of the return of the Twelfth Imam. He claimed to be a linear descendant of Ali and took the title of Imam, encouraging his followers to believe that he might be the long-awaited *mahdi*. After leading the successful ouster of Mohammad Reza Pahlavi, shah of Iran, Khomeini recreated Iran to conform to his ideology and structured the government so that the clergy would have absolute control.

Khomeini was not content in changing Iran alone. He sought to export his concept of religious government to other nations. His first step was to call for the downfall of Saddam Hussein in Iraq. To bring things to a boiling point, Khomeini declared that Saddam Hussein was Muawiyah—the original antagonist of Ali from fourteen centuries ago, returned from the grave to kill Khomeini. The result was an eight-year border war. The Shiite majority in Iraq, however, was not prepared for Khomeini's authoritarian style of government, and they supported Hussein—perhaps more out of fear of Hussein's dictatorial powers than out of loyalty to him as a leader.

Iran sent every able-bodied male into battle. At the Ramadi prisoner of war camp sixty-five miles west of Baghdad, Iraq, prisoners ranged in age from thirteen-year-old boys to white-haired old men. One of the youngest prisoners described in tears how he had been given three months of training before being sent to the front line. He and his fellow boy-soldiers had been told the Iraqis were all heathens and the Iranians had a holy duty to fight them.

Both nations paid a heavy toll for the conflict—not only financially but also in lives. The war lasted from September 1980 to August 1988, and was the longest conventional war of the twentieth century. It killed or wounded as many as a million Iranians and 300,000 Iraqis, and cost each side an estimated $500 billion (or $1 trillion total). The war devastated the economies of both nations.

The economic devastation of the war was probably a key factor motivating Saddam Hussein to invade Kuwait in August 1990s. Although Iraq offered the pretext of claiming that Kuwait was rightfully the nineteenth province of Iraq, Hussein's real motive was to grab Kuwait's vast oil wealth.

A second motive for the invasion of Kuwait was the ancient rivalry between Shiites and Sunnis. Iraq has a predominantly Shiite population, and the leadership of oil-rich Saudi Arabia is Sunni. Only Kuwait stands geographically between Iraq and Saudi Arabia. Once Kuwait fell to Iraq, an open Shiite-versus-Sunni conflict seemed inevitable.

Even though Khomeini died in 1989, a well-organized network of Khomeini-type radicals was established throughout the Arab world as the result of his ideas and influence. Arabic tapes espousing Khomeini's ideas were distributed in almost every capital city across the Middle East. Engineer Muhammad Abdel Salam Farag, author of *The Missing Religious Duty* and one of the five accused assassins of Anwar Sadat, was influenced greatly by Khomeini's ideas.

In this brief survey of Islamic history, one fact becomes clear: Almost since its inception, Islam has been at war with itself. Century after century, caliphs and imams and holy men and warriors have battled each other and killed each other in order to prove themselves to be the purest, most zealous, most dogmatic Muslims of all. When you see how Muslims war against other Muslims, it is a wonder that they have any time left to wage jihad against the infidels of the West!

A SECT WITHIN A SECT: WAHHABISM

The particular brand of Islam espoused by Osama bin Laden and his Al-Qaeda confederates is Wahhabism, an austere fundamentalist branch of Islam founded by Abd al-Wahhab (1703–1787). Though this branch of Islam was instrumental in creating the Saudi monarchy, the Wahhabist sect now seems intent on bringing the Saudi monarchy down.

Wahhabism fiercely opposes anything viewed as *bidaa* (modernity). This Arabic word expresses such intense disgust toward cultural compromise that it is usually spoken only as a muttered curse. The Wahhabis despise any social or technological change that appears to deviate from the fundamental teachings of the Koran. At various times, such innovations as the telephone, radio broadcasts, public education for women, and music have all been declared *bidaa*.

The Wahhabis also believe their faith should never give up any ground in any land that Islam has conquered. For this reason, Saudi Arabia donated heavily to the Mujahidin fighters who battled the Soviets in Afghanistan. The Soviets had invaded Muslim land, and they had to be driven out and the land reclaimed for Islam.

The ferocity of Wahhabis fighters is legendary. An Arab historian in the eighteenth century wrote of the Wahhabis, "I have seen them hurl themselves on their enemies, utterly fearless of death, not caring how many fall, advancing rank after rank with only one desire—the defeat and annihilation of the enemy. They normally give no quarter, sparing neither boys nor old men."[4]

Wahhabis advocate strict punishment for violators of the Koran: Thieves have their left hand amputated. Adulterers are stoned to death. Murderers and sexual deviants are beheaded. Since King Abdel Aziz ibn Saud unified Saudi Arabia in

1932, the royal dynasty has had to balance the demands of modernization against the intolerant beliefs of the Wahhabis.

No one knows how many Muslims in Saudi Arabia adhere to Wahhabism. Estimates range from 10 percent to as high as 70 percent. At least ten of the 9/11 hijackers came from Saudi Arabia and very likely were Wahhabis.

In recent years, more moderate Sunni governments around the Persian Gulf have faced increasing opposition and unrest within their Shiite populations. In response, some of these Sunni governments have become more radical in order to appease the Shiites within their borders. The growing trend in Muslim countries around the world has been toward Islamic fundamentalist ideology, regardless of which branch of Islam is advocated.

As a result, the world is becoming an increasingly more dangerous place. Muslims of every sect are becoming more radicalized and more bold in infiltrating and challenging the Western culture. The expansive and aggressive mood of Islam today poses a growing threat to our Western civilization, to our American way of life, to Christianity—

And to the nation of Israel.

8

ALL ROADS LEAD TO ISRAEL

On the first night of the so-called "Arab Spring" in Egypt, I sat for three hours at a desk in the CNN studio in Atlanta. During those three hours, I did my best to convince an inexperienced (and not very knowledgeable) young anchor that events in Egypt were not taking the country toward the kind of American-style democracy that he and his liberal media colleagues made it out to be.

Drawing on my firsthand knowledge of the situation in Egypt, as well as academic training, I sought to give him and his viewers a clear picture of what would unfold. I warned that Islamists would soon sweep these well-meaning young demonstrators under the Egyptian sand. I was never invited back to CNN after that, and I think I know why. The events that followed in Egypt proved that I have every right to say, "I told you so."

Those of us who have watched the Middle East for decades, relying on a clear-eyed understanding of Islamic culture and history, knew what the Arab Spring was all about. We knew the forces that were arrayed throughout the Arab world against Egyptian president Hosni Mubarak. For years, the militant Islamists have longed to destroy the Egyptian peace treaty with Israel—the treaty for which they saw Mubarak as the chief guardian.

Now, let's be under no illusions. Hosni Mubarak did not guard the peace treaty out of warm and fuzzy feelings toward Israel. And when Mubarak's predecessor, Anwar Sadat, agreed to the Camp David Accords and forged peace with Israel, he didn't do so because of his deep fondness for the Jewish state. The peace between Israel and Egypt has been kept from 1978 to this day because of one thing: American dollars.

The Camp David Accords—which won Nobel Peace Prizes for Sadat and Israeli Prime Minister Menachem Begin in 1978, and for President Jimmy Carter in 2002—were made possible because America committed billions of dollars in subsidies to Israel and Egypt, subsidies which are still being paid to both nations today. According to the U.S. State Department, Egypt receives $1.3 billion annually in military aid (which Egypt must use to purchase weaponry from American arms manufacturers), plus billions in economic assistance from the U.S. Agency for

International Development (more than $28 billion from 1979 through 2010).[1] The U.S. also agreed to pay about $3 billion annually to Israel in grants and military aid.[2]

So the "peace accords" are not about peace, they're about money. And I'm not saying there's anything wrong with that. For more than three decades, the American taxpayers have been able to purchase peace in the Middle East at a cost of a few tens of billions of dollars. Compared to the trillion-dollar cost of the wars in Iraq and Afghanistan, that's a bargain. Unfortunately, the brokered peace between Israel and Egypt may soon come to an end.

The uprisings that ousted President Mubarak were led by a small group of genuine liberals among Egypt's educated student class. They loved their country and they wanted freedom and democracy in Egypt. But once Mubarak resigned, the Islamists came out of hiding and flexed their muscles. Today, the Islamists run the country through intimidation and fear.

The Obama administration didn't see this coming. The young CNN anchor didn't see this coming. Only those who truly understand the mind of the extreme Islamist knew what was coming and were not caught by surprise. Today the hardline Salafists, who are heavily funded by their fellow Wahhabis in Saudi Arabia, are literally forcing a weak and ineffective government to appoint cabinet members and governors who are sympathetic to their Islamist ideology. These events are taking place under the nose of the Egyptian military.

One of the unintended consequences of the Egyptian army's passivity and decriminalizing of militant Islamists is that thousands of Al-Qaeda jihadists have moved into the Sinai desert and have begun launching terror attacks into Israel, using the Sinai as a base. As Bruce Riedel of the Brookings Institution observes, "Al-Qaeda's presence [in the Sinai] adds another dangerous ingredient in the explosive Arab-Israeli tinderbox."[3]

On August 17, 2011, some of these Al-Qaeda fighters crossed the Egyptian-Israeli border, reportedly dressed in Egyptian army uniforms. They killed eight Israeli bus passengers and wounded 44 more. Israel mistakenly killed three Egyptian soldiers in the confusion and crossfire. The Egyptian army moved into the Sinai, supposedly to "quell the unrest," but Al-Qaeda forces continue to gather in the Sinai desert. So far, the Egyptian army has shown little inclination to remove the thousands of Al-Qaeda fighters who menace Israel—and who have the support of the extreme Islamists in Egypt.[4]

The stage is being set for disaster.

AN ISLAND IN AN ISLAMIC SEA

Israel is surrounded by twenty-six predominantly Muslim nations: Mauritania, Morocco, Algeria, Tunisia, Libya, Egypt, Sudan, Ethiopia, Eritrea, Djibouti, and

Somalia in northern Africa; and Yemen, Oman, U.A.E. (United Arab Emirates), Saudi Arabia, Qatar, Bahrain, Kuwait, Jordan, Syria, Lebanon, and Iraq in the Middle East. Further east are the Muslim nations of Iran, Afghanistan, and Pakistan. Turkey to the north is a predominantly Muslim country with a secular government.

Israel is a tiny island of a mere 8,500 square miles in a vast Islamic sea. Such a tiny nation could hardly threaten the Muslim world, with its vast oil wealth. Little Israel should go completely unnoticed by the great Arab world—yet the exact opposite is the case. To Muslims, Israel is the fly in the soup which cannot be ignored.

Today's Islamic zealots have sworn that there can be no peace or coexistence with Israel. The Islamists view Israel as a constant reminder of Islam's humiliation. As long as Israel exists, there will never be peace. The Islamist view was expressed by Osama bin Laden in a statement aired on Al-Jazeera a few weeks after the 9/11 attacks: "We cannot accept that Palestine will become Jewish. . . . I swear by [Allah] the Great, America will never dream nor those who live in America will never taste security and safety unless we feel security and safety in our land and in Palestine."[5]

A short time later, Al-Qaeda spokesman Suliman Abu Geith released a videotaped statement on Al Jazeera, saying, "We have a fair and just case. The Islamic nation more than eighty years has been suffering. The Palestinian people have been living under the Jewish and Zionist occupation. Nobody moves to help them. Here we are, this [Israel] is an Arab land. This is a land that's being desecrated."[6]

Why does this Al-Qaeda spokesman say that the "Islamic nation" (that is, the entire Islamic world) has been suffering for "more than eighty years"? What happened eighty years before 9/11 that caused "suffering" for the "Islamic nation"?

This appears to be a reference to the Sykes-Picot agreement (1916) and the Treaty of Sèvres (1920). Sykes-Picot was a secret agreement between Britain and France for dividing the Arab provinces of the Ottoman Empire; the agreement embarrassed both nations and angered the Arab world when it was exposed in 1917. The Treaty of Sèvres was an agreement between the Allies and the dying Ottoman Empire. It partitioned the Ottoman Empire, drew boundary lines that still define the Arab world today, gave France and England mandates in Mesopotamia and the Holy Land, humiliated the Muslims, and eventually led to the creation of the state of Israel. Historian James S. Robbins explains:

> *The Ottomans had ruled the region for 600 years or so, and brought varying degrees of political harmony under the Sultanate and religious unity under the Caliphate. The 1920 treaty did away with the political order. . . . In bin Laden's universe, that was*

> *when everything started to go wrong. Viewed in that context, his plots against the Saudi and Jordanian monarchies make perfect sense. They are products of this original sin, the establishment of the political order of the Middle East by the Allied powers eighty years ago.*[7]

Muslim memories are long. The Islamists don't know the meaning of the word "bygones"—especially where the state of Israel is concerned.

SHOCK WAVES IN THE MUSLIM WORLD

Former Egyptian president Mubarak has often contended that at least 50 percent (on one occasion, he said 80 percent) of terrorist incidents in the world can be attributed to the Palestinian-Israeli conflict. The establishment of the state of Israel in 1948 not only sent shock waves throughout the Arab world, but the presence of a Jewish state in the Middle East continues to ignite Islamic hatred against the United States, Israel's chief defender.

Muslims in the Middle East regard the continued existence of Israel as an extension of a long history of Western imperialism against Arab lands and the Islamic faith. They view Israel as the bridgehead of Western influence and domination in the Middle East. Zionism, they believe, is an instrument of Western imperialism. Let's take a brief look at the history of the region, leading to the establishment of the Jewish state of Israel:

The Balfour Declaration in 1917. During World War I, the Balfour Declaration was the price Great Britain paid to gain worldwide Jewish backing for the war effort. At the time, Great Britain needed every friend it could get, especially after Russia dropped out of the war effort. The Balfour Declaration was a public letter from Lord Balfour, the British foreign minister, to Lord Rothschild, a prominent leader of Britain's Jewish community. The declaration stated:

> *His Majesty's government views with favor the establishment in Palestine of a national home for the Jewish people and would use their best endeavors to facilitate the achievement of this object. It being clearly understood that nothing shall be done which may prejudice the civil and religious rights of existing non-Jewish communities in Palestine, or the rights and political status enjoyed by Jews in any other country.*[8]

This territory called Palestine, which Great Britain administered, was something of an anomaly. The Jewish and Arab populations of Palestine were among the most politically sophisticated and culturally advanced people of the Middle East in the early 1900s. Conflict between Jewish and Arab nationalism—both groups sought a political state—had frustrated all British attempts to encourage local self-government. Arab nationalists considered Palestine part of the Arab heartland and refused to surrender any of their rights or claims. Jewish Zionists envisioned Palestine as a Jewish national home.

The devious dealings of the British in the region only served to exacerbate these differences. At times, the promises of the British officer at the foreign office in Cairo were diametrically opposed to those of the foreign secretary in London. When Arab nationalists pressured British officials, the British tried to stop Zionist expansion. When the Jewish lobby in Britain counter-pressured, the British leaned on the Arabs. The result was that both Arabs and Zionists were left guessing much of the time.

Britain came to feel what it called a "dual obligation." On the one hand, Britain tried to accommodate to the Zionists whose power in England was keenly felt at the ballot box. On the other hand, Britain also tried to appease the Arabs; the British felt indebted to the Arabs for their support during World War I. Any British support of the Zionist cause was regarded with resentment by Arab leaders, who were quick to react to any affront to their political aspirations and religious views.

The Origin of Zionism. In many ways, Zionism was a direct product of the economic, political, and social climate of nineteenth-century Europe. When Jews left Palestine following the Roman conquest of the first century, they emigrated or were transported primarily to Europe. For the most part, they formed communities separate from the Europeans. In those Jewish communities, they practiced the laws, traditions, and customs of ancient Israel.

In most countries, the Jews remained "foreigners" for centuries, in spite of their business and political involvement in various nations. From time to time, the Jews were persecuted or expelled en masse. Nearly every major European nation—Spain, France, England, Poland, Germany, Romania—has exiled its Jewish community at one time or another. Jewish writer and activist Theodore Herzl once observed that the Jews "would always be persecuted no matter how useful or patriotic they were. Nowhere was their integration into national life possible; the Jewish problem, the hatred of the Jewish minority by the non-Jewish majority, existed wherever there were Jews."[9]

When the dream of a Jewish homeland became a reality after the Holocaust of World War II, hundreds of thousands of Jews streamed into Israel from Europe, and from around the world. What many people fail to realize is that Palestine was already a homeland for tens of thousands of Jews even before World War II.

Longtime White House correspondent Helen Thomas expressed her ignorance of this fact at the White House Jewish Heritage Celebration on May 27, 2010. A reporter asked for her comments on Israel, and she replied, "Tell them to get the hell out of Palestine. Remember, these people [the Palestinian Arabs] are occupied. And it's their land. . . . [The Jews] can go home to Poland and Germany and America and everywhere else.[10]

The Jewish homeland is not "Poland and Germany." That is where the Holocaust took place. The Jewish homeland has always been Israel, the land God promised to Abraham and his descendents. In fact, in 1914, some 85,000 Jews lived in Palestine, alongside some 6,000 Arabs. In other words, Palestinian Jews outnumbered Palestinian Arabs 14 to 1. This population figure is often overlooked when Westerners discuss the Jewish-Arab conflict in Israel. The land of Israel has continuously been the Jewish homeland from the time of Abraham through the centuries of the Diaspora (Dispersion) and right down to the present day. Historically, far more Jews than Arabs have lived in Palestine, even before the establishment of the state of Israel.

While Jewish sentiment was increasingly focused on the Zionist theme during the late 1800s, Arab loyalty was divided between Islam and Christianity. About 5 percent of the Arabs in Palestine call themselves Christians; they are descendants of Christians who have lived in Palestine since the time of the Apostles.

A distinct Palestinian Arab nationalist movement did not emerge until World War I. Up until World War I, Osmanlis (the people of the Ottoman Empire, or Turkey) exercised a shadowy form of control over many parts of the region. The Bedouins still roamed the hills and valleys and periodically raided the settled villages in the hill country on the north plains. Shortly after the outbreak of World War I, the Ottomans clamped rigid restrictions on Palestine and the surrounding area.

After the Balfour Declaration, Arabs became increasingly fearful that Palestine would become wholly Jewish. Winston Churchill's white paper of July 1922 was an attempt to clarify the British position. Churchill affirmed two ideas: First, the Balfour Declaration did not state that Palestine as a whole should become a Jewish national homeland, but that a homeland should be created within Palestine. Second, all citizens of the country were Palestinian, and none were entitled to any special judicial status. Churchill also affirmed that Britain would continue the political and economic development of the existing Jewish community, with the help of the Jewish community around the world.

San Remo Conference and League of Nations. At the time of the San Remo Conference in 1920, the area called Palestine, which was then under British mandate, comprised the region we know today as Israel and Jordan. From 1921 to

1923, Britain divided this mandate, drawing a line from the Dead Sea south to Elat on the upper tip of the Red Sea. The Jordan River formed the boundary from the Sea of Galilee and the Dead Sea. The Golan Heights were part of the northern area of Palestine, bordering Syria, which was under the French mandate. The area east of this line was called Transjordan and was closed to Jewish settlement. The area west of that line was designated as the Jewish national homeland. In essence, the Arabs were given all the land east of the Jordan River, the Jews were given the land west of it.

In 1922, the League of Nations assigned the Palestinian mandate to Great Britain. This mandate differed from other Middle East mandates that called for progressive development of independent states. In Palestine, the British were vested with "full powers of legislation and of administration save as they may be limited by the terms of this mandate."[11] The Lausanne Peace Treaty with Turkey in 1923 affirmed this position taken by the League of Nations. This mandate meant that Great Britain maintained authority over the region called Palestine.

Great Britain also was given control of Iraq, Egypt and modern Jordan. France claimed Lebanon, Syria, Algeria, Morocco, and Tunisia as part of its mandate from the League of Nations. The British mandate for Palestine authorized Jewish immigration and "closed settlement" on the land, which meant that Jews who decided to establish permanent residence could be assisted in obtaining Palestinian citizenship. Jewish leaders were authorized to construct and operate public works, services, and utilities not directly undertaken by the British mandatory administration.

In 1923, Britain ceded the Golan Heights to the French because Britain did not want to allocate resources to that area and the French were already in the region. Both Jews and Syrians lived on the Golan Heights. Both Jewish and Arab communities complained that the British mandatory authorities discriminated against them, and both communities objected to any measure that seemed to favor the other community.

Great Britain felt it jeopardized its friendship with the entire Arab world if it antagonized Palestinian Arabs—but Britain also worried that it might prevent Palestine from becoming modernized and democratic if it alienated the Jewish community. As a result of these conflicting concerns, Britain's policy toward Palestine tended to be uncertain and erratic. Both Jews and Arabs grew increasingly bitter toward each other and toward Britain, and each community tended to keep to itself and develop separate institutions and cultures. Sometimes, divisions between Palestinian Arabs and Jews erupted in violent clashes.

Even though Palestinian Jews and Arabs had a common citizenship and a common government, no common Palestinian community took shape. The Arab community fused Muslim and Christian communities together under the control of leading Muslim families. Arab self-governing institutions supplemented the functions of British mandate government. Jewish settlement in the area continued, and many of these Jewish settlements operated under a communal *kibbutz* system.

The United Nations Partition Plan. In 1947, the United Nations General Assembly Resolution 1981 adopted a Partition Plan that set aside a segment of the Galilee region, the West Bank, and the Gaza Strip as an Arab state. The remaining area of Palestine would become a Jewish state—the state of Israel. Jerusalem would be kept as an international zone.

Acting on this UN resolution, Israel declared its independence as a nation on May 1, 1948. The declaration states, in part, "We, the members of the National Council, representing the Jewish people in Palestine and the Zionist movement of the world . . . hereby proclaim the establishment of the Jewish State in Palestine, to be called Israel."

The War of Independence. Within hours after Israel declared its independence, five nations—Egypt, Syria, Lebanon, Iraq, and Yemen—declared war on the new Jewish state. Yemen declared war, but did not take military action; Saudi Arabia made no formal declaration, but sent a small military contingent under Egyptian command. Thus began a year-long War of Independence.

The war concluded with the 1949 armistice agreement, which gave Egypt control of the Gaza area. The West Bank region of Samaria and Judea came under Jordanian supervision. The remainder of the land was declared to belong to Israel. Jerusalem became a divided city—east Jerusalem was apportioned to the Arabs, west Jerusalem to the Jews. Jordan controlled the entire Old City of Jerusalem, including the Temple Mount and many of the most revered Christian sites.

The Six Day War. In May 1967, Egypt sent troops into the Sinai Peninsula and ordered United Nations troops out of the area, imposing a blockade of the Straits of Tiran. Egypt then entered into a military alliance with Jordan. In June, forces from Syria, Jordan, and Egypt moved simultaneously against Israel. The invasion quickly failed, and the conflict became known as the Six Day War. After Israel successfully repulsed the attack, the cease-fire lines gave Israel control of the Golan Heights, the West Bank, Gaza, and the Sinai. The Straits of Tiran were opened and Jerusalem was united under Israeli control.

The government of Israel later annexed the Golan Heights (which had been under Syrian control for a mere nineteen years, during which time more than four hundred attacks had been launched against Israel's Galilee region). Israel also annexed east Jerusalem. The remaining areas were not annexed, but were patrolled and controlled by an Israeli occupation force to ensure that no further assaults would be launched against Jews in the region.

The Yom Kippur War. In 1973, while the vast majority of Jewish civilians and soldiers were at Yom Kippur services, Egypt and Syria launched simultaneous attacks against Israel. Egyptian tanks crossed the Suez. Syrian tanks rolled into the Golan. The Israel Defense Force (IDF) was initially caught off-guard, but ultimately rallied and turned the tide of the attack. Israeli forces in the south crossed the Suez Canal into Egypt. In the north, IDF forces advanced to within twenty miles of Damascus.

The Soviet Union under Leonid Brezhnev threatened to enter the war, raising the specter of World War III. A cease-fire was reached within three weeks after the initial attack. Under the terms of the cease-fire, Israel withdrew to its 1967 borders, making no claim to the new territories it had taken in Egypt and Syria while defending itself against the sneak attack. Both Israeli and Arab forces suffered heavy casualties.

THE ARAB PERSPECTIVE: "A MISTREATED PEOPLE"

The British role in creating the State of Israel and later, America's recognition of Israel, left a deep scar in the Arab psyche. Many Arab Muslims believe to this day that the Christian West planted Israel in their midst as a means to exert control over the Middle East. They see the existence of Israel as a new manifestation of the ancient Crusade against Islam.

Muslims, unlike Westerners, do not easily forget the past. To Muslims, the Crusades of the Middle Ages might just as well have happened yesterday. In the Muslim mind, colonialism is alive and well—and the existence of Israel is proof. Muslim militants still resent the British and the French for dividing the Arab lands between them like a loaf of bread after World War I. The end result is that Muslims regard Israel as a direct affront to their claim to the area and an act of disrespect for the dignity of the Arab people. These are deeply held convictions in the Arab world.

The thought that "the House of War"—the Muslim designation for the non-Muslim world—should occupy a land that once belonged to the House of Islam is no small matter to the people of the Middle East. It strikes at the very heart of Islamic ideology—and Arab pride. That's why Muslims will not rest until the Jews leave Palestine, accept Muslim rule, or are eliminated.

Establishment of the PLO. The Palestine Liberation Organization (PLO) was formed specifically to "liberate" Palestine from Jewish control and place it under Arab rule. PLO headquarters were initially in Jordan, but Jordan expelled the PLO in 1970 and the organization moved to Lebanon. Yasir Arafat rose to prominence during that transition time.

The Oslo Accords. The Oslo Accords—the agreement struck between Israeli Prime Minister Yitzak Rabin and Yasir Arafat—created the Independent Palestinian Authority (IPA). The IPA was given jurisdiction over Gaza and Jericho, and in subsequent years, has received governmental authority over Ramallah, Bethlehem, and several other areas. The PLO has demanded, and continues to demand, the whole of the West Bank—including those areas settled and cultivated as farms by Jews. The PLO also demands the entire old city of Jerusalem.

THE HEART OF THE REGION: JERUSALEM

Jerusalem has been the international capital city of the Jewish people since King David gained control of the city in 1996 B.C.—more than four thousand years ago. Jewish people have lived in the city since before the final conquest by King David.

Jerusalem in Muslim History. Jerusalem is not mentioned in the Koran, and the name Jerusalem does not figure in early Muslim writings. When the city is mentioned at all, it is called Aelia, the name imposed by the Romans to obliterate its Jewish and Christian associations.

While the city is not mentioned in the Koran, the al-Aqsa mosque on the Temple Mount is mentioned several times in the "sayings" of Muhammad. Muhammad supposedly declared:

- the reward or blessing for a Muslim who prayed in the al-Aqsa mosque was multiplied five hundred times;
- the al-Aqsa mosque was the second mosque established on earth;
- Muslims should not undertake difficult journeys except to reach three destinations—the al-Haram mosque in Mecca, the prophet's mosque in Medina, and al-Aqsa mosque in Jerusalem.

The Koran refers to God taking Muhammad on a journey by night from the mosque in Mecca to the al-Aqsa mosque. The journey ended with Muhammad ascending directly into heaven from the rock now located in the Dome of the Rock shrine.

The Dome of the Rock. The Dome of the Rock was built by Abd al-Malik on the Temple Mount in Jerusalem in 692 A.D. It was the first great religious building complex in the history of Islam and marked the beginning of a new era. It was a declaration to the world that Islam was to be the supreme religion of the world. This verse of the Koran figured prominently in the design of the building: "There is no God but God alone, he has no companion. Muhammad is the Prophet of God, who sent him with guidance the religion of truth to make it prevail over all religion" (Koran 9:33).

The Crusades and Following—Various Groups in Control. After the Crusaders entered Jerusalem in 1099, all Jews in the city were murdered, sold into slavery in Europe, or ransomed to the Jewish community of Egypt. The Crusaders then brought in Christian Arab tribes from east of the Jordan River and settled them in the Old City. The Dome of the Rock, constructed on the Temple Mount by the Umayyad Caliph Abd al-Malik ibn Marwan in 691, was renamed the Templum Domini by the Crusaders.

PRAYING FOR THE PEACE OF JERUSALEM

What should our response be as Christians?

First, let us voice our concern that Christian sites in Israel be protected, and that the rights of Christians to worship at those sites be respected.

Second, let us continue to support Gospel missions to both Jews and Muslims, for all people desperately need to know that Jesus, the Prince of Peace, is humanity's only hope for lasting peace.

Third, let us become informed about the historical and current events in Israel and Jerusalem. Let's boldly speak the truth in love whenever we hear misinformation presented as fact. We should never hesitate to speak God's truth with confidence and grace.

Fourth, let us heed the admonition of the psalmist:

> *Pray for the peace of Jerusalem:*
> *"May those who love you be secure.*
> *May there be peace within your walls*
> *and security within your citadels."*
> *For the sake of my brothers and friends,*
> *I will say, "Peace be within you."*
> *For the sake of the house of the LORD our God,*
> *I will seek your prosperity. (Psalm 122:6-9)*

9

OIL—THE FUEL THAT FUNDS OUR DESTRUCTION

The world economy is driven by oil.

Our Western society depends on oil for energy, manufacturing, and transportation. The United States is the world's largest importer of foreign oil, and has become dependent—some would say addicted—to oil that comes from some of the most politically volatile parts of the world. A serious interruption in the flow of oil could bring the world's strongest economy to its knees.

According to Senator Richard Lugar of Indiana, author of The Lugar Energy Initiative, America now consumes 20.7 million barrels of oil every day—and imports about 60 percent of its oil from foreign oil producers. The top suppliers of our oil imports are Canada, Mexico, Saudi Arabia, Venezuela, and Nigeria. About 40 percent of our oil imports come from nations in the Organization of Petroleum Exporting Countries, or OPEC.[1]

America's dependency on oil has transferred vast sums of wealth to oil-producing Muslim nations. The price of oil has seesawed wildly in recent years, soaring to a record peak of $145 per barrel in July 2008, and dropping to a mere $30 per barrel just five months later in December 2008. It hit $100 per barrel again on January 31, 2011, due to concerns about the stability of Egypt and other Muslim nations during the Arab Spring uprisings. OPEC nations have seen their revenues grow from $50 billion in 1974 to $200 billion in 1980 to $750 billion in 2010. By 2012, OPEC oil revenues are expected to top $1 trillion.[2]

This represents a staggering flow of wealth from the Western nations to the Arab world. We have created a situation which may prove to be our undoing. We show no signs of lessening our dependence on foreign oil, even though we have enormous undeveloped petroleum reserves within our own borders or just offshore. We show no inclination to explore them. Yet we know that OPEC nations have the ability to generate an "oil crisis" that can trigger a massive upheaval in our society and our economy.

Every American president since Richard Nixon has promised to take action to make America "energy-independent," yet America's dependency on foreign oil has only grown, not decreased. The problem of keeping the oil flowing from such an unstable region should motivate our leaders to find ways to wean America from its addiction to foreign oil—yet our leaders never seem to focus on the problem until it reaches the crisis stage. By then, of course, it's too late.

MUSLIM BELIEFS REGARDING OIL

The West may flood OPEC nations with geologists, petroleum engineers, economists, and diplomats, but until those "experts" come to grips with Islamic ideology, their understanding of the Middle East oil picture will be woefully incomplete. To understand the Islamic mind, we must grasp how Muslims view wealth and oil.

A Sign of God's Pleasure. Economic success is regarded by Muslims as a sign of God's pleasure. Prior to the rise in oil consumption and increased drilling in Muslim nations, Muslims tended to measure Allah's blessing by whether a war was won or lost. From the beginning of Islamic history, Muslims have held to a belief that Allah reveals the weaknesses of other faiths through victory and defeat. If my nation defeats your nation in battle, this means that Allah has revealed the weakness of your nation and your religion. When the armies of Islam defeated "infidel" nations, this was viewed as a sign that the victory was authorized by Allah for the advancement of Islam.

This view of victory as proof of Allah's favor was often reinforced in the early history of Islam, as Muslim armies won victory after victory, beginning with the Battle of Badr in western Arabia in A.D. 624. This conviction deepened during Islam's first millennium—from A.D. 600 to 1600—as Islam spread across the Middle East and North Africa, and as far west as Spain.

In recent decades, Muslims have interpreted financial success as evidence of Allah's blessing. This belief is one of the reasons that even moderate Muslims—as embarrassed as they might have been by the Ayatollah Khomeini's excesses during the Iranian revolution—would not totally disown him. The economic success of Iran under his leadership was proof to most in the Islamic world that Khomeini enjoyed the approval of Allah.

A Means of Gaining World Superiority. Oil is also regarded by many in the Islamic world as a material gift from Allah so that Muslims (and Islam as a religion) might achieve world superiority. J. B. Kelly, author of *Arabia, the Gulf and the West*, observes:

> *Racked thus by powerful sentiments of grievance and resentment against the West, the Arabs see the oil weapons as a gift sent by God to redress the balance between Christendom and Islam. It enables them to act as though the might and grandeur of the Umayyad and Abbasid caliphates has been restored, to lay the Christian West under tribute to the Muslim East, and to fulfill the destiny which God in his infinite wisdom has ordained for those to whom he has chosen to reveal the one true faith. Extravagant though these fancies may appear to Western eyes, they are very real to those who entertain them, and infinitely more appealing than the calmer dictates of reason.*[3]

Oil in the twenty-first century is tantamount to the sword of the seventh century. It is a means of exerting the greatest possible force on non-Muslim adversaries. It is a means of forcing the Christian West to pay tribute to the Islamic nation, the Muslim caliphate. This way of thinking follows this progression:

> *Economic success is proof of Allah's favor . . .*
> *Success results in Islamic superiority . . .*
> *Other religions and cultures must be subjugated . . .*
> *Oil is Allah's appointed means of controlling—and humiliating—the Christian West.*

OIL AS A WEAPON

After the 1973 Yom Kippur War, the Arab nations blamed their loss on Western support for Israel. The war took a heavy toll on Israeli fuel stocks, but a U.S.-led supply effort kept fuel flowing to Israel to power the tanks and planes that defeated Egyptian and Syrian forces. The Arab world realized that the oil they had sold to the United States had been refined and shipped to Israel for the war effort. So an infuriated OPEC imposed the 1973 oil embargo against the United States and Western Europe as retribution. The result: American drivers sat in gasoline lines that stretched for blocks and the price of gas shot sky-high.

The OPEC oil embargo resulted in a 366 percent increase in oil prices. The price of oil jumped from $3 a barrel to $12 a barrel, with the total world energy bill rising to $20 billion in 1973 and $100 billion by 1976. The high cost of oil dealt a harsh blow to the world's major economies, wiping out a half million jobs. The global GNP fell by nearly $20 billion.

We have seen similar interruptions in the oil supply, resulting in major price spikes. For example, after the Iranian Revolution in 1979, the price of a barrel of oil went from $12 to $24. After the Iraqi invasion of Kuwait in 1990, the price shot to more than $35 a barrel.

And there are other ways the Arab world demands tribute from America, the "Crusader nation." For example, the American taxpayer sends $50 to $60 billion a year in military and economic aid to Middle Eastern nations with a goal of maintaining peace and the free flow of oil in the Persian Gulf region. Our dependency on foreign oil is far more expensive than most of us realize!

WHERE DOES THE OIL MONEY END UP?

What have the Arabs done with the money earned from their oil fields? Many tales of the nouveau riche oil barons have been outrageous and amusing—from the Saudi Arabian princes who casually gamble away millions in a single evening in European casinos to the sheik who tried to buy the Alamo as a birthday present for his son.

For the most part, the Arab OPEC states have invested enormous amounts of their oil money in domestic development programs—from schools to housing to road systems. Much of that wealth has also been channeled into foreign investments, primarily in oil-consuming nations. At latest count, Saudi Arabia was estimated to have more than a trillion dollars invested in other countries—though accurate figures are hard to come by.

The largest portion of surplus oil money has been invested in the United States, though the exact ownership of these holdings is often hidden behind multiple corporate layers. Since the United States government doesn't know how much Arab money is involved in its economy, it has no means of measuring the impact of those investments on our economy.

For a long time, oil-rich Arabs knew to keep their financial holdings just below the level at which disclosure to the United States Securities and Exchange Commission is required. But no more. The Kuwaitis operated in this fashion for years, and eventually amassed nearly five percent ownership in some of America's top firms.[4] Today individuals and Muslim nations own banks and corporations outright such as Barclay Bank.

The stealthy Arab economic offensive is potentially more alarming than any "oil crisis" OPEC might inflict on our economy. The rise in Arab investments in our economy could be a far more effective way of manipulating the economy and affecting U.S. foreign policy than we realize.

Muslim Money in Many Sectors of American Business and Government. In the past, Arab oil money has been loaned in amounts of billions of dollars to such U.S. corporations as American Telephone and Telegraph (AT&T), International Business Machines (IBM), Dow Chemical, and Kimberly-Clark.[5] Arab oil money has been invested in American real estate, commercial ventures, hotels, shopping centers, tourist resorts, banks, and other financial institutions. It has been loaned to major U.S. corporations, including aerospace giant Lockheed. Much OPEC investment in America is in the United States government itself, in the form of United States Treasury securities.

It is little wonder that former political officials—including those with State Department and Defense Department experience—have become consultants to OPEC nations upon leaving government service. There are big dollars to be earned by helping OPEC investors find suitable places to put their wealth.

Arab oil wealth is often used to affect U.S. foreign policy. When the Saudis felt Iraq could function as a buffer against the radical Iranian revolutionaries, they used their influence to push the United States into supporting Iraq in the Iran-Iraq war. When the tides changed and the Saudis felt threatened by Iraq's invasion of Kuwait, the Saudis swung their support behind American efforts to push the Iraqis—the Saudis' former allies and Arab brothers—out of Kuwait.

We often learn that Arab oil wealth is used in contradictory ways. For example, while our "friends" the Saudis were selling us oil and investing in our economy, they were also funding the Taliban in Afghanistan. The reason has to do with the internal politics of Saudi Arabia. Because the radical Wahhabis are such a powerful cultural and political force in Saudi Arabia, the Saudi government has aided the anti-American Taliban in a bid to appease the radicals within its own borders.

At what point might Arab governments use oil as a means of disrupting Western economies in a bid to choke off support for Israel? What pressures, subtle or overt, might oil-rich Arab governments use to affect how American companies do business in the Middle East? What would happen to our economy if Arab wealth were suddenly withdrawn from U.S. financial institutions? These are questions we must consider—and contingencies we must plan for.

THE DANGEROUS CONCEPT OF UMMAH

Ummah is the Islamic concept of the "community of believers." In many ways, *ummah* is the philosophy that keeps OPEC nations united when it comes to pricing oil and making investment decisions. For decades, Muslim leaders have flirted with the idea of creating a "common market" built on the *ummah* philosophy.

Whereas Europe's common market exists for trade, a common market in the Arab world is more likely to be used as a religious and political tool. The first leader to openly espouse this idea was Gamal Abdel Nasser of Egypt.

For the most part, *ummah* has functioned as a way for oil-rich nations to preserve their wealth. Radical Muslims would like to see an Islamic common market so that all the wealth of the Arab world could be shared more equitably. Rich Muslims, however, want a common market only if it helps protect their personal fortunes.

A common market requires more structure and discipline than is needed by OPEC. For example, a common market would need a centralized banking system. The danger of creating an Islamic common market with its own banking system is that the banking system would be politicized due to close ties between the banks and Arab governments. Many U.S. corporations are partially owned by Arab investors. In some cases, these investors are actually "investment banks," such as the Kuwait Investment Office or the Saudi Arabian Monetary Agency. The result is that *foreign governments* are actually part owners of American companies. Should these nations form an alliance, the result would be that a block of nations could acquire a controlling interest in leading American firms.

The political ramifications are enormous. At what point might the Arab world decide to dictate American economic policy or foreign policy—such as our policies toward Israel? A European banker once observed, "It took the Arabs ten years to learn how to wield their oil power, but it isn't going to take that long to wield their money power."[6] He was right. The Arabs caught on very quickly.

NOT ANSWERABLE TO NON-MUSLIMS

The concept of *ummah* establishes a sense of community. A related concept deals with how Muslims are to relate to those *outside* the Muslim community. In short, this concept says, "No Muslim should be answerable to a non-Muslim."

What happens in a corporation in which Muslims have acquired a controlling interest? In fact, isn't that the intent of Muslim investment—to gain control so that no Muslim is answerable to a non-Muslim? What happens if top management is replaced with Muslim personnel who are accountable only to one another in the corporation?

It is not inconceivable that a day will come when a company might require its personnel to convert to Islam in order to win a Middle Eastern contract. The West makes a clear distinction between business and religion. Oil-rich Muslims do not.

One way Muslims subjugate non-Muslims is to humiliate them. What better way for the Muslim world to humiliate the West than to instigate practices that result in runaway inflation and unsustainable budget deficits, which in turn lead Western nations into decline and collapse?

Oil fuels the engine of the Western economy. But oil is also a weapon of jihad. The goal of jihad is to defeat Christianity, to collapse the "Crusader nation," and to bring about the subjugation and surrender of the West—and oil is a potent weapon in that struggle. One of the great ironies of our age is that the very oil that runs our economy may ultimately fund our destruction.

10

THE SPREADING ISLAMIC WILDFIRE

Six months after seizing power in Iran, the Ayatollah Khomeini declared, "The governments of the world should know that Islam cannot be defeated. Islam will be victorious in all the countries of the world, and Islam and the teachings of the Koran will prevail all over the world."[1]

Khomeini only reiterated what Muslim leaders and holy men have voiced for centuries. We must never be so naïve as to assume that the Muslim zone of influence is limited to the Middle East. It is a worldwide influence. Muslims are the predominant power in Indonesia, the world's fourth most populous nation, and they are increasing in power in the Philippines. Both nations are economic powerhouses in Southeast Asia. Muslim leaders in both of these countries clearly see the big picture of world domination, and they are beginning by establishing a religious hegemony in Asia. Their rising power in Europe can only be described as dizzying.

GROWING AND BUILDING AT A RAPID PACE

Muslims are on track to make Islam the world's largest religion. They are currently winning 50 million people annually to their faith.[2] Muslims are building mosques, which are the greatest symbol of power, at a rate unprecedented in world history. Muslim extremism is also on the rise in most Arab nations, in spite of the War on Terror.

In the 1980s, Mirza Khizar Bakht, the secretary-general of the First Interest-Free Finance Consortium—Great Britain's Islamic bank—expressed his dream of establishing a Muslim shopping center in central London's Regent Street or in Knightsbridge. The aim of the center was to "unite the whole Muslim world in London."

If you have been to London recently, you know that his dream has largely become a reality. Arab money and Arab influence is on full display on the streets of London. The Islamic Council of Europe, which is based in London, spends large sums on propaganda among Muslims and Christians, and has built mosques in each major European city. The Central Mosque in London has a minaret that competes with the city's cathedrals on the city's skyline and seats 2,800 people. Now they are planning a 70,000 seating capacity mosque with British tax payers' money. It is only one of hundreds of mosques that have been constructed in England, largely in the last thirty years. In fact, England went from having one mosque in 1945 to having more than 1,500 today. Great Britain presently has more Muslims than Baptists and Methodists combined.

While London is a major base of operations for the expansion of Islam in Europe, the greatest numbers of European Muslims live on the Continent. France has the largest Muslim population—well over 3 million. Muslims are the nation's second-largest religious group in France (Roman Catholics are the largest), and there are more French Muslims than French Protestants (all denominations combined).

There are about 4.3 million Muslims in Germany, constituting more than 5 percent of the population—and that number is growing rapidly. Spain has a growing number of Muslims, as does Italy. In Rome, a new mosque was constructed at an estimated cost of $20 million. According to an ABC News report, more than 5,000 mosques were built in the southern republics of the former Soviet Union within two years after the collapse of the Soviet government. In Kenya, Muslims are currently building mosques so that one mosque can be found in every ten square kilometers, whether there are any Muslims living in the area or not.

ISLAMIC EXPANSION IN THE UNITED STATES

Islam has expanded with great fervor in the United States in the last century. In the decade of the 1970s alone, Islam grew by 400 percent in the United States. Today, the number of Muslims in America is estimated at 2.6 million, and that number is expected to more than double to 6.2 million by 2030.[3] The three main reasons for this rapid growth are:

Increased immigration. Since the ratification of the 1965 Immigration Act by President Lyndon Johnson, waves of Muslim immigrants have flooded the United States. Several hundred thousand Afghan refugees who had fought the Soviets fled persecution and war to come to America. More than 2 million Iranians, the majority of them highly educated and prosperous, fled Iran. Muslims from Lebanon and the former Yugoslavia made their way to America to escape civil wars in their homelands. The majority sought political freedom and economic opportunity—but we are also seeing militant Muslims coming to America to infiltrate our society and undermine our way of life.

One such immigrant is the late Ismail Al-Faruqi, a Palestinian immigrant and founder of the International Institute of Islamic Thought. Al-Faruqi taught Islamic studies at Philadelphia's Temple University. In the early 1980s, he wrote, "Nothing could be greater than this youthful, vigorous, and rich continent [North America] turning away from its past evil and marching forward under the banner of *Allahu Akbar* [God is great]."[4]

Ahmad Nawfal, a leader of the Jordanian Muslim Brethren, is a frequent speaker at Muslim rallies in the U.S. He urges militant Muslims to rise up. "With the ideology that we possess," he says, "it will be very easy for us to preside over this world."[5]

Zaid Salim Shakir is a co-founder of Zaytuna College in Berkeley, California, and the former Muslim chaplain at Yale. He took part in the National Prayer Service for President Obama's inauguration. Shakir has openly stated his desire to see America become a Muslim nation, ruled by Sharia law. He said, "Every Muslim who is honest would say, I would like to see America become a Muslim country." Muslims, he adds, cannot accept the legitimacy of the American constitutional order because it goes "against the orders and ordainments of Allah."[6]

The archbishop of Izmir, Turkey, Giuseppe Germano Bernandini, reported to his synod of bishops that a renowned Muslim leader told him, "Thanks to your democratic laws we will invade you. Thanks to our religious laws we will dominate you." That Muslim leader's prediction is being fulfilled before our eyes.

High birth rate among Muslims. A second reason for Muslim expansion in the U.S. is that Muslim immigrant families have high birth rates, especially those who come from the Middle East. Muslim parents are diligent in passing the teachings of Islam down to their children.

Large families and high birth rates have long been viewed as part of the Islamic plan for world domination—and Muslim leaders have made no secret of their plans. In 1974, Algerian leader Houari Boumedienne told the United Nations, "One day, millions of men will leave the Southern Hemisphere to go to the Northern Hemisphere. And they will not go there as friends. Because they will go there to conquer it. And they will conquer it with their sons. The wombs of our women will give us victory."[7]

Conversion, especially among African-Americans. A significant number of African-Americans have converted to Islam since the 1960s. Many rejected the values and ideals they viewed as belonging to a hypocritical white Christian society. Muslim leaders see the African-American population as ripe for conversion, and they repeatedly make such claims as, "Christianity is a racist religion; Islam is a religion of peace." Nothing could be further from the historical truth. In fact, Islamic cultures have a long tradition of slavery which continues to this day. For example, the city of Dubai in the United Arab Emirates boasts a towering skyline that was built in large part by slave labor imported from Asia.[8]

The message espoused by militant black Muslims is much the same as the message preached by militant Arab Muslims: America must be subjugated. In June 1991, an African-American convert to Islam, Siraj Wahaj, became the first Muslim to offer the opening prayer in the U.S. House of Representatives. He quoted the Koran and appealed to Allah to grant the lawmakers guidance, righteousness, and wisdom.

A year later, however, Wahaj addressed a Muslim conference in New Jersey where he sounded far less moderate. The goal of Muslims, he said, is to replace the Constitution with the Koran and the caliphate. "If we were united and strong," he said, "we'd elect our own emir [as president] and give allegiance to him. . . . If six to eight million Muslims unite in America, the country will come to us." In 1995, the U.S. attorney for New York listed Wahaj as an unindicted co-conspirator in the case of the blind sheik Omar Abdel Rahman in his trial for conspiracy to overthrow the U.S. government.[9]

Overall, some 60 to 90 percent of all converts to Islam in the United States are African-Americans. Sadly, 80 percent of these converts were raised in the Christian church. In 1994, an article published in *Christianity Today* predicted, "If the conversion rate continues unchanged, Islam could become the dominant religion in Black urban areas by the year 2020."[10]

One sociologist has noted that in the 1960s when Eastern religions first became popular in the United States, the rich turned to Zen Buddhism and the poor turned to Islam. The rich sought enlightenment, knowing that riches do not bring spiritual satisfaction. The poor sought power, believing that power could bring all forms of satisfaction.

The Black Muslim movement in America started during the days of segregation. The movement became popular, in part, because African-Americans saw the Islamic movement as standing against oppression. They believed that Islam would help restore dignity to African-American people. The Nation of Islam was founded in 1930, and grew to produce such black American leaders as Elijah Muhammad, Malcolm X, and Louis Farrakhan. Other Black Muslim groups arose alongside the Nation of Islam, including the Five Percenters, Ansaar Allah, the Islamic Party of North America, Dar ul-Islam, Islamic Brotherhood, and the Hanafi Movement.

Prison populations seem ideally "ripe" for the message of Islam. Most Black Muslims do not turn to Islam because they are attracted to its theology, its laws, or its history. Rather, they are attracted to Islam's offer of power for the powerless and inclusion in a "brotherhood" of power. In recent years, Islam has experienced a surge in popularity in our nation's prisons. A 2007 report commissioned by the U.S. Department of Justice found that many previously non-religious prisoners were "converted during their imprisonment. According to the FBI, some of these prisoners may be vulnerable to terrorist recruitment."

Islam is spread in prison primarily by charismatic Muslim prisoners who recruit and convert their fellow prisoners and are often able to graft an Islamic spiritual identity onto the history and identity of existing prison gangs. The author of the report, Dr. Mark S. Hamm of the Department of Criminology at Indiana State University, writes:

> *Intelligence officers agree that most inmates are radicalized by other radical inmates, and not by outside influences. Radicalization occurs through a process of one-on-one proselytizing by charismatic leaders. . . . Gang dynamics have become extremely complex in recent years as members are now crossing racial lines to increase their numbers for protection. Former rivals, like the Crips and Bloods, are joining forces under Islamic banners. Neo-Nazis are becoming Sunni Muslims. Meanwhile, there is growing conflict within inmate Islam as various factions of the faith compete for followers, thereby pitting the Nation of Islam against Sunnis, Sunnis against Shiites, and Prison Islam against them all. Moreover, radicalization is developed on a prison gang model.*[11]

Black Muslims in the United States have only marginally integrated with the wider community of orthodox Islam. The American movement has taken the title of "World Community of Islam in the West." Historically, Orthodox Islam did not recognize Black Muslim Americans because of their belief in black supremacy and "other heresies." Today, however, that is changing as orthodox Muslims discover the benefits of joining forces with less orthodox groups in order to magnify their power and influence.

WHO IS TARGETED FOR CONVERSION?

American converts to Islam tend to fall largely within the twenty- to thirty-something age group. Since the late 1960s, several important Islamic organizations have been established to strengthen and support American Muslims, and to propagate their message in our culture. They are making their greatest inroads among our youth and college-age students. The Council of Imams trains local mosque prayer leaders, and the Association of Muslim Students has at least two hundred active chapters on college campuses across the United States. Similar organizations can be found in England, Australia, Canada, and other Western nations.

These organizations have boldly stated their goals:

- To disseminate Islam through publications geared to both Muslims and non-Muslims;
- To establish Islamic institutions, including places of worship, community service centers, and educational facilities;
- To assist Muslims in practical aspects of religious observance (the Five Pillars of Islam);
- To propagate and facilitate Islam's faith-sharing effort among non-Muslims; and
- To encourage the "unity of Muslim conscience" through a heightened sense of belonging and Muslim identity.

Vast sums of money have been made available to Islamic Americans to pursue these goals. These organizations are aggressively building facilities, publishing books and newspapers, and creating web sites that espouse Islamic teachings. In this way, the Islamists seek to gain control of American minds and hearts. They are taking advantage of our constitutionally guaranteed freedom of religion in a bid to ultimately undermine our Constitution and take away our freedom of religion.

IN THE END—NO FREEDOM OF RELIGION

We in America are so accustomed to our religious freedom that we assume that such freedom is universally respected. But Islam does not respect or tolerate differences of belief. Arab Islamic nations consider Christian missionary activity to be a crime; those who engage in Christian evangelism are punished as criminals.

Many Muslims who converted to Christianity in North Africa and the Middle East are languishing in prisons at this moment, convicted of a crime against the Islamic state. What is their crime? Apostasy—the crime of forsaking Islam. Ismail Al-Faruqi, who taught Islamic studies at Temple University, explained the reasoning behind this view:

> *To convert out of Islam means clearly to abandon its world order, which is the Islamic state. That is why Islamic law has treated people who have converted out of Islam as political traitors. . . . [The state] must deal with the traitors, when convicted after due process of law, either with banishment, life*

> *imprisonment, or capital punishment. The Islamic State is no exception to this. But Islamic political theory does allow converts from Islam to emigrate from the Islamic state, provided they do so before proclaiming their conversion, for the state does not keep its citizens within its boundaries by force. But once their conversion is proclaimed, they must be dealt with as traitors to the state.*[12]

Apostasy—the act of forsaking what Muslims consider to be the one true religion—is an offense punishable not only by imprisonment, but often by death. There is no religious tolerance in Islam, though some Muslim governments maintain a pretense of tolerance and "religious freedom." Many Islamic nations, for example, have a "religious freedom" clause in their constitutions. However, "religious freedom" in those countries is always interpreted as (for example) the right of a Christian or Jew to convert to Islam; it is never interpreted as the right of a Muslim to convert to another religion.

We in the West need to remove our rose-colored glasses and recognize clearly that when a nation declares itself to be an Islamic state, religious liberty vanishes in that moment. Non-Muslims instantly become second-class citizens in that society.

THREE CONSEQUENCES OF AN ISLAMIC STATE

When an Islamic government takes power, we invariably see three painful consequences that affect Muslims and non-Muslims:

Personal freedom is purged. Once Muslims gain political control of an area, they move quickly to eliminate personal freedoms—especially freedom of speech and freedom of association. They also eliminate all external signs and symbols of non-Muslim culture.

Immediately after the Taliban seized power in Afghanistan in 1996, the Islamist regime banned employment and education for women, music and "equipment that produces the joy of music," movies, videos, TVs, computers, dancing, wedding parties, statues and framed pictures, applause at sports events, kite flying, pool tables, chess games, card games, children's toys and dolls, fireworks, jewelry, wine, and much more. Women were required to cover themselves head to toe in shroud-like burqas and were ordered to stay in their homes unless accompanied by a male relative. Men were required to wear beards that extended a minimum of the width of one's fist.[13]

The religious police in Afghanistan, who enforced Sharia law, were trained by radical Wahhabis in Saudi Arabia. A sign posted on the wall of the Taliban's police headquarters read, appropriately enough, "Throw Reason to the Dogs. It Stinks of Corruption."[14]

The soccer stadium in Kabul became an arena for public spectacles of punishment. Thieves had hands amputated in front of cheering crowds. Fornicators were flogged and adulterers were stoned to death. Men accused of homosexual activity were partially buried in the ground, then a stone wall was pushed over on them by a bulldozer. These sadistic punishments, clearly the product of a diseased mind, were devised by Mullah Mohammad Omar, the supreme leader of the Taliban.[15]

Personal freedom is practically unknown in Saudi Arabia, the "holy land" of Islam. Like the Taliban, the Saudi government carries out Sharia law with floggings, amputations of hands and feet, stoning, beheading with a sword, and even crucifixion.[16] Suhaila Hammad, the spokeswoman for Saudi Arabia's National Society for Human Rights, defended the practice of beheading condemned prisoners, saying, "Allah, our creator, knows best what's good for his people."[17]

Women's rights are almost nonexistent in Saudi Arabia. Women comprise only 5 percent of the Saudi workforce, the lowest percentage of any nation in the world.[18] It is against the law for women to drive cars in Saudi Arabia (an odd loophole in the law permits women to pilot airplanes, but they must be driven to the airport by a man).[19]

A tradition called *purdah* requires a complete separation between the sexes. The world of men and the world of women must never come in contact in Saudi society. Both men and women are required to cover most of their bodies, and Saudi women can never be seen in the company of a man who is not either her husband or a kinsman by *mahram*. A *mahram* relative is related either by blood (parent, grandparent, sibling, uncle, aunt) or related by marriage (parent-in-law or step-parent).

There is an odd provision by which a man who is not related to a woman can become *mahram* through what is called "milk kinship." A woman must provide five meals of breast milk to the man in order to create this "kinship." For example, an aunt might provide five meals of breast milk to a young nephew-by-marriage so that the families can freely mingle when the nephew becomes a man. Though this custom seems grotesque to Western sensibilities, Islamic clerics take the matter very seriously, and continually debate such issues as whether a man should drink the milk from a bowl or straight from the woman's breast.

In 2010, a group of Saudi women in Riyadh attempted to use the "milk kinship" custom to gain the right to drive. Threatening to breastfeed their foreign-born chauffeurs, the women declared, "We either be allowed to drive or we breastfeed foreigners!"[20]

The Saudis also do not grant basic human rights to non-Muslim visitors to their country—including American servicemen who are defending the Saudi Kingdom. The Saudis were pleased to accept help from the U.S. military when the Iraqi forces threatened to invade. But the Saudis also imposed stifling restrictions on the 400,000 American soldiers who defended Saudi territory during Operation Desert Shield. The soldiers were told that if they wanted to celebrate religious holidays, they were to do so in remote areas where the local citizens could not observe them. Chaplains, both Christian and Jewish, were told not to wear any religious symbols in public (including head coverings for Jews and crosses for Christians). There are no Christian churches or synagogues anywhere in Saudi Arabia. In fact, the Saudi government refuses to permit a single room in a single building to be used by Christians for Christian worship within Saudi Arabia.

Because Saudi Arabia is considered the home of "pure Islam," the religious practices and icons of "infidels" are considered an abomination. What an irony! American soldiers were in Saudi Arabia to help defend this nation and its oil wealth, yet Islamic intolerance toward Christians and Jews is as repressive as it was in the days of Muhammad, 1,400 years ago.

When Idi Amin was the president of Uganda during the 1970s, he slaughtered an estimated 300,000 Christians before he was overthrown in 1979. Once out of power, he slipped out of Uganda and ran to the protective arms of his Muslim brothers in Libya and Saudi Arabia. In exile, Amin was applauded throughout the Islamic world—not *in spite* of his massacre of Christians, but *because* the slaughter of "infidels" was seen as a forward move for Islam in Uganda.

An end to innovation. The second painful consequence we see when Islamic governments take power is that modernization and technological advances come to a grinding halt.

Apart from the oil-producing nations, most Islamic nations are poor. Wealth in the modern world has been strongly linked to modernization, and Islam as a whole stands against innovation, creativity, and progress. There's a saying attributed to Muhammad (though it is not in the Koran): "The worst things are those that are novelties. Every novelty is an innovation, every innovation is an error, and every error leads to hellfire." Sunni Islam defines observance of tradition or sayings of Muhammad as good, departure from tradition as bad.

Enough innovation has trickled into the Islamic world to show poor Muslims that they do not have the conveniences and material prosperity of the West. Muslims know that they are missing out on many of the advanced blessings of the modern world. This only aggravates their anger toward the West. They feel a paradoxical mixture of jealousy for the innovations we enjoy, mingled with a rejection of the "heresy" of all ideas and inventions that depart from the simple, impoverished purity of seventh century Islam.

The message of the Islamists to poor Muslims is never an outright denunciation of luxuries or technology. Rather, they say, "We know you live in a police state and you live in poverty. The reason for this is that Satan is doing this to you. Satan is the West. Satan is America. Come join our holy war. Join the army of Allah to defeat the West."

Islamic governments tend to be highly autocratic regimes in which the rich get richer and the poor get poorer. Economic mismanagement and corruption are widespread. A comment by an Algerian interviewed in a French news magazine is typical of opinions held throughout the Muslim world: "Algeria was once the granary of Rome, and now it has to import cereals to make bread. It is a land of flocks and gardens, and it imports meat and fruit. It is rich in oil and gas, and it has a foreign debt of twenty-five billion dollars and two million unemployed."[21]

A policy of appeasement. The third painful consequence we see when Islamists take power is that bureaucratic governments fear the wrath of radical Muslims. So, in order to maintain their popularity and power, these governments often appease the hardliners and zealots in their society. This is one reason why you almost never hear moderate Muslims speak out against Muslim terrorists. If they speak out, they will have to face the wrath of the extremists. So they keep silent. They appease the hot-headed extremists to avoid trouble.

Appeasement is the policy of most Middle East governments. Let me give you an example of how a policy of appeasement works to placate radical factions:

Years ago, a church was seized by radical Muslims in the town of Basateen, near Cairo. The Muslims converted the building into a mosque. When Christians complained to the authorities that their property had been unlawfully taken, police demolished the building on the pretext that the Christians had not acquired the proper construction permits. Rather than confront the actions of the Muslim militants, the government adopted a hide-behind-the-law approach. This happens again and again.

Egyptian law states that no church may be built or have any alterations, repairs, or improvements without a presidential decree. This law was enacted in 1856 following the outline of the "Covenant of Umar"—a statute that was placed on the books by the Ottoman Empire when Egypt was an Ottoman colony.

In 1972, President Anwar Sadat promised Coptic Christian leaders that he would grant fifty permits a year for church building. However, from 1973 to 1979, he granted a total of fifty permits (rather than the three hundred promised). In 1978 and 1979, he gave five permits. By 1990, hundreds of applications for permits were outstanding. They had gathered dust in government bureaucratic offices for decades. Some Christian churches had waited as long as twenty-seven years for a building permit, even though the government builds mosques almost daily and pays the salaries of mosque leaders. After President Mubarak came to power, he reactivated and tightened the 1856 law, making it virtually impossible for new churches to be built or old churches renovated.

Here is the irony: the policy of appeasement on the part of both Sadat and Mubarak brought about the death of one and the ousting of the other.

Since 1973, Egypt has engaged in a continual effort to appease radical Muslims by passing laws paving the way for the Koran to be used as the primary source of law in Egypt. Court decisions have set precedents that push non-Muslims more and more into the role of *dhimmi*—non-Muslims granted extremely limited rights under Sharia law.

What happens when Christians speak out against unfair treatment? We found out when Coptic Christians in Egypt spoke out in 1980. As an act of protest, Pope Shenouda of the Coptic Church canceled all official Easter festivities in 1980 and restricted the celebration to simple prayers. He refused to accept President Sadat's annual Easter greetings. The members of the Holy Synod (the governing body of the Coptic church) retired to the desert monastery of St. Bishay.

Angered by the worldwide press attention caused by these actions, President Sadat attacked Coptic leaders in a speech delivered on May 14 of that year. He accused them of plotting to overthrow his government, of slandering both him and Egypt, and of attempting to foster social discontent. He then placed the Christian leaders under house arrest and ousted leaders of the synod from their positions of authority within the church. In their place, he appointed a council of bishops, which was to be more responsive to governmental policies.

After Sadat was assassinated in 1981, his successor, Hosni Mubarak, released virtually all of Sadat's political prisoners except the Coptic leaders who were held under house arrest. It was several years before President Mubarak finally released them and allowed them to resume their duties as ruling elders of the church in Egypt.

These events in Egypt are not unusual. In fact, this is typically what happens in so-called "moderate" Muslim states. Only Muslims are regarded as full citizens with all the rights of citizenship. In Saudi Arabia (which many in the West mistakenly view as a "moderate" Arab state), non-Muslims cannot be citizens at all.

The official Saudi "Tourism Guide" webpage lists all the items which you, as a tourist in the Kingdom of Saudi Arabia, are forbidden to bring into the country. Items which are (in bold red letters) "**not allowed**" include "Bibles, crucifixes, statues, carvings, items with religious symbols such as the Star of David, and others." In other words, you must respect the Islamic faith while the Saudis disrespect your faith and forbid you to even read your Bible while you are a guest of the kingdom. This is very perplexing, because the Koran admonishes all Muslims to read the Gospels!

When Queen Rania of Jordan appeared on the Oprah Winfrey program a few weeks after 9/11, she said, "The important thing is the spirit of Islam. That is all about tolerance, about doing good, diversity, equality, and human dignity. The fact that Islam is very tolerant means that it doesn't impose anything on other people."[22]

The queen might just as well be speaking in nonsense syllables, because the truth—as we have amply documented—is the complete opposite of everything she has said. Even when "moderate" Muslims are in power, the Islamists demand absolute submission and surrender—and they wield the power of the Islamic state to enforce their demands.

11

OUR RESPONSE AS AMERICANS

Safoorah Khan was hired in November 2007 to teach middle-school math in the tiny Berkeley, Illinois, school district. After just nine months on the job, she asked for a three-week leave of absence to take part in the Hajj, the Muslim pilgrimage to Mecca. All Muslims are expected to make the pilgrimage at least once in their lives as one of the Five Pillars of Islam. Yet Khan, who was only twenty-nine at the time, would likely have many years ahead of her to fulfill that goal. In fact, in eight years, the Hajj would occur during a school vacation, which would make it the ideal time for her to fulfill her obligations both to her faith and her employer.

Khan insisted on making the Hajj at the worst possible time for the school—and for her students. Taking the leave of absence during December 2008, as she wanted, would deny the school its only math-lab teacher just before exams. Her request, the school claimed, was unreasonable and wasn't permitted under the school's contract with the teachers' union. The school refused Khan's request. Khan resigned, made the pilgrimage to Mecca, and then filed a complaint with the Equal Employment Opportunity Commission, claiming to be a victim of "religious discrimination."

Safoorah Khan's attorney, Kamran A. Memon, said that the school's refusal was evidence of "anti-Muslim hostility." One has to wonder why the school hired Khan in the first place if it was such a hotbed of "anti-Muslim hostility." Common sense tells us that the school's refusal of her request is evidence of nothing more than a desire to have students receive math instruction and to have teachers perform the duties for which they are hired. Khan was treated no differently than any other teacher in the district.

Khan's case was taken up by the Obama administration's Justice Department, led by Attorney General Eric Holder and Assistant Attorney General Thomas Perez. Holder and Perez are clearly convinced that America is a cauldron of anti-Muslim bigotry. As Perez puts it, "our Muslim-American brothers and sisters" have been "victims of a post-9/11 backlash" and "a real head wind of intolerance against Muslim communities."

The Justice Department filed suit against the school district alleging discrimination and violation of Khan's civil rights. The government demanded back pay, money damages, and reinstatement for the Muslim teacher. Berkeley, Illinois, is a tiny community of five thousand people, mostly blue-collar African-Americans and Hispanics, and the school district didn't have the resources to fight the federal government. So the school settled the case for $75,000. The district also agreed to Justice Department demands that it formulate a new "religious accommodation policy" which will undoubtedly be tilted heavily in favor of Islam.[1]

Why is the Justice Department going out of its way to criminalize a commonsense personnel decision? Why is the Justice Department so intent on finding "intolerance" and a "backlash" where it is clear that none exists? It is becoming commonplace for people in the leftist media and the government to throw around accusations of Islamophobia.

"ISLAM IS ISLAM AND THAT'S IT"

But it seems to me that the "politically correct" segment of our society is afflicted with the opposite disorder. I call it "Islamophilia." It's the irrational and self-destructive desire to show how enlightened and morally superior you are by bending over backwards to embrace the Muslim cause.

We even see rampant Islamophilia in the highest levels of the U.S. military—and it has cost some of our brave U.S. servicemen and servicewomen their lives. We all remember the attack at Fort Hood, Texas, when Army Major Nidal Malik Hasan entered the Soldier Readiness Center, shouted "Allahu Akbar!" ("Allah is greater!"), then opened fire on scores of unarmed soldiers, including a pregnant woman who later died.

By the time Major Hasan was brought down by civilian police officers (he survived with paralyzing injuries), he had killed or mortally wounded 13 people and left 29 others injured. It was the worst shooting incident on a military base in U.S. history.

Soon after the attack, we learned that U.S. intelligence agencies had actually monitored emails between Hasan and the radical Al-Qaeda imam Anwar al-Awlaki. Hasan had been setting off alarms in the intelligence community for months, but the politically correct military bureaucracy ignored the warning signs.[2]

Hasan, who had trained as a psychiatrist at the Uniformed Services University of the Health Sciences in Bethesda, Maryland, was a frequent disciplinary problem, yet his superior officers promoted him to the rank of major, apparently to avoid appearing "intolerant" or "Islamophobic." During his residency in psychiatry at

Walter Reed Army Medical Center, he required extra supervision because of his extreme views.

While at Walter Reed, Hasan delivered a PowerPoint talk to a roomful of mental health staff members. His subject was Muslims in the U.S. military. Among the points listed in his presentation: "We [Muslims] love death more [than] you love life!" and "Fighting to establish an Islamic State to please God, even by force, is condoned by the Islam."[3]

One of Hasan's classmates recalled that presentation: "We asked him pointedly, 'Nidal, do you consider Shari'a law to transcend the Constitution of the United States?' And he said, 'Yes.' We asked him if homicidal bombers were rewarded for their acts with seventy-two virgins in heaven and he responded, 'I've done the research—yes.' Those are comments he made in front of the class. . . . I was astounded and went to multiple faculty members and asked why he was even in the Army. . . . Political correctness squelched any opportunity to confront him."[4]

The political correctness continued even after Hasan killed more than a dozen soldiers at Ford Hood. Army Chief of Staff George W. Casey, Jr., sent a mass email to soldiers expressing his concern about a potential "backlash against our Muslim Soldiers and civilians." Casey went on NBC's *Meet the Press* and said, "Our diversity, not only in our Army, but in our country, is a strength. And as horrific as this tragedy was, if our diversity becomes a casualty, I think that's worse."[5]

Now, that is an astonishing statement. If our "diversity" ever becomes a "casualty," that will be a worse loss than the *real* casualties—the dead and wounded victims of the Fort Hood shooting! At the very highest levels of our military, our leaders are so anxious to be thought of as "tolerant" and "politically correct" that they openly value cultural "diversity" above the lives of our fighting men and women. That is why the military kept promoting Nidal Malik Hasan, even though he was clearly a threat to his fellow soldiers. The military bureaucracy bent over backwards to keep the Army from appearing to be "Islamophobic."

Political correctness in the upper echelons of the Pentagon literally killed those soldiers at Fort Hood. And political correctness in the highest echelons of our government is likely to kill many more people and may ultimately cost us our American way of life.

Since his election as president of the United States, Barack Obama has been on a campaign to ingratiate himself with the Wahhabis, the Muslim Brotherhood and other militant Islamist groups. Some examples:

- President Obama invited Ingrid Mattson, a Canadian-born Muslim with ties to Hamas and the Muslim Brotherhood, to offer prayer at his inaugural prayer service.[6]

- Newly inaugurated President Obama gave his first formal television interview to Al-Arabiya, an Arabic network, and he began by saying that "all too often the United States starts by dictating" to other nations, and that the U.S. had "made mistakes" in the Arab world.[7]
- President Obama skipped the National Day of Prayer, but recorded a special message to Muslims at the start of Ramadan.[8]
- In his June 2009 Cairo speech, President Obama spoke approvingly (three times!) of the Muslim practice of covering women with hijabs and niqabs. He reiterated his approval of the practice at a White House celebration of Ramadan.[9]
- At the White House Ramadan dinner, President Obama also said, "Islam, as we know, is part of America."[10]
- On Thanksgiving Eve 2009, Mr. Obama issued a Hajj message to all Muslims.[11]
- In June 2011, the Obama administration announced that it would formally recognize and resume diplomatic contact with Egypt's Muslim Brotherhood, even though the Brotherhood denies Israel's right to exist.[12]

President Barack Obama's love affair with the Muslim world runs deep. In 2007, early in Mr. Obama's race for the presidency, *New York Times* columnist Nicholas D. Kristof wrote a laudatory profile of the candidate called "Obama: Man of the World," based on a wide-ranging interview Kristof had conducted with the candidate. In the interview, Mr. Obama recalled being a "street kid" in Jakarta, Indonesia, and getting in trouble for misbehaving during Koran study classes in his elementary school. Kristof noted that Mr. Obama could still speak the Indonesian language he had learned as a child.

Kristof went on to observe, "Mr. Obama recalled the opening lines of the Arabic call to prayer, reciting them with a first-rate accent. In a remark that seemed delightfully uncalculated, . . . Mr. Obama described the call to prayer as 'one of the prettiest sounds on Earth at sunset.'"[13]

President Obama has treated the Saudi king as if he were a moderate Muslim and a force for peace in the Middle East. On April 2, Mr. Obama attended the G20 Summit in London. While there were many heads of state at the summit, Mr. Obama singled out King Abdullah of Saudi Arabia for special honor, bowing deeply from the waist as he took the hand of the king in both hands—a gesture in which Mr. Obama symbolically placed the office of the president of the United States under subjection to the Saudi Royal House.

The *Washington Times* called the bow a "shocking display of fealty to a foreign potentate,"[14] but the Saudi-backed newspaper *Asharq Alawsat* suggested that the reason for President Obama's bow was that "Obama wished to demonstrate his respect and appreciation of the personality of King Abdullah Bin Abdulaziz."[15]

Whatever Mr. Obama's reasons for bowing to the king, it's clear that in many ways, throughout his administration, he has bowed and scraped before the Muslim world, currying favor with supposed "moderates" in the Islamic community, both in the United States and abroad. Yet these so-called "moderates" include the Saudi king (the sponsor and friend of the Wahhabists) and such militant groups as the Muslim Brotherhood. Whether President Obama knows it or not, these are Muslim fundamentalists, and to them the world is divided into two realms—Dar al-Islam (the House of Islam) and Dar al-Harb (the House of War, the realm of infidels).

President Obama would do well to heed the words of the Islamic prime minister of Turkey, Recep Tayyip Erdoğan. In 2007, he disparaged the term "moderate Islam," which is widely used in the West. "These descriptions," Erdoğan said, "are very ugly. It is offensive and an insult to our religion. There is no moderate or immoderate Islam. Islam is Islam and that's it."[16]

Mr. Obama is wasting his bows and his breath trying to ingratiate himself with the Muslim fundamentalists. In their eyes, he belongs to the House of War. He may bow to the king, secretly negotiate with Muslim Brotherhood, speak glowingly of Islam, disparage his own nation, and give international respectability to Muslim extremists, but their view of President Obama and the United States will not change. To be sure, they see him as a "useful idiot" who can advance their cause, but he will never get the acceptance he is seeking.

OPERATION MODERATION

With all that Mr. Obama has said and done to befriend the Muslim world, you would think that his favorability ratings would soar. In fact, his popularity in the Muslim world has plummeted—and so has the popularity of the United States. James Zogby is president of the Arab American Institute, a senior analyst in his brother John's polling firm, Zogby International, and a member of the executive committee of the Democratic National Committee. A Lebanese-American, James Zogby has found that in 2008, the last year of the George W. Bush presidency, only nine percent of Egyptians held a favorable view of the United States; by July 2011, two and a half years into the Obama presidency, that favorable rating had shrunk to just five percent.

Farah Stockman of the Boston Globe adds, "Similar figures in Morocco, Jordan, and the United Arab Emirates show that the United States is viewed less favorably now than the final year of the Bush administration." Moreover, the poll found that the policies of militant Islamist Iran "are viewed more favorably than the policies of the United States."[17]

The Gallup organization also polled the Egyptian people after the 2011 revolution, and discovered that the vast majority of Egyptians—75 percent—do not want their government to accept economic aid from the United States. This is an especially shocking statistic in view of the economic need in that nation. Why do the Egyptian people reject American money? It's because they feel that it makes Egypt beholden to the U.S. and Western interests, turning Egypt into a "puppet state." During the past three decades, Egypt received $50 billion from U.S. taxpayers—and all the taxpayers have received for their money was the resentment of the Egyptian people.[18]

Despite these findings, the Obama administration continues to pump aid into various organizations in Egypt that were (supposedly) pursuing "democratic reform." The White House supposedly gave this aid directly to "reform" organizations to prevent the interim government from "skimming the cream" off the aid. The problem is that the Obama team can't tell the difference between an extremist and a moderate. As a result, much of the indirect aid under Mr. Obama's "operation moderation," is going to the militant Muslim Brotherhood and similar organizations. It is almost a dead certainty that some of these funds will be used to increase the level of persecution of Egyptian Christians, as well as to undermine the security of Israel.

It's tragic enough that Christians in Egypt must reconcile themselves to suffering and persecution for Christ in their homeland—but must Christian taxpayers in America subsidize that injustice? Instead of this misguided effort to fund "moderate" elements in the Middle East (which are not moderate at all), wouldn't it be wiser to simply honor the wishes of the Egyptian people and stop sending our unwanted dollars to their country?

WHAT CAN ONE PERSON DO?

America is under attack by Islamists in both overt ways (terror attacks) and covert ways (stealth and infiltration). What can we as Americans do to fight the overt and covert plans to convert America into an Islamic state and to subjugate all of Western civilization? Here are a number of suggested actions our nation should take, plus actions that you and I as individual citizens can take:

Demand that your leaders fight terror as a war, not a crime. Before 9/11, the United States treated terrorism as a criminal act to be solved by the FBI and prosecuted by the Justice Department in civilian courts. After 9/11, our leaders realized that this was an inadequate response to terrorism. That's why President George W. Bush responded by declaring a full-fledged "War on Terror."

After President Obama was inaugurated, America's stance toward terrorism changed, almost as if we had turned back the clock to September 10, 2001. Even though the terrorists were still at war with America, America was no longer at war with terror. The Obama administration replaced the term "War on Terror" with the Orwellian euphemism "overseas contingency operations." Homeland security director Janet Napolitano replaced the term "terrorist attack" with "man-caused disasters."

It could be said that the 2010 British Petroleum oil spill in the Gulf of Mexico was also a "man-caused disaster"—yet it wasn't an act of terrorism. Why replace a perfectly good English term like "terrorism" with meaningless bureaucrat-speak? When the government wants to change our language, it is because the government wants to change the subject. When politicians talk in meaningless, politically correct terminology, they are trying to change the way we think. They are trying to make us forget that militant Islamists are at war with us, and that those Islamists are trying to destroy our way of life.

The government isn't merely trying to change the way we think about terror. It's trying to change the way America deals with terror. On November 13, 2009, attorney general Eric Holder announced that a number of accused 9/11 terror suspects—Khalid Sheikh Mohammed, Ali Abdul Aziz Ali, Ramzi Bin al-Shibh, Walid bin Attash, and Mustafa Ahmed al-Hawsawi—would be moved from the military tribunal justice system to the United States District Court for the Southern District of New York. In other words, these enemy combatants would be tried in civilian courts just a few blocks away from Ground Zero.

Immediately, a storm of protest erupted. Everyone in America with an ounce of common sense found Holder's decision to be the height of insanity. One of those who spoke out was Senator Lindsey Graham of South Carolina. The decision, he said, "makes no sense to most Americans—including me. . . . These Al-Qaeda terrorists are not common criminals. Their attacks resulted in the biggest loss of American life from an act of war on our homeland since the Civil War. Never before have we allowed non-citizen, enemy combatants captured on the battlefield access to our civilian courts providing them with the same constitutional rights as American citizens. Al-Qaeda terrorists should not receive more rights than a Nazi War criminal."

Senator Graham then recounted an incident to illustrate his point. U.S. District Court judge Michael Mukasey (who later became attorney general under George

W. Bush) was the presiding judge in the 1995 trial of Sheikh Omar Abdel-Rahman, the "blind sheik" who conspired to blow up the World Trade Center with a truck bomb in 1993. During the civilian court trial, the government was required by court rules to disclose the identity of all of Sheikh Abdel-Rahman's known co-conspirators.

The government handed over the list, and one of the names on the list was that of a fairly obscure Muslim radical named Osama bin Laden. U.S. intelligence agencies later learned that the list of co-conspirators was passed along to bin Laden himself—and that knowledge gave bin Laden a lot of information about U.S. surveillance methods. From then on, bin Laden was more careful about his movements and communications—and he was much harder for our intelligence agencies to track. Though our government successfully prosecuted the blind sheik, the U.S. was hindered in its ability to get bin Laden—and prevent 9/11.

Judge Michael Mukasey later wrote in an opinion piece in the *Wall Street Journal* that the civilian courts and civilian statutes "are not well suited to even the limited task of supplementing what became, after September 11, 2001, principally a military effort to combat Islamic terrorism." Terrorism trials, he concluded, do not belong in the "strained and mismatched legal system" of the civilian courts.[19]

As Senator Graham concludes, "Civilian trials create confusion. Our soldiers and intelligence services are already uncertain as to what rules apply. . . . Is reading Miranda Rights to terrorists any way to fight a war? . . . These trials should not take place in New York or any other civilian court. To do so, ignores the fact we are at war. . . . Military tribunals are the best way to render justice, win this war and protect our nation from a vicious enemy."[20]

Finally, in April 2011, Attorney General Holder admitted what the rest of us have known all along—terrorists must be tried by military tribunal. America is engaged in a life-and-death struggle against extreme Islamist terror. The terrorists themselves know that this is war. Now if we could only convince our own government of that!

I encourage you to contact your elected representatives by phone, mail, or email. Be assertive yet courteous. Tell your representatives that America must continue to fight the War on Terror—not "overseas contingency operations" against "man-caused disasters." Whenever you see a story in the news or hear a statement from your representative that demonstrates a lack of resolve to meet terrorism head-on and call it by it's rightful name, let your voice be heard in Washington, D.C. To contact the president or vice president, visit www.whitehouse.gov/contact/. To obtain contact information for your congressperson, visit writerep.house.gov/writerep/welcome.shtml; get contact information for your senator at www.senate.gov/general/contact_information/senators_cfm.cfm.

Enter those phone numbers into the speed dialer of your cell phone. Then anytime you want to let your elected representatives know what you think about an issue, give them a call. Instead of staring at the wallpaper at the doctor's office, take out your cell phone and make your wishes known. Your representatives work for you—and they will do a better job if they know you are watching what they do.

Support true moderate Muslims and marginalize radical Muslims. As American citizens, we need to urge our government to stop appeasing radical Islamists and start marginalizing them. This includes radical Muslims in the United States and in other countries (such as the Muslim Brotherhood).

Our government and the media have a dismal track record of picking out certain prominent Muslims, dubbing them "moderates," and giving them a platform to propagandize for a radical, pro-Sharia point of view. Here are just two prime examples:

- Anwar Al-Awlaki was born in New Mexico and, soon after the 9/11 attacks, was hailed by the *New York Times* as part of a "new generation of Muslim leaders capable of merging East and West." He served as the Muslim chaplain at George Washington University, and was consulted as an expert on Islam by the *Washington Post* and *National Geographic*. In 2002, he led a prayer service for Muslim congressional staffers in the U.S. Capitol.[21] Al-Awlaki even appeared as a guest speaker at a luncheon for military brass at the Pentagon because (according to a Defense Department document) "the secretary of the Army . . . was eager to have a presentation from a moderate Muslim."[22]

  In short, Anwar Al-Awlaki presented the perfect picture of a "moderate" Muslim. Yet at that same time, Awlaki was being investigated by the FBI because he had close ties to three 9/11 hijackers. Ironically, those three hijackers were all aboard Flight 77—the plane that flew into the Pentagon, the very building where he was invited to give a luncheon speech! In late 2002, Awlaki fled to Yemen, his ancestral homeland, where he openly spouted jihad against the United States—and he helped inspire or direct a number of terror attacks in the U.S., including the Fort Hood massacre in Texas, the Christmas 2009 in-flight "underwear bombing" attempt, the failed Times Square bombing attempt in May 2010, and more. It turned out that this supposedly "moderate" Muslim was a senior Al-Qaeda leader. He was killed by a U.S. drone strike in Yemen on September 30, 2011.

- In 2009, an investment group led by Imam Feisal Abdul Rauf purchased 51 Park Place in lower Manhattan, about 600 feet from the site of the 9/11 attacks at the World Trade Center. In fact, the landing gear of United Airlines Flight 175 actually flew out of the South Tower and crashed into the roof of 51 Park Place, falling through the top two floors of the five-story building. So this building was truly part of Ground Zero. Rauf's plan was to convert that building into an Islamic cultural center and mosque—a plan that has come to be known as the "Ground Zero Mosque."

  Though Rauf portrays himself as a "moderate" Muslim, interested only in interfaith harmony and understanding, he once told CBS newsman Ed Bradley, just weeks after 9/11, "United States policies were an accessory to the crime that happened" on 9/11.[23] He refuses to acknowledge that Hamas is a terror organization.[24] And he once said "Christians in World War II . . . bombed civilians in Dresden and Hiroshima."[25]

  Rauf's original name for the Park Avenue project was "the Cordoba Initiative," a name with an interesting historical significance. As former Speaker of the House Newt Gingrich pointed out:

> *"Cordoba House" is a deliberately insulting term. It refers to Cordoba, Spain—the capital of Muslim conquerors who symbolized their victory over the Christian Spaniards by transforming a church there into the world's third-largest mosque complex. . . . Every Islamist in the world recognizes Cordoba as a symbol of Islamic conquest. It is a sign of their contempt for Americans and their confidence in our historic ignorance that they would deliberately insult us this way. . . .*
>
> *America is experiencing an Islamist cultural-political offensive designed to undermine and destroy our civilization. Sadly, too many of our elites are the willing apologists for those who would destroy them if they could.*[26]

Despite widespread objections to the Ground Zero Mosque from the public and from families of the 9/11 victims, President Obama, then-Speaker Nancy Pelosi, and New York Mayor Bloomberg all spoke out in support of the project and in support of the "moderate" imam, Feisal Abdul Rauf. In fact, in the very midst of the heated debate over the Ground Zero mosque, the State Department sent Rauf on a *taxpayer-funded* "goodwill tour" to the Muslim world. It was as if the government was deliberately insulting its own concerned citizens.

Though we have seen our media and our government officials fawn over so-called "moderate" Muslims who are anything but, it's important that we openly applaud and publicly support those *genuine* moderate Muslims who sincerely condemn terrorism and call upon their fellow Muslims to demonstrate peace, tolerance, and love for America. A few examples worth noting:

- Raheel Raza, is a Pakistan-born Canadian, a devout Muslim, a board member of the Muslim Canadian Conference, and author of *Their Jihad, Not My Jihad*. She is an outspoken opponent of terrorism and an equally outspoken supporter of equality for Muslim women. Because of these stances, she often receives death threats. She also strongly opposed the "Ground Zero Mosque" in lower Manhattan. In an August 2010 appearance on *The O'Reilly Factor*, she said:

  > *I oppose the idea. . . . It's confrontational. It is in bad faith. And it doesn't really set up any kind of dialogue or discussion on tolerance. . . . How does building a mosque in the very place where Muslims murdered so many other Americans . . . create any kind of respect? . . .*
  >
  > *Building a mosque or a place of worship . . . across the street from Ground Zero is a slap in the face upon Americans. . . . I can't begin to imagine how [Rauf and his partners] would even conceive an idea that building a mosque there . . . [would] build tolerance and respect. . . .*
  >
  > *Mayor Bloomberg and other bleeding-heart white liberals like him don't understand the battle that we moderate Muslims are faced with in terms of confronting radical Islam . . . in North America, which has only grown since 9/11 because of political correctness.*[27]

- Zuhdi Jasser is a doctor, a retired Lieutenant Commander in the United States Navy, and staff physician to the U.S. Congress. He is also president of the American Islamic Forum for Democracy, and is a frequent guest on the Bill O'Reilly, Glenn Beck, and Sean Hannity shows. He is the son of Syrian-born parents who fled oppression in their homeland and settled in Wisconsin. Jasser is a devout Muslim, an advocate for Israel, and an opponent of the "insidious supremacism" of militant Islam.[28] In 2010, Jasser spoke out strongly against the "Ground Zero Mosque," writing in the *New York Post*:

  > *Ground Zero is the one place in America where Muslims should think less about teaching Islam and "our good side" and more about being American and fulfilling our responsibilities to confront the ideology of our enemies. . . . This is about a deep, soulful understanding of what happened to our country on 9/11.*

> *When Americans are attacked, they come together as one, under one flag, under one law against a common enemy that we are not afraid to identify. . . . Ground Zero is purely about being American. It can never be about being Muslim.*[29]

- Not long after 9/11, Arab journalist Ahmad al-Sarraf appeared on an Al Jazeera TV program and chided radical Muslims for their extreme rhetoric. He said, "Why don't we have tolerance? This rhetoric of hatred is in all sermons, in all schoolbooks. . . . We don't need America to interfere and teach us how to worship, but we need a certain element to force us to change our curriculum that calls for extremism."[30]
- On another occasion, Al Jazeera ran a televised debate between a Kuwaiti political scientist, Shafeeq Ghabra, and two anti-American Islamist hardliners. When the two militants tried to excuse Osama bin Laden and put the blame for 9/11 on America, Mr. Ghabra responded boldly, "The Lebanese civil war was not an American creation; neither was the Iran-Iraq war; neither was bin Laden. These are our creations. We need to look inside. We cannot be in this blame-others mode forever."[31]

Truly moderate Muslims such as these, who courageously voice support for America and condemnation of extremism and terror, need to be acknowledged and supported as role models for all Muslims.

Support energy independence and alternatives to OPEC oil. The United States is the world's largest oil importer. Though most of our oil imports come from Canada and Mexico, we still import a significant amount of oil from troubled parts of the world, including the Middle East. It only takes a cut in supply of a few percent to cause price spikes and serious economic repercussions. Our energy supply is a matter of national security. Our economy was severely affected by the Arab oil embargo of the 1970s, which was triggered by Arab dissatisfaction with American support of Israel during the Yom Kippur War. We should never allow ourselves to be blackmailed again because of oil.

As a nation, we have the innovative ability and technological skills to come up with scores, if not hundreds, of alternatives to foreign oil. The only question is: Do we have the wisdom and the will to do so? America has enormous domestic energy resources which we thus far refuse to exploit. We have centuries-worth of recoverable oil and gas in Alaska, in offshore oilfields, in the western United States, and much of it has been placed off-limits because of far-left politics, environmental extremism, and bureaucratic over-regulation.

We also have the technological know-how to extract enormous quantities of energy from the sun, the wind, hydrogen, and the atom. We are constantly improving technologies for burning coal more efficiently and cleanly. And yes, we can do so much more in the way of conservation.

I frequently encounter people who believe that America need not strive for energy independence. They say, "Let Americans produce wheat and computers, and let the Arabs provide the oil. We can maintain the status quo." This is an incredibly shortsighted view, and it fails to take into account the fact that many Islamic states actually wish to see the West come under the domination of Islam. It's not only the terrorists who believe this way, but the leaders of Islamic states, Islamic institutions, and Islamic organizations like the now-ascendant Muslim Brotherhood. What the terrorists are willing to kill and die for, these other extremists are willing to accomplish gradually, stealthily, using any weapon at their disposal—including the economic weapon of oil.

When Osama bin Laden and his fellow conspirators were planning the 9/11 attacks, they chose their targets with care. They selected the great symbols of American power. They targeted the World Trade Center as the great symbol of American economic power. They targeted the Pentagon as the hub of American military power. And don't forget that Flight 93, which was brought down by heroic passengers in a field in Pennsylvania, was almost certainly intended to strike at either the U.S. Capitol or the White House—a planned blow to our democratic, constitutional form of government.

Oil profits funded the attacks of September 11, 2001. Every barrel of oil we import from the Middle East transfers American wealth to the Muslim world, and some of that wealth inevitably ends up in the bank accounts of terrorists and others who want to subjugate us and destroy us. Our dependence on foreign oil is funding our own destruction. But we can do something about it. Here are some examples:

- Learn about energy. Read books about energy—books like *Power Hungry* by Robert Bryce, *Oil 101* by Morgan Downey, *The Quest: Energy, Security, and the Remaking of the Modern World* by Daniel Yergin, and *Drill Here, Drill Now, Pay Less* by Newt Gingrich. Read up on all sides of the issue, then make up your own mind.
- Once you are well-informed on energy, become an outspoken defender of energy independence. As a knowledgeable citizen, share your knowledge and wisdom with others in casual conversations, in letters to the editor, in blogs, and in social media.
- Contact your legislators and inform them of your concerns regarding energy policy and legislation. Talk to federal, state, and local representatives, because

your governor and state legislature make a lot of decisions about the energy industry in your state. Tell them that you want energy legislation and regulation to be based on proven science, not emotionalism or political ideology.

Advocate for tighter foreign investment laws. The American economy would be severely disrupted if OPEC investors suddenly liquidated their assets, dumped their United States Treasury bills on the market, or transferred their liquid assets away from the United States. I don't claim to be an expert in economics, but I believe that we, as individual citizens, must demand that our elected representatives put strong safeguards in place to protect our economy from manipulation by foreign investors.

I believe that one consequence of the Arab Spring uprisings and revolutions of 2011 may be that the fragile anti-terror coalition President Bush assembled following 9/11—a coalition that included a number of Islamic nations—may collapse. Arab nations that were at least nominally friendly to America may become openly hostile—and OPEC nations may decide that it's time, once again, to use oil and oil wealth as a weapon against the West. When that happens, I hope America is prepared for the economic consequences that will occur.

Press for full human rights and religious freedom in Islamic nations. Encourage your elected officials to hold Islamic nations accountable for the rights and welfare of non-Muslim people, such as the Copts in Egypt. Christians and Jews should be allowed to practice their religion, to build houses of worship and schools, and to be protected from harm. They should be allowed to advertise their activities and to distribute materials related to their faith. These are fundamental human rights that are routinely violated in many Islamic countries.

American aid to other countries should be conditioned on the human rights records of religious freedom of those nations. Aid, in the form of goods and services, should go to the people who need it—not to the Swiss bank accounts of corrupt leaders. We should openly ask oil-rich Muslims why they don't use their wealth to lift up their brothers in needy Muslim countries.

Whenever the federal government grants money to universities, foundations, and other institutions, it attaches requirements that the funds be used in ways that are free of racial, ethnic, and religious prejudice. Shouldn't the United States place similar restrictions on the use of foreign aid? This is taxpayer money, and it should be used in a way that is consistent with American values. As private citizens and taxpayers, we have a right and a duty to voice our concern about how our tax dollars are used on the international stage.

The nations of the Christian West, and particularly the United States, have long declared themselves to be protectors of the oppressed. Are we doing enough to protect the oppressed minorities in the nations of the Middle East? Our policies regarding human rights should be clear, firm, and coherent. Christian missionaries should be allowed to speak openly about the Injeil (the Gospels) in Muslim lands, inasmuch as the Koran itself urges Muslims to study the Injeil. We should construct our foreign policy on the firm basis of justice, not economic gain or political interests. America should demand freedom of speech and freedom of religion in nations that receive our aid—and press for these same freedoms in nations that do not.

Speak up! Tweet, blog, and post on Facebook. Become an influencer and an opinion leader. Share your ideas, opinions, beliefs, and values via podcasts, YouTube videos, blogs, and social networking. Be honest and careful with your facts, and avoid passing along unconfirmed "Internet rumors" and "urban legends." Back up everything you say with sources. Be polite, don't spread hate—but be bold as you "speak the truth in love."

As you receive information from the news, the Internet, and other sources, be skeptical. Fact-check everything you see and hear before making up your mind. Hold the news media accountable for slanted stories and biased reporting. Blog or write letters to the editor whenever you catch the news media distorting the truth.

Support America's homeland defense efforts. Be alert to suspicious activity by potential terrorists. We have to be continually aware that America is no longer far-removed from the rest of the world by two oceans. America is now a battlefield on the front lines of the War on Terror. The terrorists are trying to hit us again, and they can strike anywhere.

As an Egyptian-born American, I am willing to do my part to defend this homeland—and I encourage all Americans with a Middle Eastern name or background to join me in this. To my adopted and beloved homeland, I say, "Profile me!"

That's right. I pass through a lot of airports every year, and I want the hardworking people of the transportation safety system to know that I hereby volunteer to be racially profiled.

In recent years we have seen absurd incidences where women in their nineties and frightened little children have been subjected to humiliating searches that—had they been done by anyone other than agents of the Transportation Security Administration—would be prosecutable as sexual assaults. Such searches defy reason and do not make air travel any safer.

So I say: Profile me—and profile everyone like me who has a Middle Eastern name and appearance. I can already hear the howls of protest from everyone from CAIR to the ACLU, that profiling is a violation of civil rights. But how does the present system preserve the civil rights of children and old ladies who are needlessly manhandled because of some misguided allegiance to political correctness?

I think any American of Middle Eastern extraction should be willing to prove he or she loves America and the values America stands for. Some people think that patriotism means standing up for your rights. I say patriotism also means being willing to sacrifice your selfish interests for the sake of your country.

So many Americans gave their lives to purchase the freedom we so often take for granted. Should we Middle Eastern Americans be willing to spend an extra few minutes at the airport out of love for our country?

As a boy I dreamed of living in "the land of the free and the home of the brave." Now that I am here, I want to do my part to keep America free.

What are you willing to do for America today?

12

OUR RESPONSE AS CHRISTIANS

It's said that no good deed goes unpunished.

Catholic University of America in Washington, D.C., has graciously opened its doors to students of all faiths, including Muslims. And it is being punished for it.

John Banzhaf III, an activist attorney and professor at George Washington University Law School, has filed a complaint with the Washington, D.C., Office of Human Rights. He claims that Catholic University has violated the human rights of Muslim students by not sanctioning a Muslim student group and by not providing Muslim students a place to pray without Christian symbols on the wall.

Banzhaf alleges that Muslim students "must perform their prayers surrounded by symbols of Catholicism . . . a wooden crucifix, paintings of Jesus, pictures of priests and theologians which many Muslim students find inappropriate." He adds that students are particularly offended at having to pray and meditate in Christian chapels and "at the cathedral that looms over the entire campus—the Basilica of the National Shrine of the Immaculate Conception." The students want to be able to "pray without having to stare up and be looked down upon by a cross of Jesus."

One wonders if the students happened to notice the sign in front of the campus—the one that reads "Catholic University." It's not as if the University has tried to hide its religious orientation.

Banzhaf admits that the university's stance is "technically" legal—"but it suggests," he adds, "they are acting improperly and probably with malice. . . . [The Muslim students] have to pray five times a day, they have to look around for empty classrooms and to be sitting there trying to do Muslim prayers with a big cross looking down or a picture of Jesus or a picture of the Pope is not very conducive to their religion."

Catholic University was founded to be conducive to the *Catholic* religion, not the Muslim religion. If Muslim students wanted to attend a university that endorses their religion, shouldn't they have enrolled at, say, a *Muslim* university?

Islam has a name for this strategy—the strategy of moving into a non-Muslim organization, then trying to *force* that organization to change itself and accommodate Islam. This strategy is called *dawah*. In a broad sense, *dawah* refers to inviting non-Muslims to convert to Islam. A person who practices *dawah* is called a *dai*—in essence, a Muslim missionary. But there is also a clandestine form of *dawah* that is focused on moving into a non-Muslim culture, infiltrating that culture, and forcing it to become more receptive to Islam. Here are some examples of this infiltration form of *dawah*:

- For a number of years, the Islamic Society of North America (which has ties to the Muslim Brotherhood and Hamas) and the Islamic Council on Scouting of North America (ICSNA) have partnered with the Boy Scouts of America on interfaith events at the Boy Scouts National Jamboree. In short, the Boy Scouts of America—which was founded in 1910 to help instill patriotism and Christian values in boys—has been infiltrated by stealth-jihadist organizations.[1] The chairman of ICSNA, Muzammil H. Siddiqi, has been widely viewed as a "moderate" Muslim and was invited by President George W. Bush to lead in prayer at the Interfaith Prayer Service at Washington National Cathedral a few days after 9/11. However, Siddiqi tipped his hand in an October 18, 1996, newspaper column when he wrote in *Pakistan Link*:

  > It is true that Islam stands for the sovereignty of Allah *subhanahu wa ta'ala* and Allah's rules are not limited to the acts of worship, they also include social, economic and political matters. By participating in a non-Islamic system, one cannot rule by that which Allah has commanded. But things do not change overnight. Changes come through patience, wisdom and hard work.
  >
  > I believe that as Muslims we should participate in the system to safeguard our interest and try to bring gradual change for the right cause, the cause of truth and justice. We must not forget that Allah's rules have to be established in all lands, and all our efforts should lead to that direction.[2]

- Have you heard about the Sharia finance industry? It is yet another missionary (*dawah*) arm of Islam. The goal of Islamic financiers is to infiltrate the Western financial sector and persuade Western investors to use Sharia-compliant investment practices. In this way, the Islamists gain a toehold in our financial system with a goal of ultimately gaining control of the Western economy. A Sharia-compliant financial institution must tithe (*zakat*) a portion of its assets—and those tithes often end up funding jihad and terrorism. Western companies that engage in Sharia-compliant banking include Barclays,

Citibank, Credit Agricole, Deutsche Bank, Goldman Sachs, HSBC Holdings, INVESCO Perpetual, Merrill Lynch, and Morgan Stanley.

- Islamic *dawah* has even invaded the Happiest Place on Earth—Disneyland. A Muslim woman employed as a hostess at a restaurant in Disney's Grand Californian Hotel filed a discrimination complaint. She claimed the restaurant would not let her wear her hijab (head scarf) at work. The restaurant features a Chip 'n' Dale (Disney cartoon chipmunks) theme. On multiple occasions, the woman, Imane Boudlal, refused to remove her hijab and was sent home. One time, she brought a gaggle of reporters, photographers, and chanting supporters with her, clearly seeking publicity.

  Disney officials have tried to accommodate Boudlal, while still maintaining the visual theme of the restaurant. "She's been allowed to work," said a Disneyland spokeswoman. "We've given her the opportunity to work in a backstage role the last several shifts that she's come in. . . . Every role at Disneyland Resort has a specific costume." And a hijab is not part of the costume.

  Clearly, Boudlal is trying to be noticed—and she's trying to impose her culture on Disneyland. "Don't put me in the back," she insists. It should surprise no one that she is represented by a staff attorney for the Council on American-Islamic Relations (CAIR).[3]

  CAIR also represents another Disneyland employee in a near-identical case. A woman named Noor Abdallah insisted on wearing her hijab while working as a vacation planner at a Disneyland Esplanade ticket booth. Once again, Disneyland tried to accommodate their Muslim employee with a "backstage" job. Like Boudlal, Abdallah refused to take a job that was out of public view. So Disney created a specially designed hijab that fit under a beret as part of a compromise costume.[4]

  These cases are not just about employment. They are about trying to bring the Disney corporate culture into submission to the Islamic culture.

There's an Arabian proverb that expresses the Muslim concept of *dawah* well: "If the camel once gets his nose in the tent, his body will soon follow." All of these skirmishes—like the Ground Zero Mosque, the Muslim students' complaint against Catholic University, and the hijab feuds at Disneyland—are various forms of *dawah*, the camel of Islam nosing around the tent flap of Western civilization, looking for a way to get all the way inside the tent.

The institutions of our society—such as our government and the media—are reluctant to believe that our culture is actually being infiltrated and invaded by stealth jihadists. I fear that our society will not wake up until it's too late—and the camel of Islam owns our tent.

SUPPRESSING THE TRUTH ABOUT ISLAM

The mainstream media is "in the tank" for the Islamists in America. Some prime examples:

- A 2009 story on the front page of the *New York Times* was nothing more than a fawning puff piece about Imam Feisal Abdul Rauf and the Ground Zero Mosque. The article glowingly presented the proposed Islamic cultural center as a place "that strengthens ties between Muslims and people of all faiths and backgrounds," and profiled Rauf as "having built a career preaching tolerance and interfaith understanding. . . . [He is] a bridge builder . . . sometimes focused more on cultivating relations with those outside his faith than within it."[5]

  A few weeks after the *Times* piece appeared, Rauf's organization, the American Society for Muslim Advancement (ASMA), published its year-end report. It cited the *New York Times* article as a successful result of its Muslim Leaders of Tomorrow training program, boasting that the program "showed immediate results." The report added that a co-author of the *Times* piece, Sharaf Mowjood, had gone through the Muslim Leaders of Tomorrow training and had written "a compelling story about the Muslim community's plan to establish a center near Ground Zero. The story was published on the front page of the *New York Times*."

  In fact, Sharaf Mowjood, who co-wrote several pieces on the Ground Zero Mosque for the *Times*, had previously worked as a lobbyist for the Council on American Islamic Relations (CAIR). "Excerpts from Mowjood's work," writes Alana Goodman of Newsbusters.org, "could possibly pass as press releases for groups like CAIR or ASMA. His *Times* articles were extremely favorable toward Rauf and the Ground Zero mosque." Nowhere in his articles did Mowjood disclose his ASMA ties, or the fact that he had been specially trained by ASMA to write press releases disguised as news stories.[6]

- The Associated Press issued special guidelines to its reporters on how to report the story of the Ground Zero Mosque. One of the first guidelines: "Avoid the phrase 'Ground Zero Mosque.'" Instead, AP reporters were to call it the "Muslim (or Islamic) center near WTC site" or the "mosque near WTC site."

  The AP also underscored the "fact" that Ground Zero Mosque organizer Feisal Abdul Rauf is a "moderate" Muslim. "Rauf counts former Secretary of

State Madeleine Albright from the Clinton administration as a friend," the guidelines said, "and appeared at events overseas or meetings in Washington with former President George W. Bush's secretary of state, Condoleezza Rice, and Bush adviser Karen Hughes." Because the Associated Press is the most influential wire service in the country, many other print and broadcast news organizations adopted the AP guidelines.[7]

- The Media Research Center surveyed network news coverage of the Ground Zero Mosque and found that 93 percent of network sound bites portrayed Americans as harboring "Islamophobic" views. By contrast, the Arabic online news service Elaph surveyed people in the Arab world and 63 percent of respondents said that they viewed Americans as "tolerant" of Islam and Islamic people. In other words, American news networks portrayed Americans as tolerant only 7 percent of the time, while 63 percent of people in the Arab world viewed Americans as tolerant. Arabs have a much higher opinion of Americans than our own American news media![8]

- The Palestinian Authority (PA) governs parts of the West Bank and Gaza strip, and hopes someday to remove the nation of Israel from Palestine. Part of the PA's effort to delegitimize Israel is to deny Israel's history. The PA not only claims that the Holocaust never happened, but also claims that the Jews never lived in the Holy Land during Bible times, and that there was never a Jewish temple on the Temple Mount in Jerusalem. Thus the Jews have no legitimate claim to even one square inch of Israel.

  It's not surprising that the Palestinians would make such claims. What is surprising is that American news organizations would go along with them. National Public Radio, the *New York Times*, and the Associated Press have all adopted a policy of treating the historical, archaeological facts about the Temple Mount as if they were a matter of opinion.

  NPR Jerusalem correspondent Mike Shuster has reported, "Jews believe there was a temple" on the Temple Mount, and "Jews say that the Temple Mount was the site of two ancient temples in the Jewish tradition." The *New York Times* reports, "The Temple Mount, which Israel claims to have been the site of the First and Second Temples." Similarly, the AP writes, "Jews believe the mosques sit on the ruins of the First and Second Jewish temples, and revere as their holiest site a nearby wall believed to have surrounded the sanctuaries. Muslims say nothing existed on the hill before the mosques." (The "nearby wall" that the AP so casually mentions is the Western Wall, a remnant of the ancient wall that surrounded the Temple courtyard.)

> By treating historical fact as if it were just Jewish opinion, these news organizations have sided with the Palestinian propaganda machine in opposition to the well-established historical truth. It is revealing to know that these mainstream media outlets are so eager to pander to militant Islamists that they would treat documented historical fact as questionable propaganda.[9]

The tragedy of honor killings in America has gone woefully under-reported in the mainstream media. North American news outlets tiptoe around the issue of honor killings, says feminist psychologist Phyllis Chesler, because of "multiculturalism"—the "politically correct" view that one should never criticize the practices of other cultures. "Multiculturalism trumps feminism," Dr. Chesler writes, "and so the media accept a two-tier sisterhood in which Muslim girls are run over, stabbed, strangled, drowned and decapitated for wanting to live like the women they read about in *The New York Times* and *The Washington Post*." Some examples of honor killings:

- In 2006, a Canadian-Afghan young woman, Khatera Sadiqi, and her fiancée, Feroz Mangal, were gunned down by her brother because she had moved in with her fiancée's family and had disinvited her estranged father from the wedding.

- In Irving, Texas, in 2008, two Egyptian-American sisters, Amina and Sarah Said (ages eighteen and seventeen), were found shot to death in their father's taxi cab. The Irving Police Department's 911 call center had received a cell phone call from Sarah, who told the operator, "My dad shot me and my sister! I'm dying!" The girls' father, Yaser Abdul Said, had fired nine bullets into Sarah, and two into Amina. He was enraged because his daughters had boyfriends and had become "too Western." Yaser Said has not been seen since the killings, and may have fled the country. The *New York Times* devoted a single sixty-word paragraph to the story, and the *Los Angeles Times* and *Washington Post* ignored it altogether.

- In 2009, Muzzammil Syed Hassan, the Pakistani-American founder and CEO of the Bridges TV network, stabbed and beheaded his wife, Aasiya Zubair Hassan, rather than permit her to divorce him. Ironically, Hassan founded Bridges TV in order to "counter negative stereotypes of Muslims." Phyllis Chesler noted that the *New York Times* got around to covering the story five days later—"and then mainly to explain that Islam had nothing to do with it and that anyone who believes to the contrary is misguided or prejudiced."

The term "honor killing" almost always refers to the death of a female victim, typically a wife or daughter. According to Sharia law, honor killing may be applied to men as well as women, and is consistent with the Koran and the Hadiths (the collected traditional sayings and acts ascribed to Muhammad). But the reality on the ground is that such punishment is almost always meted out to females, because wives, mothers, and daughters represent the honor of the family (in Islamic thinking), and that honor should always remain pure. Even a hint or suspicion of dishonorable behavior by a woman can result in death.

Apologists for Islam, especially those who portray Islam as a religion of peace, are quick to claim that the Koran does not sanction honor killing. Yet it is impossible to deny that the zeal for honor killing is directly inspired by passages in the Koran and explicitly endorsed by the Hadiths.

For example, Koran 4:15 says, "If any of your women are guilty of lewdness, take the evidence of four (reliable) witness from amongst you against them; if they testify, confine them to houses until death do claim them. Or God ordain for them some (other) way." And Koran 24:2 states, "The woman and the man guilty of adultery or fornication—flog each of them with a hundred stripes: Let no compassion move you in their case, in a matter prescribed by God, if ye believe in God and the last day."

The Sahih Hadiths make an even more explicit case for honor killing. In the Sahih Al-Bukhari (Volume 7, Book 63, Number 196), narrator Abu Hurairah, a companion of the prophet Muhammad, tells about a man from the tribe of Bani Aslam who comes to Muhammad in the mosque and says, "O Allah's Apostle! I have committed illegal sexual intercourse." Muhammad ignores the man and turnes his face away. The man repeats these words, insisting four times that Muhammad hear his confession of sexual sin. After the man has given witness against himself four times, Muhammad asks, "Are you insane?" The man replies, "No." So Muhammad tells the others in the mosque to take the man out and stone him. So they stone him at the place of prayer in Medina. After the first stones strike the man, he flees in pain and terror, but the mob catches him and continues to stone him until he is dead.

In the Sahi Muslim No. 4206, a woman asks Muhammad for purification by punishment. He tells her to go and ask Allah for forgiveness. But the woman persists in begging for punishment, confessing her sin four times, and admitting she is pregnant. So Muhammad tells the Muslim community to let the woman give birth and nurse the child. Once the child is weaned, they are to bury her up to her chest, so that her head and shoulders are above the ground. Then they are to throw stones at her head until she dies. This method of executing women is still practiced today in the Islamic world, and is depicted in the motion picture *The Stoning of Soraya M.*

Elsewhere in the Hadiths, Hadhrat Umar, a companion of Muhammad, says,

"I fear that with the passage of time a person may say, 'We do not find mention of stoning in the Book of Allah [that is, the Koran] and thereby lead astray by leaving out an obligation revealed by Allah.'" He adds that the stoning of adulterers and adulteresses is indeed found in the Koran, "and is the truth, if the witnesses are met or there is a pregnancy or confession." (See Sahih Al-Bukhari Vol. 2, page 1009, and Sahih Muslim Vol. 2, page 65.)

There are other passages from the Koran and the Hadiths I could cite, but the point is clear: The concept of honor killings arises directly from the Islamic holy texts. Such killings occur with heartbreaking frequency across the Muslim world, where even an unproven *suspicion* of a woman's unchaste behavior may leave a stain of dishonor on the entire family—a stain that can only be removed by her death.

The American media, which worships at the altar of political correctness and multiculturalism, buries such stories in order to avoid appearing to condemn Muslim culture. As Dr. Phyllis Chesler concludes, "The media's attitude to 'honor killings' is not only shameful and dishonors the dead; it's also part of the reason why America's newspapers are sliding off the cliff: Their silence on this issue is merely an especially ugly manifestation of how their news instincts have been castrated by political correctness."[10]

Longtime Philadelphia investigative reporter Herb Denenberg described what he called "the sad state of the mainstream media." Shortly before he passed away in early 2010, Denenberg wrote: "One of the strongest supporters of Islamic terrorism is our mainstream media." The media's policy of political correctness, he adds, "means that the mainstream media doesn't give the public the truth about the threat of radical Islam. . . . If we don't kill political correctness, it will kill us by making us unaware of the ongoing war fought by radical Islam against the U.S. and the West. If you can't even identify your enemy and be honest in describing your enemy, you are a dead duck. . . . The mainstream media censors out news of radical Islam, making our enemies invisible."[11]

Again and again, the news media suppresses the truth about radical Islam. Yet that same media doesn't hesitate to attack Christians and Christianity. Some examples from recent years:

Time magazine makes an annual ritual at Christmas and Easter of publishing cover stories that attack the credibility of the nativity story and the resurrection. The History Channel aired an Easter special questioning whether the Bible is a giant hoax. The Discovery Channel aired a documentary called "The Lost Tomb of Jesus," claiming to disprove the resurrection story. *Newsweek*'s Holy Week cover asked "Is God Real?" *New York Times Magazine* ran a pre-Easter story called "Darwin's God," claiming that religious belief is nothing more than the result of millions of years of brain evolution. CNN founder Ted Turner once said, "Christianity is a religion for losers," and suggested that "Thou shalt not commit adultery" be removed from the Ten Commandments.[12]

Recent books from major publishers have attacked and ridiculed the foundational beliefs of the Christian faith, from the fiction bestseller *The DaVinci Code* by Dan Brown to such nonfiction works as *The God Delusion* by Richard Dawkins, *God Is Not Great: How Religion Poisons Everything* by Christopher Hitchens, and *Letter to a Christian Nation* by Sam Harris.

In 2006, entertainer Rosie O'Donnell ranted against Christians on ABC's *The View*, saying, "Radical Christianity is just as threatening as radical Islam!" Columnist Don Feder responded to O'Donnell with this observation:

> *Let's see if I've got this straight:*
>
> *Militant Muslims behead prisoners. Radical Christians oppose embryonic stem-cell research.*
>
> *Militant Muslims blow themselves up in crowded shopping malls, slaughtering women and children. Radical Christians defend traditional marriage.*
>
> *Militant Muslims fly planes into buildings, Radical Christians work to protect the sanctity of human life. . . .*
>
> *Militant Muslims issue fatwas. Radical Christians distribute voter guides.*
>
> *Yep, I can see the similarities all right.*[13]

THE COWARDICE OF THE MEDIA

Why are members of the secular media soft on Muslims but merciless on Christians? The answer is simpler than you might think: It is sheer cowardice.

Fear of swift Islamist retribution keeps Western journalists from speaking out boldly against Islamic extremism. They remember the worldwide uproar that greeted Danish newspaper cartoonist Kurt Westergaard after he depicted the prophet Muhammad with a bomb in his turban. Westergaard was forced to take protective measures after the cartoon sparked death threats.

In February 2008, three Muslim men were arrested for plotting to kill Westergaard. In response, the cartoonist remodeled his house, adding steel doors, reinforced glass windows, a panic room, and surveillance cameras. In January 2010, a Muslim from Somalia invaded Westergaard's house armed with an axe and a knife. Westergaard snatched up his five-year-old granddaughter and hid in the panic room until police came, wounded the intruder, and arrested him.

Since then, members of the Western media have been falling all over themselves to praise Islamic ideologies. Fear is a powerful motivator. People who seem courageous when they feel protected by the First Amendment and the American legal system suddenly feel their knees knocking when they view the terrorist video of Khalid Sheikh Mohammed beheading *Wall Street Journal* reporter Daniel Pearl in Pakistan.

I don't blame journalists for being afraid of offending the Islamists. But I do blame them for their hypocrisy when they turn right around and attack Christians, knowing they'll never have to hide in the panic room from a Christian. Journalists regularly praise Muslims for standing by their convictions—then attack Christians for stubbornly refusing to compromise their convictions.

For example, in Great Britain in 2008, a civil registrar, Lillian Ladele, refused to perform same-sex marriage ceremonies because such unions would violate her Christian conscience. Though she courageously put her job at risk because of her convictions, she was roundly condemned by the press. Yet those same media outlets praised Muslims who braved the H1N1 virus (swine flu), putting their health at risk to stand by their convictions and make the pilgrimage to Mecca.

Christians are taught to love, forgive, and live at peace with all men. Militant Islamists are taught jihad and the duty to defend the honor of Islam. Journalists know that it is safer to condemn a Christian than to condemn a jihadist.

In 1981, I met a militant Muslim who complained to me that Christians are cowards. I asked, "Why do you say that?" He replied, "The name of Jesus is used as a word for cursing in your American movies and TV. If Christians weren't cowards, you would rise up and kill every actor and movie producer who blasphemes your Jesus."

In his religion, the faithful are expected to avenge God. In the Christian religion, we expect God to avenge the faithful. Because we trust the One who says, "Vengeance is mine, I will repay," it may look to the rest of the world as if Christians are cowards. It may seem that we allow the world to walk all over us, and there will never be any consequences. But we believe in a God who will avenge his own name, so we leave vengeance in his hands.

ALLAH VERSUS THE GOD OF THE BIBLE

In order to understand militant Islam and to deal with it in an effective way, we need to recognize a few historical facts, cultural realities, and theological truths:

- Not all jihadists are terrorists. Jihad means "struggle," and some jihadists carry on the struggle in "stealth" ways. That's why many American Muslim leaders seem "moderate" in their public pronouncements—but in their private pronouncements, they talk about subverting and subjugating Western society.

  Islamists have a word for this kind of subterfuge: *taqiyya*. This word means "religious dissimulation or deception." It's the practice of concealing one's true aims in order to achieve victory for Allah. The practice of *taqiyya* is especially emphasized in the Shia Islamic sect. Because the Shiats have so often been an oppressed minority, they developed *taqiyya* as a survival technique.

  In Arabic, *taqiyya* literally means "caution." A related word that is sometimes used is *kitman*, which means "concealment." You can't always know for sure that a seemingly "moderate" Muslim is truly moderate. Some are—but some are practicing *taqiyya* or *kitman*, which means that there may be a concealed agenda at work.

  The Bush White House considered Anwar al-Awlaki to be a "moderate" Muslim. In reality, he was a skilled practitioner of *taqiyya*, a high-level Al-Qaeda operative, and a terrorist. He once spoke at a luncheon in the Pentagon—but he ended up being killed by a CIA drone in Yemen.

- Islam and Christianity differ greatly in what they teach about Jesus. Muslims regard Jesus as a prophet—but not the Son of God. Muslims view Christians as blasphemers for proclaiming Jesus Christ as the Son of God. They regard Muhammad as the only true prophet.

  Christians, by contrast, regard Jesus as fully God and fully man, and the Savior of all mankind. They see Muhammad as a misinformed and misguided founder of a false religion.

- Islam and Christianity have historically used very different means to further their cause. Islam advances by coercive power—including violence and force. Islam demands the conquest and subjugation of all who do not believe in Islam.

  Christianity, in sharp contrast, advances by means of persuasion and personal conversion. It rejects worldly power. As Jesus told Pontius Pilate, "My kingdom is not of this world." Jesus didn't come with a message of outward rituals and outward power; rather, he came in all humility with a message of the inward regeneration of the human heart. This inner renewal is demonstrated through a lifestyle of obedience to God's Word.

  Islam is a religion steeped in rules and rituals, in the observance of the Five Pillars of Islam—the creed (*Shahada*), the five daily prayers (*salat*), the fasting during Ramadan (*sawm*), giving alms (*zakāt*), and the pilgrimage to Mecca (*hajj*). Islam is a religion of legalism and works.

Christianity is a faith based on spiritual rebirth, founded on a personal relationship with God through Jesus Christ. The Christian faith is based on God's grace, not human works.

- Islam is not a religion in the same sense that Judaism and Christianity are religions. Most Westerners do not realize how their view of religion differs from the way Muslims view Islam. Western thinking divides the world into sacred and secular, into religion and government. But the Muslim mind does not make such distinctions. Islam is a religious ideology, a political ideology, and a social ideology all in one—and Islam will never subordinate itself to a secular government. Islamists are patient, and they work gradually to transform a society until that society submits to Sharia and Islam.

Because Islam proclaims itself to be the superior religion and the superior form of government, Islamists believe themselves entitled to build a mosque anywhere in the world. Applying the principle of *taqiyya*, the Islamists may present that mosque to non-Muslims (*dhimmi*) as an "Islamic cultural center" designed to "strengthen ties between Muslims and people of all faiths and backgrounds," but the reality is that the mosque exists to plant the flag of Islamic conquest.

We don't know what individuals and nations are bankrolling the Ground Zero Mosque, but it's likely that much of the estimated $100 million cost will come from Saudi Arabia. If that is so, then notice the irony: The organizers of the Ground Zero Mosque insist that it *must* be built on that site. No other site will do because the mosque symbolizes Islamic conquest. Yet Saudi Arabia does not permit Christians to build a church or even bring a Bible onto Arabian soil. That is how much contempt the Islamist mind holds for the West in general and Christians in particular.

The non-Muslim apologists for the Ground Zero Mosque—the politically correct liberals, the multiculturalists, the socialists—play down Muslim ideology. "These are tolerant, moderate Muslims," they say. "They just want to live in peace and practice their faith, the same as the rest of us." Well, many Muslims do—but not the stealth jihadists like those who are building the Ground Zero Mosque. They are laughing in their sleeves at the gullible Americans who unwittingly serve the cause of subjugating America.

WHAT CAN WE DO AS CHRISTIANS?

How should we respond as followers of Christ to the challenge of Islam? What actions can you and I take as individual believers to make a difference in the world? Let me offer some concrete suggestions:

Become fully informed. In January 2002, I was watching a congressman being interviewed on a national news program. The wounds from the 9/11 attacks were still fresh and this congressman talked about the challenge of terrorism. A well-traveled, high-ranking legislator, I expected him to share some insightful comments on the threat we face. Instead, I heard him refer to the Al-Qaeda terrorists as people who have "mischief in their hearts" and who are governed by "bad thoughts."

I was shocked! Didn't he have any understanding of how the Islamic extremists viewed their religion, how they viewed America, how they viewed history? Didn't he have anything more substantial to share with us than "mischief" and "bad thoughts"?

As a self-governing people, we Americans need an understanding of what really motivates terrorists. We must seek to understand as much as we can about the character and objectives of Islamic fundamentalism. We must become familiar with the teachings and tenets of the Muslim religion. We must understand how the militant Islamists plan to subjugate Western civilization, and we must open our eyes to the reality of the threat that radical Islam poses to Western culture.

Muslims in the West—people like the Imam Feisal Abdul Rauf and organizations like the Council on American-Islamic Relations—will only tell us what we want to hear. They will put on the front of "moderate" Islam and lull us to sleep while they infiltrate our society and our institutions.

So each of us must personally examine the tenets of Islam so that we will know what Islam has planned for us. As we become informed, we must speak out, sharing our insight with the people around us—our family, friends, neighbors, colleagues, students, teachers, fellow Christians, journalists, and government leaders. Many will not believe us when we tell them the truth about the militant Islamists' goals. So we need to back up everything we say with facts, sources, quotations, and credible information.

The truth is our ally. Learn it—then let others know.

Develop a Christian apologetic. The word "apologetics" refers to making a defense of, and a rational justification for, the Christian faith. The word comes from the Greek *apologeîsthai*, meaning "to speak in defense." As Christians, we must be prepared to explain our basic Christian beliefs. As the apostle Peter writes, "Always be prepared to give an answer to everyone who asks you to give the reason for the hope that you have. But do this with gentleness and respect" (1 Peter 3:15).

You may need, for example, to refresh your understanding of the Trinity. You need to know why you believe in the Father, the Son, and the Holy Spirit, and why this belief is (in contrast to what Muslims claim) monotheism.

One of the most popular tracts handed out by Muslim students on American university campuses is a booklet that claims that Christians believe in three gods rather than one. Many Christians don't have a good response. They don't understand one of their core beliefs, the doctrine of the Trinity. That doctrine, simply stated, is that there is only one true God, and yet within the being of God there has always existed a bond of relationship, love, and intimacy: Father, and Son, and Holy Spirit.

At least one biblical seminary is helping students to be able to defend their faith in a dialogue with Muslims. Southern Evangelical Seminary in Charlotte, N.C., launched its Institute of Islamic Studies in 2002, and offers a Master of Arts degree in that field. One of the key courses is "Islamic Apologetics," with an emphasis on answering Islam's charges against Christianity.

Muslims make up one of the fast-growing segments of our society. It's time we ask ourselves, "What would I say if a Muslim asked me about my faith? How would I respond if a Muslim tried to convert me to Islam?" We need to know think about these questions—and we need to have the answers.

Pray. As Christians we must pray and intercede for Muslims. Our first and foremost responsibility is to ask God to sovereignly and supernaturally open the door for the Gospel in the Muslim world. Now more than ever, we must ask God to manifest his power to convict people of their need of the Savior, Jesus Christ. We must pray against the fear, timidity, suspicion, resentment, and deception that keep us from reaching out to the Muslim people all around us. And we must pray that God would send forth his Spirit to release those who are held captive by the spiritual forces of false belief.

We must:

- Pray that God will defend the cause of liberty and intervene directly in mercy toward those who are oppressed and persecuted for the sake of the Gospel.
- Pray for protection and provision for all of our fellow Christians, and especially for those who are new to the Christian faith, so that they will stand firm in the faith.
- Pray that God will intervene in any way He chooses to bring terrorists to justice and to expose and foil future terrorist plots.
- Pray that for our president and other elected leaders, that God would protect

them and give them wisdom and that they would serve the nation in humility and obedience. You may say, "But I didn't vote for the president, I don't agree with him." Christians in the first century didn't have the option to vote for King Herod, or Pontius Pilate, or Emperor Nero either—but they were still commanded by God to pray for their leaders. Even wicked leaders? Especially wicked leaders! Let's pray for all of those who have authority over us, then leave the rest up to God.

- Pray against the spirit of fear that keeps many questioning and disaffected Muslims from leaving Islam. Muslims are taught that to turn from Islam is to become an infidel who will be plagued by the devil and by demons (*jinn*). Islam imprisons Muslims with a fear that leaving Islam will bring about Allah's certain wrath and hell after death.

I have heard many former Muslims recall that, upon hearing the Gospel for the first time, they felt great fear. They fear God, they fear resisting Muhammad, they fear Islam, they fear that they may have believed a falsehood in the past, and they fear the prospect of hell in the future. At least at first, the more they know about Jesus, the greater the fear they experience.

Some of the fear Muslims experience is well-founded. Those Muslims who convert to Christianity (or any other religion) take a great risk and pay a high price—especially in strict Muslim families. Leaving Islam is called "apostasy," the rejection of Islam by word or action. The prescribed punishment for apostasy is death—and many Muslims who have converted to Christ have paid that price. Even if they are not killed, those who leave Islam stand to lose every relationship they care about.

Fear is the stronghold of any false religion. Fear is the weapon that false religions use to control their people. We must confront that fear whenever we share our faith with a Muslim—and our greatest weapon against fear is earnest and prolonged prayer.

Increase Christian evangelistic efforts. We must redouble our efforts to reach the world with the Gospel of Jesus Christ. Many Christians who were once Muslims now tell me that they experienced a longstanding hunger in their hearts for the truth of God, but they didn't know Jesus because they had never heard of him. While they may have heard the name of Jesus or they had heard of Christianity, they didn't know what Jesus said and did, or what he accomplished through his death and resurrection.

Here is a very short course in becoming a witness to the Muslim people around you:

- Ask God to give you a heart full of Christlike love and compassion for Muslim people, plus an eagerness to pray for them, and the courage to speak to any Muslims God may bring across your path.
- Arm yourself with Scripture. Memorize passages of the Bible so that you will be able to speak to Muslims of the love and saving grace of Jesus Christ, the love and mercy of God the Father, and the assurance of Christ's forgiveness and the gift of eternal life.
- Pray for boldness in your witness to Muslims.
- Ask the Holy Spirit for wisdom and discernment before and while you speak to a Muslim, so that you will know what you should say, and what might be better left unsaid.
- Never berate a Muslim for his or her beliefs. Instead, speak the truth in a loving, calm, and confident manner.
- Speak boldly what you know to be true about Jesus and do not compromise or argue. Simply state what you know to be the truth. Don't fall into a "you have your beliefs and I have mine" stance. You have more than "beliefs." You have the truth of God's Word. Be gracious, but stand firm for what you know to be the truth about Jesus and salvation: "Salvation is found in no one else, for there is no other name under heaven given to men by which we must be saved" (Acts 4:12).
- If the person will allow you to pray, then pray in the powerful name of Jesus (Acts 4:12). Muslims believe that Jesus can heal, perform miracles, and even raise the dead, so don't hesitate to rely on the power of his name.
- Trust the Holy Spirit to work in the person's life. The Holy Spirit is the One who convicts. He is the One who opens the eyes of the blind. He is the One who leads a person to accept Jesus. He is the One who delivers us all from evil.

Here is what we can do as churches and Christian organizations:

- Let the Gospel speak for itself. Even as we give copies of the Gospels to Muslims, we must pray that Muslims will read it and be moved to seek God. Pray that they will discover the divine riches of the Gospel's truth. Surely Christ was speaking to all people when He said, "If you hold to my teaching, you are really my disciples. Then you will know the truth, and the truth will set you free" (John 8:31-32).

- Make a concerted outreach to Muslim women. More than 500 million Muslims are women. Most Muslim women are illiterate, poor, and living in a village. Jesus held women in high regard and gave them equal access to the Gospel. Muslim women want to hear about a Savior who will lift them up and give them a true sense of worth.
- Above all, support those on the front lines who are taking the Gospel to Islamic lands such as *Leading The Way*.

Reach out to Muslims in love. One of the greatest antidotes for fear is to convey the Gospel truth in a spirit of genuine love. We must love Muslims the way Jesus loves them. The Bible says, "Perfect love drives out fear" (1 John 4:18).

Many Muslims feel threatened and rejected in the United States. This is an ideal time for Christians to reach out to their Muslim neighbors and build a bridge of friendship. Invite Muslims to your home for a meal (no alcohol or pork). Don't be afraid to pray in their presence or invite them to a Christian Bible study. Give a Muslim neighbor a New Testament in his or her native language.

Muslims must often accept the love of God before they can grasp the salvation that Jesus Christ makes possible. So speak openly and with gentleness to Muslims about God's great love.

People often become what they fear. Muslims who fear Allah's judgment and condemnation often become judgmental and condemning in their interactions with others. According to Islam, grace and forgiveness are rare attributes of God, and they are even rarer in the lives of Muslims. A common saying in the Islamic world declares, "Islam is as arid as the deserts of its birth."

Newly converted Muslims need to be told with authority and love that they need not be afraid any longer, that God loves them, and He is not angry with them. Just as fear binds the hearts of Muslims, so love brings them release from fear. Once a Muslim has a real taste of God's divine love, fear is lifted.

We must live individually and collectively as strong Christians. We must learn the principle of loving those with whom we disagree, without being argumentative or condemning, but also without being weak or passive. We must speak with spiritual authority, yet without arrogance. In many ways, we need to learn how to do this, especially when dealing with people of other cultures.

Let us couple our expressions of love with genuine integrity and righteousness. Muslims cannot accept the truth of the Gospel if we do not live morally exemplary lives. Let us be living examples of godliness and "love in action" within our own families and in our associations with all other people, and especially toward our Christian brothers and sisters.

Above all, don't be afraid. The God of the universe goes with you. Don't be intimidated by Muslim people—but don't look down on them, either. Love them with the love of Jesus Christ. Be as patient and kind to them as your Lord Jesus has been to you.

If you can do that, and leave the results to God, it will be enough.

WHAT WOULD YOU DO IN HIS PLACE?

As I was working on the message in this book, I heard about a Christian pastor in Iran named Youcef Nadarkhani. Born to Muslim parents, Pastor Nardarkhani converted to Christ when he was nineteen. Now in his mid-thirties, he has a wife and two sons, ages nine and seven. As a member of the Protestant evangelical church of Iran, Pastor Nadarkhani oversees a network of house churches.

In 2009, he learned of a new Iranian policy that required all children, including his two boys, to read from the Koran. He went to the school and voiced his objection, based on the Iranian constitution's guarantee of freedom of religion. But when the school reported his protest to the government, the police came and arrested him. Protesting the laws of the Islamic government is a crime.

He went before a tribunal on October 12, 2009. He was found guilty of several crimes, including the crime of apostasy—renouncing the Islamic faith—and he was sentenced to death. The government offered to commute his sentence if he would recant and deny his Christian faith.

Pastor Youcef Nadarkhani refused to recant. He said, "You demand that I repent of my faith, but 'repent' means to return. What should I return to? The blasphemy that I believed in before my faith in Christ?"

When the news reached the outside world that Pastor Nadarkhani had been sentenced to death for the "crime" of being a Christian, letters of protest began pouring into the government of Iran. An international campaign was launched to save his life—a campaign that included Secretary of State Hillary Clinton, British Foreign Secretary William Hague, California pastor Rick Warren, Speaker of the House John Boehner, activist Nina Shea, the U.S. Commission on International Religious Freedom, Christian Solidarity Worldwide, Amnesty International, and many other individuals and groups.

Apparently, the government of Iran thought it could blunt international criticism by trumping up false charges against Nadarkhani, so the court added new charges of rape and extortion—but the whole world could see through these sham accusations. The court sent Pastor Nadarkhani to a prison for political prisoners, and the delivery of the written sentence was delayed for a period of time. Some Iran-watchers believe the Islamic government was buying time to pressure Nadarkhani into recanting his Christian faith.

On November 13, 2010, the sentence was finally delivered, declaring that Nadarkhani would be executed by hanging. The sentence was appealed, but the Supreme Court of Iran upheld the death sentence—yet the sentence includes a provision for suspending the death penalty if Nadarkhani would deny his faith. In an effort to force him to recant, the prison officials took him out into the prison yard and showed him the hangman's rope. He told them, "I am staying in my faith."

The death sentence is a violation of the Iranian constitution and the United Nations Charter of Human Rights, which affirms that every human being on the planet has the right to choose his or her own faith. The Iranian government insists it will carry out the execution in the name of the "religion of peace"—but Pastor Nadarkhani steadfastly refuses to deny his Lord.

As I write these words, Pastor Nadarkhani is still alive—and still under a death sentence. He may be released—or he may join the company of martyrs. Time will tell.

I see in this man the future of our own culture. Radical Islam is at war with the West. The kingdom of Christ and the Caliphate of Allah are engaged in a death struggle—and you and I are combatants in this struggle.

If events continue as they have been going, it's possible that you and I may face this same decision that Pastor Nadarkhani faces as I write these words. We may have to choose between life and death, between denying our Lord or staying true to him as the rope is placed around our necks.

Like Pastor Nadarkhani, we may be called to be separated from loved ones, from children, from all we cherish and love. We may be subjected to false accusations. We may be pressured again and again to recant.

The Sharia courts already have a toehold in Europe, and they are coming to America. How long will it be, I wonder, before you and I must stand and answer to a Sharia court? Will we have the courage to answer as Pastor Nadarkhani has?

What would my answer be? What would your answer be?

May God have mercy on us, His children, so that such a time never comes. But if it does, may God give us grace to answer as Pastor Nadarkhani answered. May He give us the boldness to praise our God and proclaim the truth that Jesus died for our sins, He rose again, and He alone is Lord.

NOTES

CHAPTER 1: THE WAR WE ARE LOSING

1. Kareem Fahim, "Slap to a Man's Pride Set Off Tumult in Tunisia," *New York Times*, January 21, 2011, http://www.nytimes.com/2011/01/22/world/africa/22sidi.html?_r=2&src=twrhp&pagewanted=all; Peter Beaumont, "Mohammed Bouazizi: the dutiful son whose death changed Tunisia's fate," *The Guardian*, January 20, 2011, http://www.guardian.co.uk/world/2011/jan/20/tunisian-fruit-seller-mohammed-bouazizi.
2. Yasmine Ryan, "The Tragic Life of a Street Vendor," Al Jazeera English, January 20, 2011, http://english.aljazeera.net/indepth/features/2011/01/201111684242518839.html.
3. Draggan Mihailovich and Nathalie Sommer, "How a Slap Sparked Tunisia's Revolution," CBS News, February 20, 2011, http://www.cbsnews.com/stories/2011/02/20/60minutes/main20033404.shtml.
4. BBC, "Tunisia Suicide Protester Mohamed Bouazizi Dies," BBC News, January 5, 2011, http://www.bbc.co.uk/news/world-africa-12120228.
5. Can Ertuna, "The Regime is Overthrown, What Now?" *Hurriyet Daily News & Economic Review*, February 13, 2011, http://www.hurriyetdailynews.com/mob_n.php?n=the-regime-is-overthrown-what-now-2011-02-15.
6. Mary Abdelmassih, "Muslims Attack Christian in Egypt, Cut Off His Ear," Assyrian International News Agency, March 26, 2011, http://www.aina.org/news/20110325223845.htm.
7. David D. Kirkpatrick, "Copts Criticize Egypt Government Over Killings," *New York Times*, October 10, 2011, http://www.nytimes.com/2011/10/11/world/middleeast/coptics-criticize-egypt-government-over-killings.html.
8. Nawar Shora, *The Arab-American Handbook: A Guide to the Arab, Arab-American, and Muslim Worlds* (Seattle: Cune Press, 2009), 291.
9. Walid Phares, "Muslim Brotherhood Riding the Crest of Arab Spring,"

Newsmax, June 3, 2011, http://www.newsmax.com/WalidPhares/muslimbrotherhood-arabspring-gadhafi/2011/06/03/id/398700.

10. Amro Hassan, "Egypt: Some Copts and Muslims Come Together during Orthodox Christmas," *Los Angeles Times*, January 8, 2011, http://latimesblogs.latimes.com/babylonbeyond/2011/01/egypt-copts-and-muslims-come-together-for-once-during-orthodox-christmas.html.

11. Meredith Birkett, "Christians Protect Muslims during Prayer in Cairo's Dangerous Tahrir Square," PhotoBlog on MSNBC.com, February 3, 2011, http://photoblog.msnbc.msn.com/_news/2011/02/03/5981906-christians-protect-muslims-during-prayer-in-cairos-dangerous-tahrir-square.

12. Maggie Michael, Associated Press, "Christians Under Siege in Post-Revolution Egypt," ABC News, October 11, 2011, http://abcnews.go.com/International/wireStory/christians-siege-post-revolution-egypt-14707870.

13. Yolande Knell, "Egypt Clashes: Copts Mourn Victims Of Cairo Unrest," BBC News, October 10, 2011, http://www.bbc.co.uk/news/world-middle-east-15242413.

14. Associated Press, "Coptic Christian Priest Killed in Southern Egypt," ABC News, February 23, 2011, http://abcnews.go.com/International/wireStory?id=12978152.

15. Reza Sayah, "Egypt's Military Begins Rebuilding Burned Coptic Church," CNN, March 13, 2011, http://www.cnn.com/2011/WORLD/meast/03/13/egypt.church/index.html.

16. Yolande Knell, ibid.

17. Nader Shokry, "Copts Present Documents to Government Regarding Burned Church," Youm7, October 6, 2011, http://english.youm7.com/News.asp?NewsID=346233; AFP, "Egpyt Copts Protest Over Church Burning, Blogger," Yahoo News, October 4, 2011, http://news.yahoo.com/egypt-copts-protest-over-church-burning-blogger-194937986.html; Chana Ya'ar, "Egyptian Muslims Burn Coptic Church in Aswan Province," Arutz Sheva 7, October 2, 2011, http://www.israelnationalnews.com/News/News.aspx/148397.

18. TRNN Report, "Egyptians Chant 'Muslims, Christians Are One' as Military Viciously Attacks Protest," embedded video, TheRealNews.com, October 12, 2011, http://therealnews.com/t2/index.php?option=com_content&task=view&id=31&Itemid=74&jumival=7439.

19. Robin Hallett, *Africa Since 1875: A Modern History* (Ann Arbor: University of Michigan Press, 1974), 139.

20. Ian Johnson, *A Mosque in Munich: Nazis, the CIA, and the Rise of the Muslim Brotherhood* (New York: Houghton Mifflin, 2010), 112.

21. Ibid., 113.

22. Klaus-Michael Mallmann and Martin Cüppers, *Nazi Palestine: The Plans for the Extermination of the Jews in Palestine* (New York: Enigma Books, 2010), 33.

23. Mehran Kamrava, *The Modern Middle East: A Political History Since the First World War* (Berkeley: University of California Press, 2011), 94-95.

24. Jihad Watch, "New Muslim Brotherhood Leader: Islam Will Invade America and Europe," JihadWatch.org, February 4, 2004, http://www.Jihadwatch.org/2004/02/new-muslim-brotherhood-leader-islam-will-invade-america-and-europe.html.

25. Lawrence Wright, "The Counter-Terrorist," *The New Yorker*, January 14, 2002, http://www.newyorker.com/archive/2002/01/14/020114fa_fact_wright?currentPage=1.

26. Associated Press, "FBI Was Warned About Flight Schools," CBS News, February 11, 2009, http://www.cbsnews.com/stories/2002/05/15/attack/main509113.shtml; Brian Ross, Lisa Sylvester, "Bush Warned of Hijackings Before 9/11," ABC News, May 15, 2002, http://abcnews.go.com/US/story?id=91651&page=1; National Commission on Terrorist Attacks Upon the United States, "The Attack Looms," August 21, 2004, http://www.9-11commission.gov/report/911Report_Ch7.htm.

27. Walid Phares, ibid.

28. Team B, "FBI Captured Muslim Brotherhood's Strategic Plan," BigPeace.com, October 26, 2010, http://bigpeace.com/teamb/2010/10/26/fbi-captured-muslim-brotherhoods-strategic-plan/.

29. Josh Gerstein, "DNI Clapper Retreats From 'Secular' Claim on Muslim Brotherhood," Politico, February 10, 2011, http://www.politico.com/blogs/joshgerstein/0211/DNI_Clapper_Egypts_Muslim_Brotherhood_largely_secular.html.

30. Raven Clabough, "Self-Avowed Muslim Marxist Says White House Tied to Muslim Brotherhood," *The New American*, August 18, 2011, http://

thenewamerican.com/usnews/politics/8656-self-avowed-muslim-marxist-says-white-house-tied-to-muslim-brotherhood.

31. Ibid.
32. Josh Gerstein, "Obama Prayer Speaker Has Hamas Tie?" Politico, January 17, 2009, http://www.politico.com/news/stories/0109/17562.html.
33. Author uncredited, "Underpublicized Threat Deep in White House," World Net Daily, August 27, 2011, http://www.wnd.com/?pageId=337321.
34. Ibid.
35. Tim Mak, "U.S. Recognizes Muslim Brotherhood," Politico, June 30, 2011, http://www.politico.com/news/stories/0611/58094.html; Robert Spencer, "Obama's Muslim Brotherhood Ties," *Human Events*, February 8, 2011, http://www.humanevents.com/article.php?id=41650.
36. Walid Phares, "US Aid to the Arab Spring Must Go to Democracy Groups Not to the Islamists," WalidPhares.com, May 25, 2011, http://www.walidphares.com/artman/publish/printer_3383.shtml.
37. Lucy Ballinger and Dan Newling, "Guilty? It's a Badge of Honour Say Muslim Hate Mob," Mail Online, January 12, 2010, http://www.dailymail.co.uk/news/article-1242335/Muslims-called-British-soldiers-rapists-cowards-scum-exercising-freedom-speech-court-hears.html.
38. Mark Thompson, "The $5 Trillion War on Terror," *Time*, June 29, 2011, http://battleland.blogs.time.com/2011/06/29/the-5-trillion-war-on-terror/.
39. Addison Wiggin, "Where Will Libya's Shoulder-Fired Missiles Land?" Forbes.com, September 29, 2011, http://www.forbes.com/sites/greatspeculations/2011/09/29/where-will-libyas-shoulder-fired-missiles-land/.

CHAPTER 2: WHO ARE WE FIGHTING?

1. Robert Siegel, "Sayyid Qutb's America: Al-Qaeda Inspiration Denounced U.S. Greed, Sexuality," *All Things Considered*, NPR.org, May 6, 2003, retrieved at http://www.npr.org/templates/story/story.php?storyId=1253796; Robert Irwin, "Is This the Man Who Inspired Bin Laden? Sayyid Qutb, the Father of Modern Islamist Fundamentalism," *The Guardian*, November 1, 2001, retrieved at http://www.guardian.co.uk/world/2001/nov/01/afghanistan.terrorism3.
2. Lawrence Wright, *The Looming Tower: Al-Qaeda and the Road to 9/11* (New York: Vintage, 2007), 33-34.

3. Ibid., 35.
4. Ibid., 36.
5. Ibid., 34.
6. Ibid., 248.
7. Ibid., 140.
8. Ibid., 146.
9. Ibid., 150-152.
10. Ibid., 165.
11. Douglas Jehl, "A Nation Challenged: Saudi Arabia; Holy War Lured Saudis As Rulers Looked Away," *New York Times*, December 27, 2001, http://www.nytimes.com/2001/12/27/world/a-nation-challenged-saudi-arabia-holy-war-lured-saudis-as-rulers-looked-away.html?pagewanted=all.
12. Michael Scheuer, *Through Our Enemies' Eyes: Osama bin Laden, Radical Islam, and the Future of America* (Washington, D.C.: Potomac Books, 2006), 158.
13. Osama bin Laden, "Bin Laden's Fatwa," PBS NewsHour, PBS.org, August 1996, http://www.pbs.org/newshour/terrorism/international/fatwa_1996.html.
14. PBS Frontline, "Who is Bin Laden? Edicts and Statements," PBS.org, http://www.pbs.org/wgbh/pages/frontline/shows/binladen/who/edicts.html.
15. Rudy Giuliani, "Rudy Giuliani on Homeland Security," *Meet the Press*, December 9, 2007, On The Issues, http://www.issues2000.org/2012/Rudy_Giuliani_Homeland_Security.htm.
16. George W. Bush, "'Islam is Peace' Says President," Remarks by the President at Islamic Center of Washington, D.C., September 17, 2001, http://georgewbush-whitehouse.archives.gov/news/releases/2001/09/20010917-11.html.
17. George W. Bush, "Address to a Joint Session of Congress Following 9/11 Attacks," September 20, 2001, http://www.americanrhetoric.com/speeches/gwbush911jointsessionspeech.htm.
18. PBS, "Interview: Osama Bin Laden," PBS Frontline, PBS.org, May 1998, http://www.pbs.org/wgbh/pages/frontline/shows/binladen/who/interview.html.

19. Ibid.
20. Ibid.
21. 21, CAIR, "Persistent and Consistent Condemnation of Terrorism," CAIR.com, June 2011, http://www.cair.com/Portals/0/CAIR%20on%20Terrorism.pdf.
22. Steven Emerson, "CAIR and Terrorism: Blanket Opposition to U.S. Investigations, Equivocal Condemnations for Plots Against America," Investigative Project on Terrorism, March 28, 2008, http://www.investigativeproject.org/documents/misc/116.pdf.
23. Ibid.
24. ADL, "Council on American-Islamic Relations (CAIR): Links to Holy Land Foundation," Anti-Defamation League, July 15, 2010, http://www.adl.org/Israel/cair/Links2.asp.
25. Queen Rania Al-Abdullah, "Transcript: Queen Rania on Oprah Winfrey Show," JordanEmbassyUS.org, October 5, 2001, http://www.jordanembassyus.org/speech_hmqr10052001.htm.
26. Marc Fisher, "Muslim Students Weigh Questions Of Allegiance," *Washington Post*, October 16, 2001, B01.
27. Ibid.
28. BBC, "Africans Split on US Strikes," BBC News, October 9, 2001, http://news.bbc.co.uk/2/hi/1586988.stm.
29. Chris Fontaine, Associated Press, "Protests Against U.S.-Led Attacks Continue Worldwide," San Bernardino Sun, October 10, 2001, http://lang.sbsun.com/socal/terrorist/1001/10/terror09.asp.
30. Ibid.
31. Ibid.
32. Ibid.
33. Ibid.

CHAPTER 3: THE PROPHET AND THE KORAN

1. George Liska, *Expanding Realism: The Historical Dimension of World Politics* (Lanham, MD: Rowman & Littlefield, 1998), 170.
2. Sir William Muir, *The Life of Mohammed* (Edinburgh: John Grant, 1923), 22.

3. Ibid., 51.
4. Brendan January, *The Iranian Revolution* (Minneapolis: Twenty-First Century, 2008), 101.
5. Reza F. Safa, *Inside Islam: Exposing and Reaching the World of Islam* (Lake Mary, FL: Creation House, 1996), 70.

CHAPTER 4: ARE ALLAH AND JEHOVAH THE SAME GOD?

1. Paul Meagher, Thomas O'Brian, Consuela Aherne, editors, *Encyclopedia of Religion* (Washington, D.C.: Corpus, 1979), I:117.
2. E.M. Wherry, *A Comprehensive Commentary on the Quran* (Osnabrück, Germany: Otto Zeller Verlag, 1973), 36.

CHAPTER 5: TWO DIFFERENT PRESCRIPTIONS FOR LIVING

1. Jon Swaine, "Steve Jobs 'Regretted Trying to Beat Cancer with Alternative Medicine for so Long,'" *The Telegraph*, October 28, 2011, http://www.telegraph.co.uk/technology/apple/8841347/Steve-Jobs-regretted-trying-to-beat-cancer-with-alternative-medicine-for-so-long.html.
2. A.S. Tritton, *The Caliphs and Their Non-Muslim Subjects* (London: Frank Cass and Company, 1970), 5-8.
3. Osama bin Laden, "Bin Laden's Fatwa," PBS NewsHour, PBS.org, August 1996, http://www.pbs.org/newshour/terrorism/international/fatwa_1996.html.

CHAPTER 6: JIHAD

1. Hasan Al-Banna, "To What Do We Summon Mankind?" *Five Tracts of Hasan Al-Banna*, trans. Charles Wendell (Berkeley: University of California Press, 1978), 80.
2. Doug Potter, "Southern Evangelical Seminary Dives into Islam," *Charlotte World*, January 2002.
3. Robin Wright, *Sacred Rage: The Wrath of Militant Islam* (New York: Simon and Schuster, 1985), 99.
4. Ibid., 83-84.
5. Hasan Al-Banna, "Between Yesterday and Today," *Five Tracts of Hasan Al-Banna*, trans. Charles Wendell (Berkeley: University of California Press, 1978), 36.

6. Baqer Moin, *Khomeini: Life of the Ayatollah* (London: I. B. Tauris, 1999), 176.

7. Ervand Abraharnian, *The Iranian Mojahedin* (New Haven: Yale University Press, 1989), 220.

8. Ayatollah Khomeini, *Islam and Revolution: Writings and Declarations of Imam Khomeini*, trans. Hamid Algar (Berkeley: Mizan Press, 1981), 305.

9. Robin Wright, *Sacred Rage*, 44-45.

10. Dilip Hiro, *Holy Wars: The Rise of Islamic Fundamentalism* (New York: Routledge, 1989), 63.

11. Robin Wright, *Sacred Rage*, 179.

12. Andrew Sullivan, "This Is a Religious War," *New York Times Magazine*, October 10, 2001, http://www.nytimes.com/2001/10/07/magazine/07RELIGION.html?pagewanted=all.

CHAPTER 7: THE GOAL OF A WORLD EMPIRE

1. Diane Alden, "Christianity Under Siege, Part II: Those Who Are Voiceless," Newsmax.com, January 10, 2002, http://archive.newsmax.com/commentmax/get.pl?a=2002/1/9/224114.

2. George J. Church, "Laying Hands on an Unwanted Guest," *Time*, July 12, 1993, 27.

3. James Cook, "Sunis? Shiites? What's That Got to Do With Oil Prices?" *Forbes*, April 12, 1982, 99.

4. Neil MacFarquhar, "Bin Laden and His Followers Adhere to an Austere, Stringent Form of Islam," *New York Times*, October 7, 2001, http://www.nytimes.com/2001/10/07/world/nation-challenged-teachings-bin-laden-his-followers-adhere-austere-stringent.html?pagewanted=all.

CHAPTER 8: ALL ROADS LEAD TO ISRAEL

1. U.S. Department of State, "Background Note: Egypt," State.gov, November 10, 2010, http://www.state.gov/r/pa/ei/bgn/5309.htm#relations.

2. Yitzhak Benhorin, "Israel Still Top Recipient of US Foreign Aid," Ynet News, February 8, 2007, http://www.ynetnews.com/articles/0,7340,L-3362402,00.html.

3. Bruce Riedel, "Al-Qaeda's New Sinai Front," Brookings Institution, August 21, 2011, http://www.brookings.edu/opinions/2011/0822_sinai_riedel.aspx.
4. Shaimaa Khalil, "Egypt to Recall Israel Envoy over Sinai Shootings," BBC, August 20, 2011, http://www.bbc.co.uk/news/world-middle-east-14600357.
5. Transcript, "Text: Osama bin Laden," *Washington Post*, October 7, 2001, http://www.washingtonpost.com/wp-srv/nation/specials/attacked/transcripts/binladen_100801.htm.
6. Transcript, "Al-Qaeda Spokesman," ABC News, October 9, 2001, http://abcnews.go.com/International/story?id=80500&page=1.
7. Explainer, "What's Osama Talking About?" *Slate*, October 8, 2001, http://www.slate.com/articles/news_and_politics/explainer/2001/10/whats_osama_talking_about.html.
8. Ibid., 101-102.
9. Ibid., 280.
10. Video, "Helen Thomas Tells Jews 'Get the Hell Out of Palestine' and Go Back to Germany and Poland," Breitbart.tv, May 27, 2010, http://www.breitbart.tv/helen-thomas-tells-jews-get-the-hell-out-of-palestine-and-go-back-to-germany-poland/.
11. P.M. Holt, *Egypt and The Fertile Crescent* 1516–1922 (Ithaca and London: Cornell University Press, 1966), 292.

CHAPTER 9: OIL—THE FUEL THAT FUNDS OUR DESTRUCTION

1. Richard Lugar, "The Story of Oil," The Lugar Energy Initiative, http://lugar.senate.gov/energy/security/questions.cfm#7.
2. U.S. Energy Information Administration, "OPEC Revenues Fact Sheet," December 2010, http://www.eia.gov/cabs/OPEC_Revenues/Factsheet.html.
3. J. B. Kelly, "Islam Through the Looking Glass," The Heritage Lectures (Washington, D.C.: The Heritage Foundation, 1980), 8, http://s3.amazonaws.com/thf_media/1980/pdf/hl-2.pdf.
4. Author uncredited, "Arab Banks Grow," *Business Week*, October 6, 1980, 70-84.
5. Ibid.
6. J. B. Kelly, ibid.

CHAPTER 10: THE SPREADING ISLAMIC WILDFIRE

1. Robin Wright, *Sacred Rage: The Wrath of Militant Islam* (New York: Simon and Schuster, 1985), 21.
2. Herbert Buchsbaum, "Islam in America," Scholastic Update, October 22, 1993, 15.
3. Pew Forum, "The Future of the Global Muslim Population," Pew Research Center, January 27, 2011, http://pewforum.org/The-Future-of-the-Global-Muslim-Population.aspx.
4. Daniel Pipes, "The Danger Within: Militant Islam in America," DanielPipes.org, November 2001, http://www.danielpipes.org/77/the-danger-within-militant-islam-in-america.
5. Ibid.
6. Discover the Networks, "Zaid Shakir," DiscoverTheNetworks.org, http://www.discoverthenetworks.org/individualProfile.asp?indid=974.
7. Robert Spencer, *Stealth Jihad: How Radical Islam is Subverting America without Guns or Bombs* (Washington, DC: Regnery, 2008), 94.
8. Jessica Caplin, "Mirage in the Desert Oasis," *Harvard International Review*, March 21, 2009, http://hir.harvard.edu/print/rethinking-finance/mirage-in-the-desert-oasis.
9. Daniel Pipes, "The Danger Within: Militant Islam in America," DanielPipes.org, November 2001, http://www.danielpipes.org/77/the-danger-within-militant-islam-in-america.
10. Andres Tapia, "Churches Wary of Inner-city Islamic Inroads," *Christianity Today*, January 10, 1994, 36.
11. Mark S. Hamm, Ph.D., "Terrorist Recruitment in American Correctional Institutions: An Exploratory Study of Non-Traditional Faith Groups," National Institute of Justice, December 2007, https://www.ncjrs.gov/pdffiles1/nij/grants/220957.pdf.
12. Abdullah Saeed and Hassan Saeed, *Freedom of Religion, Apostasy and Islam* (Burlington, VT: Ashgate, 2004), 92.
13. Lawrence Wright, *The Looming Tower: Al-Qaeda and the Road to 9/11* (New York: Vintage, 2007), 261-262.
14. Ibid., 262.
15. Jan Goodwin, "Buried Alive: Afghan Women Under the Taliban," *On the Issues*, Summer 1998, http://www.ontheissuesmagazine.com/1998summer/su98goodwin.php.

16. Terance D. Miethe and Hong Lu, *Punishment: A Comparative Historical Perspective* (New York: Cambridge University Press, 2005), 63.
17. Tim Butcher, "Saudis Prepare to Behead Teenage Maid," *The Telegraph*, July 16, 2007, http://www.telegraph.co.uk/news/worldnews/1557628/Saudis-prepare-to-behead-teenage-maid.html.
18. MEMRI, "Public Debate in Saudi Arabia on Employment Opportunities for Women," The Middle East Media Research Institute, November 17, 2006, http://www.memri.org/report/en/0/0/0/0/0/0/1793.htm.
19. Laura Bashraheel, "Women's Transport: Solutions Needed," *Arab News*, June 27, 2009, http://archive.arabnews.com/?page=1§ion=0&article=124071.
20. Abdul Rahman Shaheen, "Saudi Women Use Fatwa in Driving Bid," *Gulf News*, June 20, 2010, http://gulfnews.com/news/gulf/saudi-arabia/saudi-women-use-fatwa-in-driving-bid-1.643431.
21. Bernard Lewis, *The Middle East—A Brief History of the Last 2,000 Years* (New York: Simon and Schuster, 1995), 385.
22. Queen Rania Al-Abdullah, "Transcript: Queen Rania on Oprah Winfrey Show," JordanEmbassyUS.org, October 5, 2001, http://www.jordanembassyus.org/speech_hmqr10052001.htm.

CHAPTER 11: OUR RESPONSE AS AMERICANS

1. Jerry Markon, "Justice Department sues on behalf of Muslim teacher, triggering debate," *Washington Post*, March 22, 2011, http://www.washingtonpost.com/politics/justice-department-sues-on-behalf-of-muslim-teacher-triggering-debate/2010/07/28/ABfSPtEB_story.html; Mona Charen, "Off to Mecca She Goes With Eric Holder's Blessing," *National Review*, March 25, 2011, http://www.nationalreview.com/articles/263025/mecca-she-goes-mona-charen.
2. Philip Rucker, Carrie Johnson, and Ellen Nakashima, "Hasan E-Mails to Cleric Didn't Result in Inquiry," *Washington Post*, November 10, 2009, http://www.washingtonpost.com/wp-dyn/content/article/2009/11/09/AR2009110902061.html?sid=ST2009110903704.
3. Dana Priest, "Fort Hood Suspect Warned of Threats Within the Ranks," *Washington Post*, November 10, 2009, http://

www.washingtonpost.com/wp-dyn/content/story/2009/11/09/ST2009110903704.html.

4. Mark Thompson, "Fort Hood: Were Hasan's Warning Signs Ignored?" *Time*, November 18, 2009, http://www.time.com/time/nation/article/0,8599,1940011,00.html.

5. Jonah Knox, "Treason, Bradley Manning, and Army PC," Accuracy in Media, August 24, 2010, http://www.aim.org/aim-column/treason-bradley-manning-and-army-pc/.

6. Josh Gerstein, "Obama Prayer Speaker Has Hamas Tie?" Politico, January 17, 2009, http://www.politico.com/news/stories/0109/17562.html.

7. Barack Obama, "Full Transcript of Obama's Al-Arabiya Interview," MSNBC, January 27, 2009, http://www.msnbc.msn.com/id/28870724/ns/politics-white_house/t/full-transcript-obamas-al-arabiya-interview/.

8. Nitya, "Obama Sends 'Best Wishes' to Muslims Before the Start of Ramadan," ABC News, August 21, 2009, http://abcnews.go.com/blogs/politics/2009/08/obama-sends-best-wishes-to-muslims-before-the-start-of-ramadan/.

9. Bookworm, "Obama Again Celebrates Putting Women in Hijabs and Niqabs," BookwormRoom, September 1, 2009, http://www.bookwormroom.com/2009/09/01/obama-again-celebrates-putting-women-in-hijabs-and-niqabs/.

10. Julianna Goldman, "Obama Calls Islam Part of America at White House Ramadan Dinner," *Bloomberg*, September 1, 2009, http://www.bloomberg.com/apps/news?pid=newsarchive&sid=a7zfKGt1V_ws.

11. Andrew Malcolm, "Obama Issues Special Hajj Message to World's Muslims," *Los Angeles Times*, November 25, 2009, http://latimesblogs.latimes.com/washington/2009/11/on-thanksgiving-eve-barack-obamas-special-message-to-muslims.html.

12. Tim Mak, "U.S. Recognizes Muslim Brotherhood," Politico, June 30, 2011, http://www.politico.com/news/stories/0611/58094.html.

13. Nicholas D. Kristof, "Obama: Man of the World," *New York Times*, March 6, 2007, http://www.nytimes.com/2007/03/06/opinion/06kristof.html?_r=1&oref=slogin.

14. Editorial, "Barack Takes a Bow," *Washington Times*, April 7, 2009, http://www.washingtontimes.com/news/2009/apr/07/barack-takes-a-bow/.

15. Muhammad Diyab, "The Secret Behind Obama's Bow to the King," April 8, 2009, http://www.asharq-e.com/print.asp?artid=id16327.

16. Janet Levy, "Are We Facing 'The West's Last Chance'?" *American Thinker*, July 28, 2011, http://www.americanthinker.com/2011/02/are_we_facing_the_wests_last_c.html.

17. Farah Stockman, "Obama, US Viewed Less Favorably in Arab World, Poll Shows," *Boston Globe*, July 13, 2011, http://www.boston.com/Boston/politicalintelligence/2011/07/obama-viewed-less-favorably-arab-world-poll-shows/yIVn6f6PueWbdhZutglhoJ/index.html.

18. Hannah Allam, "Egypt Rejection of U.S. Aid a Sign of Future Rifts?" McClatchy Newspapers, June 29, 2011, http://www.mcclatchydc.com/2011/06/29/v-print/116747/egypt-rejection-of-us-aid-a-sign.html.

19. Michael B. Mukasey, "Jose Padilla Makes Bad Law," *Wall Street Journal*, August 22, 2007, http://www.americanbar.org/content/dam/aba/migrated/2011_build/law_national_security/mukasey_padilla_wsj.authcheckdam.pdf.

20. Lindsay Graham, Transcript, "Graham on trying terrorism suspects: 'There is a better way,'" CNN.com, February 13, 2010, http://politicalticker.blogs.cnn.com/2010/02/13/graham-on-trying-terrorism-suspects-there-is-a-better-way/.

21. Editorial, "Awlaki, the model moderate Muslim," *Washington Times*, September 30, 2011, http://www.washingtontimes.com/news/2011/sep/30/awlaki-the-model-moderate-muslim/.

22. Catherine Herridge, "Exclusive: Al-Qaeda Leader Dined at the Pentagon Just Months After 9/11," FoxNews.com, October 20, 2010, http://www.foxnews.com/us/2010/10/20/al-qaeda-terror-leader-dined-pentagon-months/.

23. Jeff Glor, "Proposed Mosque Near Ground Zero Stokes Debate," CBS News, July 20, 2010, http://www.cbsnews.com/stories/2010/07/20/eveningnews/main6696724.shtml?tag=mncol;lst;2.

24. Tom Topousis, "Imam Terror Error," *New York Post*, June 19, 2010, http://www.nypost.com/p/news/local/manhattan/imam_terror_error_efmizkHuBUaVnfuQcrcabL.

25. Frank Walker, "We Must Act to End Jihad: Imam," *Sydney Sun-Herald*, March 21, 2004, http://www.smh.com.au/articles/2004/03/21/1079789939987.html.

26. Newt Gingrich, "Statement on Proposed Mosque/Islamic Community Center near Ground Zero," Newt.org, July 21, 2010, http://www.newt.org/newt-direct/newt-gingrich-statement-proposed-mosqueislamic-community-center-near-ground-zero.

27. I. M. Kane, "Moderate Muslim Opposes Building Ground Zero Mosque," Transcript of the O'Reilly Factor with Guest Raheel Raza, August 15, 2010, http://imkane.wordpress.com/2010/08/15/moderate-muslim-opposes-building-ground-zero-mosque/.

28. Michelle Boorstein, "Anxiety on All Sides of Upcoming House Hearing on Radicalization of U.S. Muslims," *Washington Post*, February 27, 2011, http://www.washingtonpost.com/wp-dyn/content/article/2011/02/26/AR2011022600330.html.

29. M. Zuhdi Jasser, "Mosque Unbecoming: Not at Ground Zero," *New York Post*, May 24, 2010, http://www.nypost.com/p/news/opinion/opedcolumnists/mosque_unbecoming_QmXgG4QyGgz4ATF9v7cBDM.

30. Thomas L. Friedman, *Longitudes and Attitudes: Exploring the World after September 11* (New York: Farrar, Straus and Giroux, 2002), 131.

31. Ibid., 95.

CHAPTER 12: OUR RESPONSE AS CHRISTIANS

1. Aaron Klein, "Boy Scouts Infiltrated by Muslim Brotherhood?" October 8, 2011, World Net Daily, http://www.wnd.com/index.php?fa=PAGE.printable&pageId=352145.

2. Steven Emerson, "Apologists or Extremists: Muzammil Siddiqi," The Investigative Project on Terrorism, April 20, 2011, http://www.investigativeproject.org/profile/171.

3. Raja Abdulrahim, "Disney Restaurant Hostess Sues for Permission to Wear Hijab," *Los Angeles Times*, August 19, 2010, http://articles.latimes.com/2010/aug/19/local/la-me-0819-disney-hijab-20100819.

4. Associated Press, "Disney, Muslim Worker Agree on Hijab Substitute," NBC San Diego, September 28, 2010, http://www.nbcsandiego.com/news/local/Noor-Abdallah-Disney-Muslim-103938878.html.
5. Ralph Blumenthal and Sharaf Mowjood, "Muslim Prayers and Renewal Near Ground Zero," *New York Times*, December 8, 2009, A1, http://www.nytimes.com/2009/12/09/nyregion/09mosque.html?adxnnl=1&adxnnlx=1320471420-lvC1aW5JPBuenYmjleVeZQ.
6. Alana Goodman, "Ground Zero Imam's Group Trained NY Times Mosque Reporter," Newsbusters.org, September 21, 2010, http://newsbusters.org/blogs/alana-goodman/2010/09/21/ground-zero-imams-group-trained-ny-times-mosque-reporter.
7. Alana Goodman, "AP Orders Staff: 'Stop Using the Phrase Ground Zero Mosque,'" Newsbusters.org, August 19, 2010, http://newsbusters.org/blogs/alana-goodman/2010/08/19/ap-orders-staff-stop-using-phrase-ground-zero-mosque.
8. Lachlan Markay, "Survey Shows Arabs More Opposed to GZ Mosque Than American Media," Newsbusters.org, September 20, 2010, http://newsbusters.org/blogs/lachlan-markay/2010/09/20/survey-shows-arabs-more-opposed-gz-mosque-american-media.
9. Karin McQuillan, "NPR on a Bad Day," *American Thinker*, April 3, 2011, http://www.americanthinker.com/2011/04/npr_on_a_bad_day.html.
10. Phyllis Chesler, "'Soft' Censorship: Honor Killings That You Won't Read About," NewsRealBlog.com, June 17, 2010, http://www.newsrealblog.com/2010/06/17/soft-censorship-honor-killings-that-you-wont-read-about/.
11. Herb Denenberg, "How To Kill Political Correctness Before It Kills Us," CanadaFreePress.com, January 16, 2010, http://canadafreepress.com/index.php/articles-health/19242.
12. Discover the Networks, "Ted Turner," DiscoverTheNetworks.org, http://www.discoverthenetworks.org/individualProfile.asp?indid=2004.
13. Don Feder, "Rosie O'Donnell's Anti-Christian Smear," FrontPageMag.com, September 22, 2006, http://archive.frontpagemag.com/readArticle.aspx?ARTID=2438.